DECISION-MAKING

edited by

Henry S. Brinkers

DECISION-MAKING

CREATIVITY,
JUDGMENT, AND SYSTEMS

Ohio State University Press
Columbus   1972

Library of Congress Catalogue Card Number 71-188740
International Standard Book Number 0-8142-0165-2
Manufactured in the United States of America

To Harold A. Bolz

Marion L. Smith

Elliot L. Whitaker

For their support and guidance

CONTENTS

Preface   ix

Introduction   3

PART 1: Decision-Making Strategies

Personalistic Decision Theory: Exposition and
Critique
Peter C. Fishburn   19

The Study of Collective Decisions
Bernhardt Lieberman   42

PART 2: Decision-Making Aids

Information Science as an Aid to Decision-Making
Ronald L. Ernst and Marshall C. Yovits   69

Toward a Working Theory of Automated Design
Charles M. Eastman   85

The Generation of Form by Geometric Methods
Florencio G. Asenjo   112

PART 3: Decision Aid Applications

Decision Aids for the Planning and Development of
University Facilities
Thomas E. Hoover   127

Analytic Approaches to Facility Layout and Design
Richard L. Francis   137
Development Action Sequencing under Highly
Constrained Conditions
Francis Hendricks   147
Adaptive Diagnosis of Problems
John W. Dickey   157

PART 4: Human Creativity and Judgment
Managing Visual Information
Hoyt L. Sherman   173
Matching Decision Aids with Intuitive Styles
William T. Morris   190
Conceptual Models in Design
Donald Watson   205

PART 5: Implications
Who Looks at the Whole System?
Ian I. Mitroff   223
Decision Aids: Needs and Prospects
John M. Allderige   247

Epilogue   261
Notes on the Contributors   265
Index   267

PREFACE

The essays assembled in this volume were prepared by the authors
for presentation on the campus of the Ohio State University at the
Thomas A. Boyd interdisciplinary conference on decision-making
aids. Through the financial support of the College of Engineering,
the Thomas A. Boyd Lecture Fund, and the School of Architecture,
the conference was established as a means for bringing together
an interdisciplinary group of scientists and scholars for a wide-
ranging discussion of the many aspects of emerging decision-aid
research and applications along with their implications for professional activities and professional education. Consonant with the
excellence and achievement stimulated by Thomas A. Boyd's support for higher education, the conference and the papers presented
in this volume are dedicated to the advancement of the use of
scientific methods for decision-making within the several disciplines
concerned with enhancing environment and the well-being of
people.

The stimulus for organizing the conference and commissioning
the papers to be prepared is the growing interdisciplinary interest
in the recent work in information science and cybernetics, decision
theory and operations research, and mathematics as it relates to
the study and analysis of the behavior of complex systems and the
design of machines and processes for simulating the behavior of
such systems. Decision-making, and the closely related matter of

system behavior, constitute one of the most significant, continually reappearing components of studies of complex systems, whether they be artificial systems or living beings. The concepts and theory emerging from these fields, and the growing number of applications based upon those concepts and theory, appear to be a small though important addition to the large body of theory and methods of the physical and social sciences presently in wide use in the study of large, complex systems. It is the promise that many see in this recent work for providing additional quantitative approaches for the study of such systems that suggest that it is worthwhile for professionals in a number of fields to become aware of and examine this area of work more thoroughly. It is to that end that the conference papers have been assembled for publication.

H.S.B.

September, 1971

DECISION-MAKING

Henry S. Brinkers

INTRODUCTION

This collection of essays is devoted to the topic of decision-making aids as a relationship between decision-makers of all types, the states of the real world that form the substance and context for decisions, and a variety of concepts and technologies used as decision aids that form extensions of the intellectual apparatus of decision-makers. The intention of the volume is to increase the general awareness of the quantative, and scientifically more precise, approaches to decision-making with respect to large, complex systems.

The collection might well be termed a comprehensive treatment of the topic, but one that is strategically spotty in depth. Taken together, the essays develop in depth a limited number of important aspects of decision-making and decision-making aids while achieving a comprehensive coverage by considering the nature of decision-making and decision-making strategies, the contributions of a variety of disciplines to the development of decision aids, the role of human creativity and judgment in decision-making, and finally, the implications and prospects for the future use of decision aids within academic and professional environments.

Six highly related conditions form the practical setting for the collection. They are conditions that have crystallized relatively suddenly during recent decades. The six conditions have become apparent around the world, particularly in developed nations, and have generally affected the lives of people, both laymen and professionals, and their perception of aspects of the world around them. As such, these conditions have made it both necessary and possible to employ significant extensions of the human intellect as decision-making aids.

The first of these conditions, the one that is basic to the other five, is the perceived apparent increase in the complexity of the affairs and processes of various aspects of the real world. Of all, this condition is the most pervasive, most recognized, as it has touched almost every facet of life around the world, even in developing nations where life, relatively speaking, is still uncomplicated. The second condition is the relative shift of the focus of interest away from "things," and the significance of "quantity" as a measure of achievement, toward the "relationships between things" and the "quality" of those relationships. This condition has become significant within those societies that have an abundance of things and are realizing more and more that the accumulation of things is not contributing to enhancing their quality of life. The blacks in the United States, for example, while aspiring to possess all of the things that whites enjoy, seem to understand the critical nature of the quality of relationships exemplified best, perhaps, by the idea of equal opportunity.

The third condition, an apparent natural concomitant of the shift from "things" to the "quality of relationships," is the relative shift of interest away from technological problems toward vastly more complex social problems and the nature of complex systems in general. This shift has required changes in the way in which the real world is perceived and has, of necessity, been accompanied by the fourth condition: the increasing abandonment of the fragmentary ways of viewing the real-world that have been characteristic of the modes of scientific thought for the past three centuries, and the embracing of integrative and holistic views. This shift is exemplified in the shift of attention from parts per se toward wholes and, as now frequently referred to, systems. These two conditions are intimately connected. The emphasis given to complex social and system problems demands more than what can be provided by any single discipline. Accordingly, there have arisen such compensatory concepts as the "team approach" and the several sciences that cut across the disciplines, such as information science and general systems theory, to more adequately deal with these concerns.

While the demands that these conditions have placed upon science have been enormous—well beyond the present capability to perform in many cases, although science adequately supported has responded well in meeting new demands—the demands placed upon human intellectual capacity have been equally as great. The resulting problem may be characterized in the following way. On the one hand, though the intellectual capacity of a human being is substantial, it is nonetheless limited in information-processing and storage capacity. On the other hand, the information content of even simple aspects of the real world exceeds the capacity of a single human mind by several orders of magnitude. Heretofore, notwithstanding the wide variety of mechanical and mathematical aids that have been available, the main means for establishing a balance between the information-processing capacity of the human mind and the information content of the aspect of the real world under study has been by reducing the information content of the matter under study by dividing it into parts, aggregation of variables, simplifying assumptions, and so on. However, the establishment of the fifth condition, the general availability of low-cost, high-capacity, fast information-processing technology, has enabled men to extend and increase their intellectual capacity very considerably. The effect of this condition has been that man can now deal more effectively with complex matters on his own complex terms as against the more simplistic terms of pre–information technology man.

Similarly, science has been pressed to extend its capability for handling complexity for the purpose of moving ahead into the area of complex social and system problems. The challenge for science has been not only that of developing the means for handling wholes as against increasingly smaller parts, but also that of improved means for dealing with significantly large numbers of variables and the relationships among them. This has been accomplished, to a considerable extent, through the establishment of the sixth condition: a body of scientific knowledge, drawing from the work in several disciplines but broadly applicable to a large number of disciplines, that embodies holistic approaches and the capability for expressing in precise terms, and handling the relationships between, a large number of variables. Contributions from information science and a number of areas of mathematics have been important in this latter area.

The broadest context for the apparent increase in the complexity of world processes and affairs and the other conditions that form the setting for the collection is contained in what Harvey Cox refers to in *The Secular City* as the secularization of knowledge. The essence of Cox's argument is that only after knowledge of reality passes from the mystic realm of the philosopher and the priest, whether they be in the civil, professional, or academic sectors, to the realm of empirical science, the cultural and other restraints regulating the production of new knowledge of reality are relaxed. Through this transfer, knowledge of reality becomes less dominated by beliefs and may be subjected to the objectivity of science. The release of the objects of nature—the heavenly bodies, the plants and rocks, and so on—as objects of worship, for example, was an important precondition for the emergence of the sciences. The secularization of life, soul and intellect in more modern times is now manifest in organ transplants, birth control, molecular biology, intelligent machines, student revolutions, professional and academic reappraisals, and the like. But more importantly, it is manifest in the technology bearing upon what Marshall McLuhan refers to as media. In commenting upon the influence of media and its technological base, he summarizes it this way [4, p. 19].

> After three thousand years of explosion, by means of fragmentary and mechanical technologies, the Western world is imploding. During the mechanical ages we had extended our bodies in space. Today, after more than a century of electric technology, we have extended our central nervous system itself in a global embrace, abolishing both space and time as far as our planet is concerned. Rapidly, we approach the final phase of the extensions of man—technological simulation of consciousness, when the creative process of knowing will be collectively and corporately extended to the whole of human society, much as we have already extended our senses and our nerves by the various media.

The extended consciousness made possible by the electric technology has led men in all walks of life quite naturally to the discovery of patterns of relationships that were previously unobservable. Certainly, the new technology itself has been instrumental in establishing many new patterns of relationships. However, the emergence of the means for identifying these new relationships along with the many long-standing complex relations among living and physical systems appears to be the basic factor underlying the perceived apparent increase in the complexity of the modern world. As Stafford Beer observes in *Decision and Control*, complexity is not substantially increased by additions to the number of things; really high levels of complexity arise from the increased number of relations among things. His point is illustrated by the observation that things increase normally at arithmetic rates, and occasionally at geometric rates, whereas relations can and do increase at geometric rates of the rates of increase of things.

It is not only that the world has become more complex, but that the electric technology enables us to be more aware of the actual levels of complexity. The effect of this awareness has led to the progressive enlargement of the scope of concern for most matters of importance today, by virtue of the newly perceived relationships, to levels of complexity well beyond the information-processing capacity of the human mind; and in many cases, well beyond the practical capacity of today's fastest computers. Indeed, as W. Ross Ashby notes [1] in connection with Bremermann's computation of the total information capacity of the universe, there are many seemingly simple well-defined problems that cannot be solved. Determining the best first move in a chess game is one such problem; the order of magnitude of the information contained in the problem exceeds greatly that of the information capacity of the entire universe.

Awareness of increasing complexity arising out of newly perceived relations, and man's increasing inability to deal with it, has led naturally to seeking means of coping with this condition. The search is apparent not only with respect to personal lives but also with respect to the lives of societies, nations, corporations, science, and other social systems. This collection is a partial description of the means that are being developed and used today for dealing with modern complexity. Although the appearance of the computer— which has made generally available for the first time in history sophisticated, low-cost information-processing systems suitable for substantially increasing the intellectual capabilities of man in the McLuhan sense—underlies the topics of the several essays, it is not discussed per se. Rather, the focus of the collection is upon the implications of information-processing technology for dealing with complexity, approaches, and specific methods that are in development and use, and the kinds of insights that are stimulated by the availability of such systems.

As such, the collection serves to illustrate and discuss the means by which the significant relationships in a variety of problems may be considered. The emphasis given to relationships is consistent with the growing general awareness that the quality of relationships among things, as against the mere number of things, is a better measure of the suitability and appropriateness of a problem solution. With respect to the quality of life a society can support, for example, it is becomming increasingly clear that the number of things available for use—automobiles, Hula-Hoops, and so on—may not be a suitable measure of achievement. Indeed, in developed nations the increase of things has, in some respects, led to a decline in the quality of life. This awareness is clearly evident in the profusion of articles on environmental pollution of all types, the questioning of whether continued growth is desirable and whether the priority normally given to growth per se will ultimately lead to disaster, the efforts of the zero population growth and family-planning movements, and the like. Interestingly, the emphasis given to the quality of relations, appearing first in the developed nations, is now being seen as important in many parts of the rest of the world even though the focus of attention in the developing nations is of necessity still primarily upon the production of things due to the relative scarcity of most, even common things.

From its own point of view, each of the essays in the collection deals with the question of relationships and the means by which they may be considered. Several of the essays discuss the means for handling the many relationships involved in the solution of complex physical problems, particularly in programming, scheduling, and layout and design. Aspects of the relationship between the decision-maker, his intuition and creativity, and the decision aid, along with the relation between the choice of decision aid and the probable nature of the resulting decision or outcome, are discussed by several authors. Appearing here and there throughout the collection, the authors consider the relationship between the kinds of opportunities made available by technology and the kinds of problems we seek to solve in relation to several practical and natural limits on information storage and processing. The relationship, now seen as critical to the solution of highly complex problems, particularly social problems, between information and decision-making is considered from a number of viewpoints.

In this connection, attention has been slowly shifting recently in developed countries away from the solution of primarily technological problems such as the design of a better washing machine, a more economical automobile, a faster airplane, and the like. Instead, high priority is being given to the solution of large-scale complex physical problems having extensive relationships with social processes such as environmental pollution and regional development, and pressing social problems such as poverty and housing. These problems are being seen as ones in which the matter of relationships, and adjustments in relationships to produce a more satisfactory state of affairs, is the critical issue.

These types of problems continue to be the most challenging, and yet, in many ways, their solution appears as remote as ever despite a wide variety of concerted efforts. Those involved in seeking solutions to such problems quickly realize their enormous complexity, not only of the problem but also of viable solutions. These classes of complex problems are being seen as difficult ones to evaluate and meaningfully solve in parts or out of their dynamic context of interrelations with other aspects of the real world due to the large number of difficult to define relationships they embody. The history of federal government programs in this country aimed at providing housing for the needy is an excellent case in point.

Several essays in the collection discuss a number of approaches and models of significance in handling complex physical and social problems. Aside from the several essays concerned with the social process of design of physical systems for human use, adaptive approaches to problem-solving, effective use of conceptual models, philosophical, social and other requirements for managing the whole system, and models of social choice, the models treating decision-making as an information flow and processing problem appear to have some of the richness required for dealing with complex social problems. The promise for this approach lies in the observation that models of this type are inherently capable of handling substantial complexity and that the flow and distribution of information within a social system is the most important factor influencing system behavior.

Closely associated with the development of electric and information-processing technology has been the increased interest in the behavior of whole systems, animate and inanimate. In the scientific, business, and professional worlds, the concern for the behavior of whole systems has centered around the questions of system control—or, more properly, self-regulation, information flow and distribution as the basis for system guidance and control, and the use of information for system decision-making. McLuhan suggests that this is a natural outgrowth of the embrace of the "cool" electric technology and its implosive effect. He characterizes the implosive effect as one that provides total field awareness, social consciousness and involvement, interrelation of knowledge, decentralization with participation, consciousness of the unconscious, and so on. [4, chaps. 3, 4] Thus, by embracing new technological forms, he argues, they become extensions of ourselves, and we become, henceforth, modified automatically by them. This process, in turn, provides the basis for finding new ways of modifying and applying technology.

As the science base, particularly as it had developed in a fragmentary way with a fragmentary world view over the past three centuries, was not completely able to serve these new needs with theory and methods for understanding the behavior of whole systems—complex living systems of all types and self-controlling, mechanical-electrical systems—there have proliferated significant scientific developments beginning during the 1940s that have contributed greatly not only to the understanding of the behavior of complex whole systems but, also, to their design and construction. This new system science, tending toward unifying the traditionally fragmented disciplines, is providing the scientific base for dealing with complex wholes so essential for tackling the high priority problems of today. The essays of this collection build upon the base provided by the new system science.

Although electric technology has served to extend man's central nervous system, particularly with respect to the flow of information, and enable the conditions to be established for the emergence of system science, it was system science that took up the task of extending the information storage and processing capabilities of man's central nervous system through the development of the computer.

In the early phase of the development of electric technology, from the electric light through radio and television, there were opened up many more channels of communication. In that sense, man's central nervous system was extended. However, as noted earlier in the quotation from McLuhan, in today's advanced phase of electric technology—the computer and automation phase— man's information storage and processing capabilities are extended. (As McLuhan projects, the ultimate extension will be the technological simulation of consciousness and the corporate extension of knowledge to the whole of human society.) Clearly, the extension of man's capabilities in these two ways is an essential precondition for successfully coping with the enormous complexity in today's high priority problems. This point is an important one— one that is not specifically discussed in any of the essays, but one that is intimately threaded through the entire collection.

What has been, for convenience's sake, characterized above as system science consists of the further development of a large number of scientific contributions made over a relatively long period of time. However, these developments tended to come together in a variety of ways in recent decades as conditions, increasingly, became ripe for them to do so. Accordingly, the idea of system science encompasses today three main areas of scientific thought upon which the study of complex systems is based; viz., computer and information science, operations research and general systems theory, and the abstract fields in mathematics of symbolic logic and boolean algebra, topology, and set and graph theory.

From the branches of mathematics are derived the essential tools for dealing with relationships in a quantative and precise fashion. General systems theory, and its application in operations research, provides the applied conceptual insights required to deal with the multitude of relationships inherent in real-world problems and complex systems. Information science, and its application in the design of complex systems in computer science, provides not merely the means by which the understanding of complex systems can be acquired, the computer, but it provides also the essential scientific theory for explaining the behavior of complex systems, a scientific basis for dealing with information.

Besides providing the theory and quantitative methods for dealing with information as the physical sciences have provided the theory and methods for dealing with matter-energy, a number of important concepts have been generated within information science that are having an influence on how problems are viewed and solved. Error-controlled negative feedback, for example, is an important concept because it has demonstrated that systems can be designed that are inherently capable of responses not envisioned in detail by the designer. The rigorous mathematical proof that in order to remain viable it is necessary for viable systems, both living and nonliving, to change based upon interaction with their environment has undergirded the highly useful concept of open systems. These and other concepts drawn from system science pervade the several parts of the collection. They are most apparent in those parts that deal with decision-making as an information flow and processing problem.

This collection of essays consists of five parts. Part one serves the purpose of introducing the topic by setting forth some of the major issues imbedded in the descriptive and normative models of decision-making. The very fine essay by Peter C. Fishburn presents, through several illustrations of decision models and a tightly constructed commentary on the decision theory literature, what might be termed the anatomy of a personal decision. His thoughtful critique of personalistic decision theory sets forth several of the central difficulties involved in the formulation and use of models of decision processes and decision aids. As such, it provides a highly useful evaluative framework for decision aids and processes in general. The second essay in part one, by Bernhardt Lieberman, presents a comprehensive commentary on descriptive and normative social choice models, the central problems associated with them, and the implications for their use. The Lieberman essay is an excellent companion to Fishburn's as, together, they cover the breadth of issues involved in both individual and group decision-making.

Part two of the collection serves to acquaint the reader with the current basic efforts in the development of aids to decision-making. The three essays are an extension of the presentation of normative and descriptive decision models in part one. As a group they cover the basic work on decision models in three important areas from which the main contributions have been made, namely, information science, operations research, and mathematics. The essay by Ronald L. Ernst and Marshall C. Yovits casts decision-making as an information flow and processing problem, showing through variations of their basic model of a generalized information system that decision-making is the dominant function of information systems. The nature of their model is such that it goes beyond the descriptive and normative models presented earlier and includes such features as feedback and learning. It serves well to explain the relationship between information and decision-making. The essay by Charles M. Eastman further develops the relationship between information and decision-making in the area of problem-solving and architectural design. His essay presents several models used in problem-solving and the means for developing them. Presented also is a comprehensive commentary on automated design methods in architecture and where current efforts might lead. The final essay in this part is a fascinating one by Florencio G. Asenjo that extends Eastman's commentary on automated architectural design into the realm of mathematical methods for form generation in the arts. Although Asenjo's essay focuses on the use of mathematics by the artist, his underlying themes are the widely applicable ones of mathematics as models for exact thinking and for expressing and dealing with relationships.

Part three of the collection is devoted entirely to the discussion of applications of specific decision aids to particular situations. The four essays in this part are concerned with applications normally considered to be a part of operations research. The first three essays are concerned with a class of decision aid similar to the ones discussed by Eastman, but are distinctly different from those discussed by Fishburn, Lieberman, and Ernst and Yovits. The difference arises in the setting of the problem wherein there exists one or more measurable optimum outcomes that bear a specified relationship to inputs.

The first essay, by Thomas E. Hoover, discusses the problem of development planning and budgeting at universities and proposes a model for forecasting future demand for higher education and projecting the space needs for a large number of highly variable academic programs having different requirements. The second essay, by Richard L. Francis, presents two models for use in determining the optimum layout and design of facilities. The two models are illustrated by applications to the layout of theater seating and the location of plant sites. Because the solution of even simple facility layout problems can involve enormous amounts of computer time, he discusses the application of heuristic approaches for identifying reasonably good suboptimal solutions at a considerable saving in computation time. In the third essay, by Francis Hendricks, there is presented a model for solving directly for solutions to the problem of scheduling under highly constrained conditions. The final essay of this part, by John W. Dickey, is closely related to the models discussed by Fishburn. In this essay, Dickey presents an application of Bayes Theorem to problem identification in the field of architecture, but the model is easily generalizable for many other applications.

The purpose of the fourth part of the collection is to indicate that the use of decision aids normally places increased demands upon human creativity and judgment rather than relieving the decision-maker of the need to exercise them, as might be expected. This condition arises because the availability and use of decision aids which serve as an extension of the decision-maker's intellect provide new and interesting opportunities for utilizing his intellect.

The essays in this part consider this matter in three ways. The first essay, by Hoyt L. Sherman, is a companion piece to Asenjo's essay in that they deal with the two primary bases for form generation in the arts, the geometric and the perceptual bases. Sherman sets forth a descriptive model of the perceptual process in terms very similar to those of the model of the general information system set forth by Ernest and Yovits. Useful models treating the perceptual process as a problem in the flow and processing of information are not yet at hand owing to what Sherman describes as the lack of knowledge of what is actually going on and the inability to define exactly the relationships among the large number of variables involved. An associated problem is the enormous information content of physical environments and the lack of means to appropriately describe it. However, when models of the perceptual process are perfected, the artist or the architect will be faced with the need to generate large numbers of creative solution possibilities for evaluation by the model and to render judgments concerning the suitability and quality of form possibilities generated by the model—demanding tasks, indeed. The second essay, by William T. Morris, is a brilliant commentary on the relationship between the decision-maker and decision aids and the new obligations that the decision-maker must assume to utilize decision aids effectively. The last essay, by Donald Watson, sets forth descriptive models with which the architect as a decision-maker may enhance his creativity and judgment.

The final part of the collection is an attempt on the part of two authors to stand back and objectively view the history and trends in the use of decision aids as extensions of human intellectual capacity and project the professional and academic implications. The first essay, by Ian I. Mitroff, is a truly thoughtful exposition on four questions: what are the philosophical presupppositions concerning reality that are shared by science and engineering, and how is the practice of these professions related to them; and how does the present philosophical base inhibit scientific inquiry and engineering design, and what will or should scientists and engineers of the future be like? The second essay, by John M. Allderige, concerns itself with the past difficulties and future aspirations for decision aids from the viewpoint of a practicing management consultant. His point is: the time is ripe, the need is clear, the opportunties are available; let's get operational!

References

1. W. R. Ashby, "Some Consequences of Bremermann's Limit for Information Processing Systems," *Cybernetic Problems in Bionics,"* ed. H. L. Oestreicher and D. R. Moore (New York: Gordon & Breach, 1968), pp. 69-76.
2. S. Beer, *Decision and Control* (New York: Wiley, 1966).
3. H. G. Cox, *The Secular City* (New York: Macmillan, 1966).
4. M. McLuhan, *Understanding Media* (New York: Signet Classics, New American Library, 1966).

part **1**

DECISION-MAKING STRATEGIES

Peter C. Fishburn

PERSONALISTIC
DECISION THEORY
EXPOSITION AND CRITIQUE

In recent years interest in the ways in which decisions are made has increased sharply. "Personalistic decision theory" has been set forth as a means by which decision situations may be described and analyzed. The present purpose is to define the meaning of "personalistic decision theory" and to discuss some of the many difficulties that pervade both the theory and any attempt to use it as an aid in making decisions.

First, consider the nature of decision. What is a decision? Fortunately, a common phrase is close to an answer. It is simply: "Make up your mind." To decide is to make up one's mind. Or, as Beer [8, p. 1] suggests, "the taking of a decision is best described as the fixing of a belief."

A somewhat deeper analysis suggests that a decision is a deliberate act of selection, by the mind, of an alternative from a set of competing alternatives in the hope, expectation, or belief that the actions envisioned in carrying out the selected alternative will accomplish certain goals. Decision is the selection of a mental state: it is a commitment to certain actions or inactions. Other people may observe our actions but they do not directly observe our decisions.

Such a commitment to action is not necessarily irreversible. Along with "make up one's mind" there is another familiar phrase: "change one's mind." Decisions often have escape clauses, which can be a healthy thing. Many decisions, before they are fully implemented, are replaced by subsequent decisions in response to ever-changing circumstances and desires. Of course, we also make subsequent decisions that reinforce the commitment to action of a prior and as yet unconsumated decision.

Perhaps the first step in the decision process is an awareness of a dissatisfaction with the way things are or might be at some future time. Subsequently, we seek alternatives by which we might exert some control over our environment so that the future will be more to our liking than might otherwise be the case.

As is frequently pointed out, it is of the utmost importance (especially in those situations that most concern us) to understand the sources of, and reasons for, our dissatisfaction. The better able we are to do this the better position we will be in to understand our own objectives and to develop alternatives in response to these objectives in the situation at hand.

The process of developing alternatives or strategies occurs over a period of time and is (or should be) evaluative as well as creative. In searching for and constructing alternatives we bear in mind (or should bear in mind) the purpose of the inquiry and are constantly evaluating, often subjectively, the extent to which a course of action may be able to accomplish these purposes. As we proceed, some alternatives will be modified: others, judged infeasible or inferior, will be discarded.

The judgments of ability to accomplish purposes will, of course, depend on the beliefs, whether myopic or otherwise, that the decision-maker (and/or his staff) has about the nature of his environment and how it might respond to his actions.

As indicated here the processes of alternative creation and alternative evaluation are inseparable. Nevertheless, writers often separate out the evaluative aspect and analyze a "given" set of alternatives. Although there are dangers in this, it is difficult to discuss certain evaluative procedures without such a separation.

A decision is often considered successful if the actions made in response to it help to bring about a desired future. Beer [8, p. 211] says that "decision is effective to the extent that it is competent to modify future states of the system in a way which meets the pre-established criteria of success."

Now when an alternative is decided upon, we will rarely know before the fact how things will turn out. There are simply too many uncertainties. Despite this, the decision-maker may have faith that the alternative he selects for implementation will be as effective as any of the others in pursuing his objectives. The strength of this belief may of course depend on the effort devoted to predecision research and analysis and the involvement of the decision-maker in this analysis.

This ties in closely with the personalistic decision theory notion of evaluating alternatives on the basis of beliefs and expectations of the decision-maker. Based on whatever evidence he has available to him, he identifies his beliefs in the relative abilities of the alternatives to attain his objectives. The theory suggests ways to check the coherence and internal consistency of such beliefs. Keeping in mind that the decision-maker's objectives have been (or should be) instrumental in the development of alternatives and that they will influence his value judgments, we shall suppress them in the following presentation. In their place we shall talk about consequences of decision and the decision-maker's utilities for these. Coupled with this, belief enters in the form of his personal or subjective) probabilities for consequences as conditioned on strategies. Expected utilities for strategies are formed from the consequence utilities and the probabilities.

Expected Utility

Personalistic decision theories can be based on one fundamental concept, the notion of individual preference. The assumptions of the theories use the idea of the decision-maker's preference relation to the set of strategies (or acts or alternatives). For any two strategies it is generally assumed that either one is preferred to the other or else that neither is preferred to the other. The latter case is usually known as indifference. From sufficiently powerful assumptions on the decision-maker's preferences it is possible to define well-behaved subsidiary relations, namely, preferences between consequences and a relation of qualitative probability between propositions that reflect the aspects of the situation about which the decision-maker is uncertain. It can then be shown that numbers, called utilities, can be assigned to the consequences so that one consequence is preferred to a second consequence if, and only if, the utility of the first exceeds the utility of the second. In addition, numerical probabilities can be assigned to the uncertainty-based propositions in such a way that one proposition is qualitatively more probable to the decision-maker than a second if, and only if, the numerical probability of the first exceeds the numerical probability of the second. The expected utility of a strategy is then defined as the sum of the consequence utilities weighted by their respective probabilities of occurrence under that strategy. Finally, the consequence utilities and the probabilities can be defined in such a way that one strategy is preferred to another if, and only if, the expected utility of the first exceeds the expected utility of the second.

Using obviously simplified examples we shall now look at two expected utility models.

Using the phrase adopted by Luce and Krantz [27] in their derivation of our first model from basic preference assumptions, we shall call it the conditional expected utility model. This form of the expected utility model has been used before [16], but the Luce-Krantz theory is the first that I know of that derives the general model from basic preference assumptions.

To consider the structure of this model, we shall consider the following situation. A young man, classified IV-F by his draft board, is in his last year of college. He has applied to two universities, A and B, for graduate school and has been unconditionally accepted by both; however, he is not sure that he wants to go to graduate school. If he does not enter graduate school, he plans to accept a job offer from company Z and enter their one-year training program. If he does this, his year will terminate with one of three responses from the company:

1. "Get lost."

2. "Stay on as an assistant junior engineer."

3. "Stay on as a junior engineer."

By referring to Figure 1 you will see how a decision tree for his situation is starting to take shape from the information given thus far. A solid square on the tree represents a decision point. His first decision, at the left, is among A, B, and Z. If he takes Z, then one of the three responses noted above will occur and this is shown on the tree.

If he goes to work for Z and either 2 or 3 occurs, he must then decide whether to quit and

a. enter University A, or

b. enter University B, or

c. look for a job with another company, or

d. stay on with Z.

On the other hand, if 1 occurs, he must choose a, b, or c. These three potential decision points are shown midway through the tree.

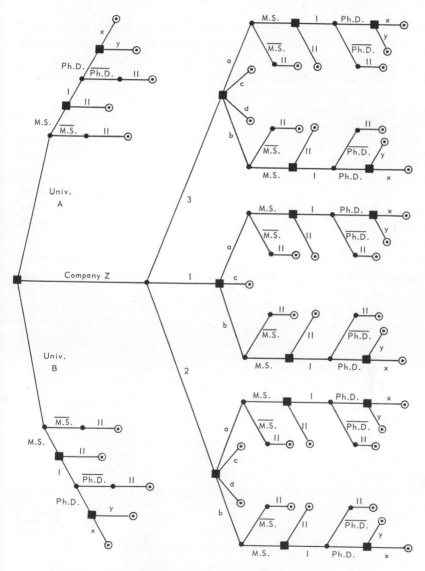

Fig. 1—Decision Tree for College Student

If he enters either graduate school at any point, he plans to work for a master's degree. If he succeeds in this he will either

I. try to earn his Ph.D. at the same school, or

II. look for a job with some company.

If he is unsuccessful at either the M.S. or Ph.D. level (shown by a bar above these letters in the tree), he will do II. If he earns his Ph.D. he will either

x. embark on an academic career, or

y. take a job with some company.

Insofar as a situation is projected into the future, a *strategy* is a complete program for action. It sets forth what to do at the initial decision point and at each succeeding decision point that could possibly be reached under the prior directions indicated by the strategy. Figure 2 codifies several of the 454 strategies that arise from Figure 1. For example, the first one shown on Figure 2 is "Go to A; if you get an M.S. degree, then look for a job with some company." The last one shown is "Take Z's job; if 1 occurs, then look for a job with another company; if 2 occurs, then enter University A and look for a job with some company if an M.S. degree is earned; if 3 occurs, then enter University B and if you earn an M.S. degree go on for your Ph.D.; if you earn your Ph.D., then begin an academic career."

Consequences

Strategies	$(A, \overline{M.S.}, II)$	$(A, M.S., II) \ldots (Z, 3, b, M.S., I, Ph.D., y)$
$(A; M.S. \to II)$		
$(A; M.S. \to I; Ph.D. \to x)$		Each entry in this matrix is for the probability of occurrence of a consequence given a strategy. E.g., $P(A, M.S., II \mid A; M.S. \to II)$ is the probability he will earn a masters degree if he goes to Univ. A next year.
$\vdots$		
$(B; M.S. \to I; Ph.D. \to y)$		
$\vdots$		
$(Z; 1 \to c; 2 \to a (M.S. \to II);$		
$\quad 3 \to b (M.S. \to I; Ph.D. \to y))$		

Fig. 2—Conditional Probability Matrix

A *consequence* is, in the ideal, a complete description of the future insofar as it is affected by, or concerned with, the decision situation at hand. In terms of our decision tree we can represent a consequence as a complete path through the tree, from the initial decision point to a terminal point. Three of the 45 consequences for Figure 1 are shown at the top of Figure 2. The last of these is, "You go to Company Z, and at the end of one year they invite you to stay on as a junior engineer, whereupon you enter University B, earn your M.S., and embark on an academic career."

Figure 2 illustrates the probability matrix for the $454 \times 45 = 20,430$ propositions of the form, 'if strategy j is followed, then consequence k will result." Many of these conditional probabilities will equal zero since some consequences are impossible under certain strategies. The sum of the probabilities in any row will equal one since the consequences are (ideally) exhaustive and mutually exclusive.

Each conditional probability is a personal or subjective probability representing the decision-maker's degree of belief in the truth of the corresponding proposition or event. This interpretation of the meaning of probability has been discussed at length elsewhere [13, 16, 25, 42, 43, 44, 45], and I shall not go into it in detail here.

Along with the conditional probabilities, the theory assumes that it is possible for the decision-maker to assign a numerical utility to each consequence so that the expected utilities of the strategies reflect the decision-maker's preferences among them. For Figure 2, the expected utility of a strategy is computed by multiplying each consequence utility by its corresponding probability under that strategy and taking the sum of these products.

Probably the best-known derivation of our second expected utility model from preference assumptions is the one given by Savage [42] although, as Savage points out, Frank P. Ramsey [37] outlined a similar derivation about twenty-five years before Savage's book was published. A number of other publications [2, 4, 10, 17, 21, 34, 40, 48] present alternative derivations of the Ramsey-Savage model.

This model differs from the preceding one by the use of states of the world. In Savage's words the *world* is "the object about which the person is concerned" and a *state of the world* is "a description of the world, leaving no relevant aspect undescribed." The decision-maker is presumed to be uncertain only about which state of the world obtains (or is the "true" state). The assumptions imply that his beliefs about which state might obtain do not depend on the strategy he might select. Thus, in this model, there are personal probabilities on the different states and these are independent of the strategies.

The interdependence between strategies and states lies in their joint determination of consequences. This is shown in the example of Figure 3, where we suppose that a judge must either

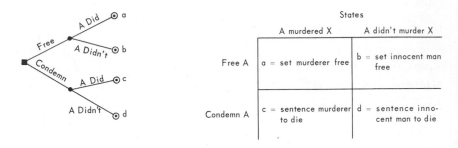

Fig. 3—Consequence Matrix for States Model

free or condemn to death an accused murderer. The judge's two strategies are shown on the left of the matrix, and the two states of the world are along the top. Note that the strategy that is used will have absolutely no effect on which of the two states is the "true" state. The consequences for each strategy-state pair are shown in the matrix.

The expected utility for a strategy in the states models is obtained by multiplying each state probability by the utility of its associated consequence for the given strategy and then summing these products.

As indicated elsewhere [16] on a suggestion from Russell Ackoff, the two models presented above are potentially isomorphic. For example, given the states model, we can write a conditional probability matrix as in Figure 2 by placing all the distinct consequences along the top of the matrix and entering in position (j, k) of the matrix the sum of the probabilities for those states and yield the kth consequence when the jth strategy is used. On the other hand, if we start with the conditional expected utility formulation, states can be defined as functions on strategies to consequences.

For example, one state might be: (if strategy 1 is used, then consequence k_1 will result; if strategy 2 is used, then consequence k_2 will result; . . .). Defined in this way, the state that obtains will not depend on the particular strategy that is used. But in this case, the state probabilities will generally not be computable from the conditional probabilities for consequences given strategies.

Suppose George, a bachelor, is dating two girls, Ann and Sue, who apparently are good friends. He plans to propose marriage to one of the girls. Whether she accepts or rejects, the other girl will learn of the proposal. If his initial proposal is rejected, he could then propose to the other girl or else forget about marriage for the time being. George's decision tree is shown in Figure 4, where his four strategies are indicated by the circled numbers. George's probabilities for the girls' responses are shown on the tree. He figures that if he proposes to Ann first, then there is a 70 percent chance that she will accept; but if he proposes to Ann after Sue has rejected his initial proposal, he figures only a 50 percent chance for an acceptance from Ann.

cond. p

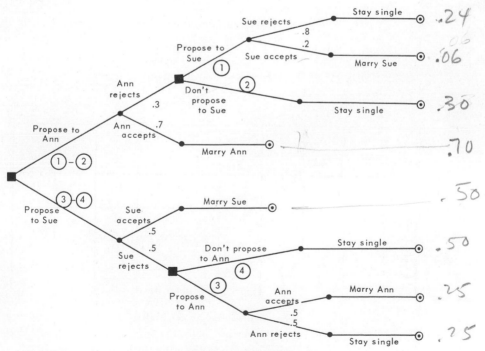

Fig. 4—Decision Tree for Marriage Example

The conditional expected utility formulation for this example is shown at the top of Figure 5. The probabilities in the matrix are obtained from those given in Figure 4. For simplicity only the three terminal consequences are used.

A states-of-the-world formulation is shown in the lower part of Figure 5. Using terminal consequences, there are $81 = 3^4$ potential

Terminal Consequences

	A = Marry Ann	S = Marry Sue	B = Stay Single	Sums
①	.70	.06	.24	1.00
②	.70	0	.30	1.00
③	.25	.50	.25	1.00
④	0	.50	.50	1.00

Conditional Probability Matrix

Nine States and State Probabilities:

0 = will reject any proposal
1 = will accept only if asked first
2 = will accept any proposal

	1	2	3	4	5	6	7	8	9
Ann:	0	0	0	1	1	1	2	2	2
Sue:	0	1	2	0	1	2	0	1	2
	P_1	P_2	P_3	P_4	P_5	P_6	P_7	P_8	P_9
①	B	B	S	A	A	A	A	A	A
②	B	B	B	A	A	A	A	A	A
③	B	S	S	B	S	S	A	S	S
④	B	S	S	B	S	S	B	S	S

Terminal Consequence Matrix

Fig. 5—Marriage Example with Both Models

states of the kind described above (functions on strategies to consequences), but if we assume that it is never true that a girl will accept only if she is proposed to after her friend has rejected a previous proposal, the situation reduces to the nine possible states described on Figure 5. The probabilities for these nine states cannot be determined completely from the probabilities in Figure 4, although it is possible to conclude that $p_3 = .06$, $p_1 + p_2 = .24$, $p_7 = .25$, and $p_1 + p_4 = .25$.

Critique

A multitude of criticisms have been leveled at both the fundamental theory of personalistic decisions and its potential usefulness. Perhaps the best way of describing some of these criticisms lies in the formulation of a decision situation.

In the first place, the reader may question whether it is ever possible to formulate a decision situation in the manner outlined above because our world and our lives are in continual flux and our experience and perhaps even our goals are subject to constant change. It might be argued that if sufficient time is set aside to attempt to spell out strategies, consequences, and perhaps states of the world, by the time that process is completed the decision is obsolete or no longer necessary. Time and experience simply do not stand still, and any theory of decision that pretends that they do is bound to be of little practical use.

In addition, it should be noted that, in practice, it is generally impossible to formulate strategies, consequences, and states with anything like the exactness suggested in our previous definitions. In the states model there will always be some residual uncertainty in the consequences, and our states will necessarily be imperfectly formulated due to our limited foresight. Strategies, although they may look ahead at a sequence of future decisions, are always subject to implementation difficulties and unforeseen or unforeseeable events that may indicate the need for new formulation and evaluation before any particular strategy has been pursued very far. Because of such things one may wonder when, if ever, it is worthwhile to attempt to formulate and evaluate a situation in the manner described above.

Suppose, however, some potential can be seen in formulating a decision situation in the manner here described. It is then necessary to decide on the extent of this formulation. How far into the future should strategies be projected? How much of the universe should we include and in how much detail? Is it in fact possible to isolate a decision situation in a satisfactory way?

Many writers have commented on such questions. In speaking of his basic theory, Savage [42] conceives of it as completely holistic, relevant in one bold stroke to the entire future, whatever it might be, of the person to whom the preference assumptions are directed. He is very much concerned, however, with how his general "look before you leap" principle might apply to manageable segments of one's future, for which he uses the phrase "small worlds." In direct connection with the preceding questions, Savage [42, p. 16] confesses at one point, "I am unable to formulate criteria for selecting these small worlds and indeed believe that their selection may be a matter of judgment and experience about which it is impossible to enunciate complete and sharply defined general principles. . . . On the other hand, it is an operation in which we all necessarily have much experience, and one in which there is in practice considerable agreement." Later in his book, in a further analysis of small worlds (pp. 82-91), he says that "any claim to realism made by this book—or indeed by any theory of personal decision of which I know—is predicated on the idea that some of the individual decision situations into which actual people tend to subdivide the single grand decision do recapitulate in microcosm the mechanism of the idealized grand decision. . . . The problem of this section is to say as clearly as possible what constitutes a satisfactory isolated decision situation."

De Jouvenel [14] also is concerned with the "look before you leap" idea, and he cites numerous historical examples in which the failure to look sufficiently far ahead or to consider with sufficient seriousness a spectrum of possible reactions by nature and other people has led to disastrous consequences. Future writers will no doubt say similar things about some of the major problems we face today, such as pollution, population control, racial injustice, and the arms race.

The potential dangers inherent in not adopting a sufficiently broad outlook in decisions involving large-scale systems have been discussed by Churchman [11], who realistically recognizes the tremendous difficulties in understanding large-scale systems.

To many readers, remarks such as these indicate a need for what so-called objective approaches to predecision analysis have been trying to provide in recent years: namely, ways to identify the more important and relevant factors in decision situations and to understand how these interact with the environment at large. According to my understanding of personalistic decision theory, there is nothing in it that denies this need. Indeed, I would suggest that much of the efforts of operations research, cybernetics, systems analysis, and related activities are conducted to provide decision makers with potentially valuable information inputs to their decisions. Although some people would disagree on this point, there does not seem to be any compelling reasons to suppose that personalistic decision theory and these other activities are not compatible.

Having considered some of the difficulties in the formulation suggested by personalistic decision theory, we shall now turn our attention to some of its ethical aspects.

To the extent that the preference assumptions are viewed as criteria that an individual's preferences ought to satisfy and that maximization of expected utility be used as a guide for decision, the theory is normative. Insofar as some other principle for decision is in conflict with this, the sponsor of the alternative will surely take issue with personalistic decision theory. There are, of course, several points at which such conflict can arise. For example, one might take issue with one or more of the assumptions of the theory (more about this later) or he might dislike its general personalistic orientation.

It might be argued that people frequently do not know what is good for them. Most parents act this way toward their children, and we find a similar attitude reflected by various organizations and governments. Other people frequently attempt to impose their preferences on our decisions. When this is the case, we might suspect that people will still behave in a manner reminiscent of personalistic decision theory with due cognizance taken of (or in spite of) others' "impositions."

Personalistic decision theory is sometimes accused of being narrowly self-centered, but that is not true. An individual may be concerned only for his own welfare, but the theory itself is "ethically neutral." This means that the theory passes no judgments on the goodness or rightness of a person's objectives (although it generally recognizes Singer's universal objective or desire [46, 47], which is the desire to obtain a greater ability to attain one's objectives). Because of this, some advocates of particular ethical systems [41] are bound to dislike the theory.

Nevertheless, because it is ethically neutral in the sense indicated, the theory can accommodate any of a large number of ethical systems. One person may be highly motivated to increase his material wealth; another may try to follow the Christian love ethic; another may like Jeremy Bentham's "principle of utility" [9, 31]. Whatever the motivation, the theory remains open as a potential guide for decision.

In considering how the theory might be of use, it might be useful to note first that the very process of formulating a decision situation can be helpful to a decision-maker. It may uncover factors and possibilities for action that might otherwise be overlooked, and it may lead to a deeper examination of objectives. A knowledge of the theory's approach may help decision-makers to structure their situations more efficiently and thereby lead to better understanding.

If a formulation leads to a manageable decision tree, or at least to a manageable skeleton of a decision tree, this can be used for analysis even when no explicit attempt is made to measure utilities or probabilities. To do this, the decision-maker begins with the final decision points and asks, for each one, what he would do if he should arrive at that point. The branches from these points that are not chosen are then deleted and the decision-maker moves back to the penultimate decision points, asking the same question for each of these. Thus he works his way back through the tree, deciding as he proceeds and crossing off those branches that he would not choose. This eventually brings him to the initial point, where he will only have to consider a greatly reduced part of the original tree. This procedure might be referred to as introspective dynamic programming. Minus explicit utilities and probabilities, it is similar to what Raiffa [36] refers to as "averaging out and folding back." If utilities are assigned to the consequences (entire paths) and listed at the terminal points in the tree, and if conditional probabilities are specified at each non-decision branch point in the tree for the branches that proceed from that point (as in Fig. 4), then one can work backward through the tree as before, using conditional expectations as the guide for selection.

As already noted, the theory leads to a definition of expected utility that preserves the decision-maker's preference order on the strategies. If this is so, why bother to use an expected utility model or the backward approach discussed above? Why not simply select a most preferred strategy and be done with it? Anatol

Rapoport [38, 39] feels that the assumed correspondence between preferences and expected utilities makes the models useless.

This criticism seems to exclude the idea of viewing the assumptions as criteria of consistency and coherence that a person's preferences ought to satisfy, a viewpoint held by most personalistic theorists. Savage [42, 43, 44, 45] for example, suggests that the theory may be used to check a decision-maker's supposed preferences. If an assumption is violated by the supposed preferences, the decision-maker may wish to "correct" his "inconsistency" before proceeding further. An expected utility model can aid this examination, as Savage demonstrates [42, pp. 101-3] on an example from Allais [1].

Other writers [16, 18, 19, 34, 51] suggest the use of the model for uncovering or "discovering" preferences between complex alternatives on the basis of judgments between simple (and probably hypothetical) alternatives. To do this, procedures for estimating utilities [18, 34, 51] and personal probabilities [54, 55] are applied to simplified alternatives. The data thus obtained are used to compare expected utilities of more complex alternatives.

However, the sheer size and complexity of many situations often causes enormous difficulties in estimating utilities and personal probabilities. I have discussed these difficulties elsewhere [16] and will not pursue them here. Let it suffice to note that the models can be used effectively in many situations only if major and often unwarranted simplifying assumptions are first made.

No critique of a theory would be complete without some discussion of its central core, that is, its assumptions or axioms. Since a thorough analysis cannot be made in the space available here, only an outline will be presented.

For discussion purposes the axioms of the theory may be divided into our general categories:

> Structural axioms
> Preference order axioms
> Sure-thing and independence axioms
> Archimedean axioms

Most of the axioms in the final three categories are defended either as realistic preference assumptions and/or as reasonable criteria of consistency and coherence.

On the other hand, the two types of structural axioms, those that say nothing about preferences and those that include the preference relation, are seldom defended as "reasonable criteria." Their purpose is to provide a sort of internal cohesiveness among the basic sets used in the formulation (strategies, consequences, states, events, and so on). In many cases they are not required by the expected utility model, but help greatly in deriving the model from themselves and the other axioms.

It is interesting to note that, of all the axioms in personalistic decision theories, many theorists are most troubled by the structural ones. For example, Savage's theory supposes that there is a strategy or act for each consequence such that that consequence will occur regardless of which state obtains. Such "constant acts" are seldom present in real situations [17, 27, 48, 49]. Moreover, his axioms require the set of states to be infinite. In a structural-preference axiom, Ramsey [37] and Suppes [48] require the set of consequences to be infinite and, for any two nonindifferent consequences, there must be a third consequence "midway" in preference between the two. The Luce-Krantz theory [27] uses several structural assumptions that may present difficult problems of interpretation with respect to the basic situation.

In essence, no extant theory of any generality is free from troublesome structural conditions. In some cases [2, 5, 10, 17, 21, 28, 34, 40] part of the trouble is avoided by embedding the actual situation in a larger structure that introduces "known" probabilities and/or random events that can be associated with chance devices. Whether such augmented theories are thought to be more realistic than unaugmented theories seems open to personal judgment.

Several things are included in the second category of axioms, the preference order axioms. One of these is the assumption of completeness, which says that of any two strategies, one will be preferred to the other or else they are indifferent. This is usually extended to the consequences where, so long as "indifference" is interpreted as "of approximately equal value," problems may arise. Many people would think that the following two consequences are not directly comparable:

1. Take your umbrella with you to the office tomorrow, which turns out to be a very rainy day, and stay safely dry beneath your umbrella.

2. Leave your umbrella at home tomorrow, which turns out
   to be a beautiful sunny day.

Some work has been done with incompleteness (or incompar-
ability) [6, 7, 24], but this is only partially related to the situations
considered in this paper. Models that do not assume comparability
of consequences for different states are presented in [12, 20].

A second order assumption is transitivity: if one strategy is
preferred to a second that in turn is preferred to a third, then the
first is (should be) preferred to the third. Some question has been
raised about the reasonableness of this axiom [29, 30, 53]. It has
been defended with the "money-pump" argument: if you are
intransitive, preferring A to B, B to C, and C to A, then you will
surely pay something to have the opportunity of doing C instead
of A. But given C you would surely pay to be able to switch from
C to B, and likewise from B to A, so that you end up where you
started (with A) minus some cash.

Indifference also is assumed to be transitive, and a number of
people [3, 4, 22, 26, 29, 50] suggest that this is an untenable
assumption. To use an example suggested by May [29], can one
see anything unreasonable about an individual who, in looking for
a new car, prefers (Buick at $3,195) to (Buick at $3,200) but finds
that he is indifferent about (Buick at $3,195) and (Chrysler at
$3,300) and about (Chrysler at $3,300) and (Buick at $3,200)?

If the possibility of intransitive indifference is accepted, the
foregoing models are not applicable in the form stated. A
"weaker" theory might be developed to accommodate intransitive
indifference. An alternative to this is to accept the original model
as an idealization and to use only strict preference judgments in
its analysis, so that strict equality of expected utilities is never
employed when an indifference judgment arises. To some extent,
I have used this approach in comparing expected utilities of
strategies in [16].

There are a number of axioms in the third category. In the
states model the sure-thing axioms' principle effect is to permit
the derivation of numerical probabilities for the states. If someone
does not like the idea of personal probability (and many people
do not) and if he feels generally favorable toward most of the
axioms of the theory, then it is likely that he will direct his criticism
at axioms in the third category.

An example of a sure-thing axiom is: if, for each state, an individual likes the consequence that arises under strategy A as much as the consequence that arises under strategy B, then he will like A as much as B. A more subtle independence axiom is: if you prefer A to B when they give the same consequence under one particular state and if C and D are respectively obtained from A and B by changing the common consequence under the particular state, then C will be preferred to D. Allais [1] and Ellsberg [15] criticize the latter axiom, and Savage [42] and Raiffa [35] respectively answer these criticisms.

Figure 6 presents one of Ellsberg's examples. An urn contains 30 red balls and 60 black and yellow balls, the latter in an unknown

	30 balls	60 balls	
	Red	Black	Yellow
A	$100	$ 0	$ 0
B	$ 0	$100	$ 0
C	$100	$ 0	$100
D	$ 0	$100	$100

Fig. 6—Amounts You Might Win

proportion. One ball is to be drawn at random from the urn after you make your choice. If you had to select A or B, which would you choose? If you had to select C or D, which would you choose? Ellsberg says that a frequent response pattern is (A,D). Is it yours? If so, and if these choices reflect strict preference, then you violate the second axiom for this situation in the preceding paragraph.

In responce to this, Raiffa [35] notes that if you prefer A and D, then you would surely prefer a composite gamble that gives you A if a flipped coin lands heads up or D if the coin lands tails up in preference to the composite that yields B with heads (H) or C with tails (T). Since the order in which the coin is flipped and the ball is drawn should not make any difference, we can represent this situation as in Figure 7. Assuming that you regard H and T as equally likely, Figure 7 shows that, regardless of which composite

	Red		Black		Yellow	
	H	T	H	T	H	T
(A, D)	$100	$ 0	$ 0	$100	$0	$100
(B, C)	$ 0	$100	$100	$ 0	$0	$100

Fig. 7—Composite Gambles

you choose and regardless of which color ball is drawn, you will be equally likely to get $100 or $0. Hence it seems reasonable to suppose that, in fact, you will be indifferent between (A,D) and (B,C) in violation of the strict preference noted above.

The general purpose of the axioms in the final category is to ensure that the numerical utility model is one-dimensional. Without such axioms it may be necessary to characterize a utility by a sequence of numbers rather than by a single number with the understanding that one consequence or strategy is preferred to a second if, and only if, the first position in the two utility sequences for which the two position numbers are not equal has the larger of the two position numbers in the first sequence. The classic paper in expected utility that does not use an Archimedean axiom is Hausner's paper [23] on multidimensional utility. In a companion paper Thrall [52] presents some situations where one-dimensional utility may seem unrealistic.

An example that would violate a typical Archimedean assumption is the following. A newly minted penny will be flipped n times. You are offered a choice between A and B:

    A. Receive $1 regardless of the results of the n flips,

    B. Be executed if every flip results in a head, and otherwise receive $2.

If, no matter how large n is taken to be, you prefer A to B, then you will violate the axiom, assuming of course that you prefer $2 to $1 to execution. If the coin is flipped 100 times, then under B there is only one sequence of the more than 1,000,000,000,000,000, 000,000,000,000,000 possible sequences under which you would be executed. In view of such numbers many people might find a satisfactorily large value of n for which they would choose B. It is often claimed that the willingness that many people show toward small risks such as crossing the street or driving a car is sufficiently convincing evidence in favor of the axiom.

References

1. M. Allais, "Le comportement de l'homme rationnel devant le risque: Critique des postulates et axiomes de l'école américaine," *Econometrica* 21 (1953), 503-46.

2. F. J. Anscombe and R. J. Aumann, "A Definition of Subjective Probability," *Annals of Mathematical Statistics* 34 (1963), 199-205.

3. W. E. Armstrong, "The Determinateness of the Utility Function," *Economic Journal* 49 (1939), 453-67.

4. ———, "Uncertainty and the Utility Function," *Economic Journal* 58 (1948), 1-10.

5. K. J. Arrow, "Exposition of the Theory of Choice under Certainty," *Synthesis* 16 (1966), 253-69.

6. R. J. Aumann, "Utility Theory without the Completeness Axiom," *Econometrica* 30 (1926), 445-62.

7. ———, "Utility Theory without the Completeness Axiom: A Correction, *Econometrica* 32 (1964), 210-12.

8. S. Beer, *Decision and Control* (New York. Wiley, 1966).

9. J. Bentham, *An Introduction to the Principles of Morals and Legislation* (1823; reprinted in part in 32).

10. H. Chernoff, "Rational Selection of Decision Functions," *Econometrica* 22 (1954), 422-43.

11. C. W. Churchman, *Challenge to Reason* (New York: McGraw-Hill, 1968).

12. D. Davidson, P. Suppes, and S. Siegel, *Decision Making: An Experimental Approach* (Stanford, Calif.: Stanford University Press, 1957).

13. B. de Finetti, "La prévision: Ses lois logiques, ses sources subjectives," *Annales de l'Institut Henri Poincaré* 7 (1937), 1-68. Translated by H. E. Kyburg in 25.

14. B. de Jouvenal, *The Art of Conjecture,* trans. N. Lary (New York: Basic Books, 1967).

15. D. Ellsberg, "Ambiguity and the Savage Axioms," *Quarterly Journal of Economics* 75 (1961), 643-69.

16. P. C. Fishburn, *Decision and Value Theory* (New York: Wiley, 1964).

17. ———, "Preference-Based Definitions of Subjective Probability," *Annals of Mathematical Statistics* 38 (1967), 1605-17.

18. ———, "Methods of Estimating Additive Utilities," *Management Science* 13 (1967), 435-53.

19. ———, "Utility Theory," *Management Science* 14 (1968), 335-78.

20. ———, "An Abbreviated States of the World Decision Model," *IEEE Transactions on Systems Science and Cybernetics* 4 (1968), 300-306.

21. ———, "A General Theory of Subjective Probabilities and Expected Utilities," *Annals of Mathematical Statistics* 40 (1969), 1419-29.

22. ———, "Intransitive Indifference in Preference Theory: A Survey," *Operations Research* 12:2 (1970), 207-28.

23. M. Hausner, "Multidimensional Utilities," *Decision Process* (New York: Wiley, 1954).

24. Y. Kannai, "Existence of a Utility in Infinite Dimensional Partially Ordered Spaces," *Israel Journal of Mathematics* 1 (1963), 229-34.

25. H. E. Kyburg and H. E. Smokler, eds., *Studies in Subjective Probability* (New York: Wiley, 1964).

26. R. D. Luce, "Semiorders and a Theory of Utility Discrimination," *Econometrica* 24 (1956), 178-91.

27. ———, and D. H. Krantz, "Conditional Expected Utility," (mimeo., January 1968).

28. ———, and H. Raiffa, *Games and Decisions* (New York: Wiley, 1957), chap. 13.

29. K. O. May, "Intransitivity, Utility, and the Aggregation of Preference Patterns," *Econometrica* 22 (1954), 1-13.

30. A. C. Michalos "Postulates of Rational Preference," *Philosophy of Science* 34 (1967), 18-22.

31. W. C. Michell, "Bentham's Felicific Calculus," *Political Science Quarterly* 33 (1918), 161-83. Reprinted in 32.

32. A. N. Page, *Utility Theory: A Book of Readings* (New York: Wiley, 1968).

33. J. Pfanzagl, "Subjective Probability Derived from the Morgenstern-von Neumann Utility Concept," *Essays in Mathematical Economics in Honor*

of *Oskar Morgenstern,* ed. M. Shubik (Princeton, N.J.: Princeton University Press, 1967), pp. 237-51.

34. J. W. Pratt, H. Raiffa, and R. Schlaifer, "The Foundations of Decision under Uncertainty: An Elementary Exposition" *Journal of the American Statistical Association* 59 (1964), 353-375.

35. H. Raiffa, "Risk, Ambiguity, and the Savage Axiom," *Quarterly Journal of Economics* 75 (1961), 690-94.

36. ———, *Decision Analysis* (Reading, Pa.: Addison-Wesley, 1968).

37. F. P. Ramsey, "Truth and Probability," *The Foundations of Mathematics and Other Logical Essays,* (New York: Humanities Press, 1950). Reprinted in 25.

38. A Rapoport, *Strategy and Conscience* (New York: Harper & Row, 1964), pp. 19 ff.

39. ———, "Game Theory and Human Conflicts," *The Nature of Human Conflict,* ed. E. B. McNeil (Englewood Cliffs, N.J.: Prentice-Hall, 1965).

40. H. Rubin, "Postulates for the Existence of Measurable Utility and psychological Probability" (abstract), *Bulletin of the American Mathematical Society* 55 (1949), 1050-51.

41. W. S. Sahakian, *Systems of Ethics and Value Theory* (New York: Philosophical Library, 1963).

42. L. J. Savage, *The Foundations of Statistics* (New York: Wiley, 1954).

43. ———, "The Foundations of Statistics Reconsidered," *Proceedings of the Fourth Berkeley Symposium on Mathematics and Probability* 1 (1961) (Berkeley: University of California Press). Reprinted with changes in 25.

44. ———, "Bayesian Statistics," *Recent Developments in Information and Decision Processes,* ed. R. E. Machol and P. Gray (New York: Macmillan, 1962).

45. ———, *The Foundations of Statistical Inference* (New York: Wiley, 1962).

46. E. A. Singer, Jr., *On The Contented Life* (New York: Henry Holt, 1936).

47. ———, *In Search of a Way of Life* (New York: Columbia University Press, 1948).

48. P. Suppes, "The Role of Subjective Probability and Utility in Decision-making," *Proceedings of the Third Berkeley Symposium on Mathematical Statistics and Probability* 5 (Berkeley: University of California Press, 1956), 61-73.

49. ———, "Some Open Problems in the Foundations of Subjective Probability," *Information and Decision Processes,* ed. R. E. Machol (New York: McGraw-Hill, 1960).

50. ———, and J. L. Zinnes, "Basic Measurement Theory," *Handbook of Mathematical Psychology,* ed. R. D. Luce, R. R. Bush, and E. Galanter (New York: Wiley, 1963) pp. 1-76.

51. R. O. Swalm, "Utility Theory-Insights into Risk Taking," *Harvard Business Review,* November-December, 1966, pp. 123-36.

52. R. M. Thrall "Applications of Multidimensional Utility Theory," *Decision Processes,* ed. R. M. Thrall, C. H. Coombs, and R. L. Davis (New York: Wiley, 1954).

53. A. A. Weinstein, "Individual Preference Intransitivity," *Southern Economic Journal* 34 (1968), 335-43.

54. R. A. Winkler, "The Assessment of Prior Distributions in Bayesian Analysis," *Journal of the American Statistical Association* 62 (1967), 776-800.

55. ――――, "The Quantification of Judgment: Some Methodological Suggestions," *Journal of the American Statistical Association* 62 (1967), 1105-20.

Bernhardt Lieberman

THE STUDY OF
COLLECTIVE DECISIONS

In the past thirty to fifty years, here in the United States, society's pressing problems have changed from being technological ones to social ones. It is certainly not necessary to catalog those of current concern; they are obvious to all, and to some degree, all social problems are decision problems. Society is concerned with which of two general approaches to the alleviation of poverty it should adopt; which of many specific programs designed to increase minority group employment should be funded; which of several plans for the improvement of urban housing should be pursued; which of a number of weapons systems should be developed; and which program for the solution of air pollution problems should be advocated? Although there are technological problems involved in all of these decisions, it is generally believed that the technical problems can be solved; the social problems and the questions of value are the perplexing ones.

Decision-makers, the men charged with the responsibility for making these choices, usually have insufficient evidence, differing values, a variety of personal, regional, and differing interests, and external pressures—all of which serve to make them very uncertain at decision time. Given these weighty, and apparently unsolvable, problems, decision-makers frequently turn to others for help with the solution of the problems, hoping that a detached, more objective observer with special or unusual training may offer assistance that the decision-maker's own staff cannot give. With the precedents of the physical and biological sciences, the accomplishments of medicine and engineering obvious to all, the decision-maker calls for analogous help from the social scientist. When he does call for help, he is faced with the array of social science traditions and approaches that have all the outward appearances of objective inquiry: journals, mathematics, monographs, laboratories, and computers—artifacts that in the past have solved so many problems. It is no surprise that the practical man of affairs comes to believe, and is led to believe, that the social sciences are able to solve his problems, much as the natural and biological sciences solved problems in earlier years. And fortuitously, and perhaps surprisingly, the decision-maker, the man plagued by doubts and difficulties, discovers that a body of knowledge exists specifically designed to understand how one should make proper decisions, and another body of knowledge exists describing how people actually do make decisions. This knowledge appears to be particularly impressive—it is mathematical; some of the most able and distinguished mathematicians, statisticians, psychologists, sociologists, and economists have contributed to it. It must appear to be interdisciplinary, mysterious, and wondrous.

When the decision-maker seeks help, much is offered to him. Most frequently he gets his aid from applied social scientists, either working for him or whose services he employs in either a contractual or consulting arrangement. He presents these men with a specific problem, and they either offer him a solution to the problem he originally raised or demonstrate to him that his definition of the problem is defective and that the problem must be redefined. They then proceed to offer solutions to the new, redefined problem.

Sometimes the decision-maker is satisfied with the solutions offered; other times he is not. The current urban-racial situation provides examples of problems that have been studied by social scientists for many years, but contributions to the solution of such problems have not been strikingly successful. And the disorders in American universities and colleges, the home of social scientific expertise, seem to have been solved most effectively by the use of force and administrative intuition rather than by the use of the social scientific knowledge resident in the universities.

It seems to be agreed that the behavioral sciences have not been as successful in solving social problems as the natural sciences have been in solving technical problems—though it should be asserted that the social sciences have had many dramatic successes. Various reasons have been offered for this relative failure; among them are that the groups that set out to solve the problems are too small, that large teams of workers are necessary for the solution of large social problems, and that too much time and effort is spent on useless basic research. Others hold the view that too much time and effort is spent on useless applied research done by groups of investigators, when we do not have an adequate knowledge base of fundamental theory and empirical findings. These questions will not be argued here.

Recently, some very sophisticated persons have begun to suggest that social scientists should proceed directly to solve urban problems just as the biological and natural sciences solved the problems of agricultural and rural America in the past century. Social scientists should do for urban society, it is said, what biologists, geneticists, and agricultural scientists did for rural soicety in an earlier day. The problems of air pollution, substandard housing, inadequate education, unemployment, and inadequate income should be solved just as it was possible to increase the yield of wheat, corn, and barley and to improve the quality of cattle and hogs. This admonition does not specify what the balance of basic and applied research work should be; it calls for both in some proper balance and a concerted effort to help decision-makers solve urban problems, using the power of objective, scientific inquiry.

Who can oppose a request to become involved even when it is offered as an admonition—it is virtue itself. What behavioral scientist is so mean that he will not attempt to solve the problems of air pollution, unemployment, housing, education, and poverty, particularly when his contribution may be in the acquisition of the basic knowledge that will enable others to solve the practical problems. There seems to be employment for all; handsome support can be offered to those with a taste for abstract work, and there are numerous challenging questions for those who wish to solve applied problems. The solution, then, is simple; let us begin the task.

This belief in the efficacy of social science, if held and offered naïvely, is at least erroneous and is perhaps dangerous. It is dangerous because the decision-makers whose problems are to be solved may react with displeasure and mild vengeance when the more stubborn urban problems are not solved quickly. And more and more behavioral scientists are becoming dependent upon decision-makers for their support, men who quite naturally want to understand the relationship of social science work to social problems. It is dangerous at this point—when scientists, including social scientists, are beginning to justify their efforts and support by showing the relationship of scientific effort to the public benefit—to offer the questionable hope that the problems of urban society can be solved in the future just as the technical problems of rural society were solved in the past.

This naïve view of the efficacy of social science is erroneous because it confuses technological problems and collective decision problems. The problem of increasing agricultural productivity was primarily a problem of understanding and manipulating a passive, neutral nature. When the scientist tries to solve technological problems, nature is not his opponent. She may be indifferent, enigmatic, or reluctant; but if the scientist is ingenious, he can understand her and solve his problem. This is not the case with our current social problems. They are to some extent technical problems. The antecedents of behavior must be understood; but even when this is done, a successful solution is not guaranteed, for current social problems are more political than they are technical. They are problems whose solutions involve conflicts of interests among different groups. A potentially successful solution may be satisfactory to one group and disadvantageous to some other very influential group, and so it is no surprise that such a solution is not adopted. In the language of decision theory it can be said that technical, technological problems are one-person games against nature, whereas most social problems are n-person, non-zero-sum games or collective decision problems.

Analyses of the structure and properties of one-person games against nature and of collective decision problems indicate clearly that the former are far simpler than the latter. Mathematical probability theory tells us much that is valid about one-person games, but the n-person game and collective decision problems present much more stubborn and intractable problems, both practically and mathematically.

Some examples may help to clarify these remarks. Consider the successful attempt to reduce air pollution in Pittsburgh after World War II and the unsuccessful attempt to implement Daniel Moynihan's plan to strengthen the structure of the Negro family. For the sake of this discussion the former can be considered a successful resolution of a collective decision problem, and the latter an unsuccessful resolution of such a problem, though some will want to disagree with this statement.

After World War II, Pittsburgh was still plagued by an air pollution problem so severe that on the very worst days the sky over the city became so dark in the middle of the day that street lights were frequently turned on at noon. Pittsburgh, for better or worse, has a rather centralized power structure. When that power structure became determined to eliminate the grossest aspects of the air pollution problem, they were remarkably successful: Pittsburgh was transformed in a relatively short time from a city with a unique and severe pollution problem to a city no sootier than many American cities. This was accomplished, not as the result of any startling research program that developed unusual, new technical knowledge, but by using the available technology and solving the collective decision problem. An analysis of power is essential to the understanding of social choice processes.

This example of ridding the Pittsburgh air of much of its pollution is an unusual one because in most social choice situations power is not so centralized; more usually it is unevenly spread among a number of participants, and many conflicting interests operate to prevent the solution of societal problems. Whatever the technical difficulties involved in the solution of air pollution problems are, it appears to be quite obvious that some of the difficulty in solving these problems can be traced to the interests of automobile companies and other industries located in or near our cities. These remarks are not meant to be condemnatory; they are offered in a descriptive spirit, pointing out the importance of considering the material interests and power relations when one is concerned about the solution of societal, social choice problems.

The controversy over the Moynihan Report, which resulted in the rejection of his suggestions, is an example of a social choice problem that was not solved because it was seen to be contrary to the interests of groups that could and did wield a veto power. Moynihan's report called for attempts to alter the family structure of underclass Negroes who have disorganized, or unconventionally organized, patterns of family life.

The report was not adopted for many reasons. Some argue that its arguments were based on propositions about behavior, and propositions about the economy, that were and are invalid. This may be true, but it is very difficult to know; it is far more clear that the proposal was defeated because a number of groups saw that the plan was contrary to their interests. Government officials administering other welfare programs saw that it was clearly contrary to their interests. Some of the most vociferous opponents of the plan were civil rights leaders who saw the plan as being contrary to their strategy of stressing the value of the customs of blacks—even if these customs might be disfunctional. These black politicians may have perceived that although the report, if implemented, might have led to short-run benefit, it would have been contrary to their own interests, and the interests of their constituencies, in the long run. Specific proposals that might have been developed from the logic of the Moynihan Report were not adopted.

The controversy over the Moynihan Report illustrates that the solution of societal decision problems is a twofold process. First, valid propositions that describe and explain human behavior must be discovered, and then programs based on these propositions must be implemented. This latter task requires that political, collective decision processes be understood. Thus, valid propositions that describe and explain behavior in social choice or collective decision situations must be discovered.

Since many believe this latter task to be a central question, a number of investigators have been studying the collective decision problem, trying to understand both how such decisions are actually made and how they should be made. Investigators have been examining the question of how persons combine their individual preference patterns into a social choice. It is a fundamental question about which there has been much speculation and an amount of mathematical work; but there have been few, if any, empirical studies dealing directly with the question. The problem is ubiquitous, and examples abound. The members of the Security Council of the United Nations must decide to take or not take some action; a president of the United States must be selected from the millions of eligible citizens, but particularly from the dozen or so likely possibilities; a university research institute must plan a research program that will interest its members who have diverse preferences and satisfy its sources of support; consumer goods must be produced and distributed to satisfy the preferences of millions of consumers; Congress must apportion the defense budget among the army, navy, air force, and marines; and a family must decide whether to live in the city or a suburb. All of these diverse decisions have something in common; in some way the preferences of different individuals or groups must be summed or amalgamated into a social or group choice.

Societies, groups, and organizations have produced a variety of decision-making procedures: the majority vote with veto power;

the majority vote without veto power; the economic market mechanisms; the dictatorial father who decides unilaterally where the family will live; bargaining and persuasion among the joint chiefs of staff; the advisors to the secretary of defense who use techniques of modern mathematical economics; the executive committee or governing board that reaches a consensus and imposes its decisions on a larger group; and the system of primary elections and conventions for the selection of the presidential candidates. Group decisions are made in these and many other ways.

Some Brief Historical Remarks

Mathematical work dealing with these election and social choice problems appears to have had its origins in the second half of the eighteenth century in the work of Borda and Condorcet. An anomalous situation that has been termed variously the paradox of voting or the Condorcet effect has intrigued thinkers for almost two hundred years. Its fascination stems from the fact that it illustrates that the very structure of a social choice situation can produce a perplexing or disturbing result. Consider the following situation.

Let 1, 2, 3 be three alternatives; let A, B, C be three individuals and let (A,B,C) be the community. Let $1 > 2$ mean 1 is preferred to 2. If for A, $1 > 2$, $2 > 3$, and we assume transitivity, then $1 > 3$. Similarly for B, if $2 > 3$, $3 > 1$, then $2 > 1$. For C, if $3 > 1$, $1 > 2$ then $3 > 2$. Since a majority, A and C, prefer 1 to 2, and a majority, A and B, prefer 2 to 3, we would hope that a majority also prefers 1 to 3. But this is not the case, B and C prefer 3 to 1.

This perplexing situation becomes more vivid if we consider an analog of it, the following game, *where side payments, payoffs among players, are not allowed.* The game is described by the payoff matrix shown in Table 1.

In this situation the three players, A, B and C, must select a single alternative among 1, 2, and 3. If they choose 1, A receives 30 dollars (or jobs if the payoff is patronage in a political situation), B receives 10, and C receives 20. If alternative 2 is chosen, A receives 20, B receives 30, and C receives 10. If they choose 3, A receives 10, B receives 20, and C receives 30. Examining this situation, we can see that A prefers 1, B prefers 2, and C prefers 3. Since side payments are not allowed, there is nothing in the structure of the situation that will enable the three participants to come

TABLE 1

	PAYOFF TO:		
ALTERNATIVE	A	B	C
1	30	10	20
2	20	30	10
3	10	20	30

to some agreement about the selection of the alternative. If side payments were permitted, the three could agree on alternative 1, for example, and A could give B a payment of 10; there would then be an equal division of the rewards, one possible and common outcome. The situation is indeed perplexing; nothing in its structure gives a clue to its solution. As we have defined the situation, even the decision rule is not specified; we have not said whether a majority vote or a unanimous choice is required to select the alternative.

Another possible way of obtaining a group choice in this situation would be to present two of the three alternatives, have the three players choose the one they prefer, and then have them compare the third alternative with the alternative they preferred from the first pair. However, if this is done, the order of presentation of alternatives will affect the outcome. For example, if 2 and 3 are compared first, 2 will be preferred by a majority. Then, if 2 is compared with 1, 1 will be preferred by the majority and will be the group choice. If, however, the first pair considered is 1, 3 and then 2 is compared with the survivor, the group choice will be 2. For theorists seeking a rational, universal social choice procedure, the fact that the order of presentation of alternatives affects the outcome is highly unsatisfactory.

Situations such as this one and similar aberrant ones helped to stimulate mathematicians to investigate the formal properties of election processes. The general problems the theorists attempted to solve can be stated as, "How can we design an election procedure that will produce a result consistent with the preference patterns of the participants? How can we design an election procedure so that the order of the presentation of alternatives does not spuriously determine the outcome? How can we assure ourselves that the 'wrong' candidate is not selected?" Borda, Condorcet, Laplace, Frances Galton, the Reverend C. L. Dodgson (Lewis Carroll), and others have considered the problem [3].

In the late nineteenth century and in this century, economists set themselves the task of discovering a social welfare function, a general rule or process by which any given set of individual preference patterns could be merged into a social choice.

For the purpose of this discussion, we define the social welfare functions as [1]

> a rule or process which produces a group or social choice from the individual orderings of alternatives, or from the preferences of the individuals involved. The rule must produce a satisfactory social choice, in every case no matter how contradictory the preferences of the individuals involved.

In a work that has since become a classic, Arrow demonstrated that given a number of reasonable conditions about the choice structure—where there are at least two persons involved and three or more alternatives to choose from—it is not possible to construct a general social welfare function. He also demonstrated that where the alternatives are limited to two, no matter how many persons are involved, the majority decision rule is a satisfactory social welfare function. Arrow's work served as a stimulus to a variety of theoretical studies of the normative question.

The Normative and the Descriptive Problems

The problem of combining individual preferences into a social choice has both normative and descriptive aspects. The normative question is, briefly, how *should* we combine individual preferences to obtain sensible, consistent, or rational results? The descriptive question is, essentially, how *do* individuals, groups, and economists actually amalgamate their preferences?

For two reasons it seems appropriate to raise the descriptive question. First, Arrow has shown that, if we allow only ordinal measurement, or ranking, it is not possible to obtain a general social welfare function. But the fact that Arrow has demonstrated the impossibility of the abstract task does not prevent individuals from actually merging their preferences. Each day innumerable decisions of this kind are arrived at. In fact, attempts to circumvent the Arrow paradox raise behavioral or descriptive questions. Luce and Raiffa discuss a number of ways of overcoming the difficulties presented by Arrow. These include obtaining more data about the values or preferences of the participants. This process involves utilizing behavioral scaling methods and also gives some information about the strengths of preferences of the participants. Where we can obtain measures of the strengths of preferences by utilizing risky alternatives, lotteries, and also by utilizing well-established behavioral scaling techniques, we can often obtain a satisfactory resolution of a difficult social decision question [16].

Consider the following example of two persons, A and B, and two alternatives, 1 and 2. A ranks the alternatives 1, 2, and B ranks the alternatives 2, 1. If we assume that neither party has sufficient power to determine the outcome, the preference structures lead to a stalemate, an irreconcilable conflict. However, if we can take into consideration the strengths of preferences of the participants, the following example makes it clear how trivial the case can be. Consider the case of a husband and wife who are considering going to a movie (1) or a concert (2). The husband prefers 2, the wife prefers 1. If the husband's preference of 2 to 1 is only slight, but the wife's preference is very great—she actively dislikes the music being performed on that night—in all likelihood, the conflict will be resolved in favor of going to the movie, and with relatively little effort and little ill feeling.

Even this brief example reveals that people in actual social decision situations have a variety of techniques for resolving difficult problems of social choice. These resolutions may or may not be optimal or particularly rational, however, it is of considerable interest to examine these techniques carefully.

How Decisions Are Actually Made

In the discussion above we saw that Arrow demonstrated that, given certain reasonable conditions, it is not possible to obtain a general social welfare function; but we also saw an example of a husband and wife who, with little effort, were able to make a satisfactory social choice, although they had contradictory preference patterns, by taking into account each other's strengths of preference.

Difficulties arise when preference patterns are contradictory; often, but not always, persons involved in making a choice have consistent preference patterns that enable them to make a large number of group choices with little difficulty. In addition, persons who cluster together often have similar preference patterns over a wide range of choice domains prior to their interaction in a group;

and as they function together and interact, their preference patterns become more similar, resulting in a large number of social choices that are concluded with little difficulty. However, many situations yield a constellation of preference patterns that lead to disagreement about social choice, and it is these perplexing situations that present the intellectual and practical challenges.

The conduct of international affairs provides us with situations in which numerous anomalous and paradoxical preference patterns exist; often, in international affairs, it is difficult to make side payments. Husbands and wives, political leaders in a legislature, faculty members in a university department, and the employees of complex organizations often have many ways in which they can bargain, negotiate, and effect side payments to enable them to effect satisfactory social choices in difficult situations. But in the conduct of international affairs the fundamental interests of the participants are often in intractable conflict, and internal constraints—national politics, for instance—may operate on the leaders to prevent them from striking what might be desirable bargains.

If we examine just how group decisions are arrived at, we may note that a variety of behavioral processes or factors influence the outcome; these vary from the power of the various members—a single member of the group may have sufficient power to determine the group choice—to the strength of preferences of the participants, and the personality and intellectual characteristics of those involved. We will discuss the various determining behavioral processes under the following headings:

1. The distribution of power
2. The joint welfare function
3. Bargaining and coalition formation processes
4. Individual differences of the participants
5. Group processes and phenomena
6. Previous experiences and commitments of the group members, and the possibility of future social choices

The Distribution of Power

In many situations the social choice is effected rather simply and directly; a single person has the power to determine the decision, and where the preference patterns of those involved are contradictory or anomalous, he exercises that power. The dictatorial father who decides where the family will live; the president of a small college who makes an appointment when his deans and faculty cannot agree; the president of a small company holding 51 percent of the stock of the company, who makes a decision by himself when his employees are in hopeless disagreement—all of these are examples of the exercise of dictatorial power.

At the opposite extreme from the situation of dictatorial power is a situation in which power is equally distributed among all participants involved in the decision process. Perhaps the most vivid and detailed example of such a situation is the election described in C. P. Snow's novel *The Master*. In this piece of fiction Snow describes in detail the bargaining, personal preferences, unconscious processes, and other considerations that exist when a group of eleven men, all with equal power and the desire to exercise it, produce a social choice.

However, in most decision situations the power is not so simply distributed among the participants in the decision; in the large number of social choice situations power is neither equally dvided among all participants nor does a single person hold sufficient power to determine the decision. More often power is diffused among participants, with some having a great deal, others having very little, and some having a moderate amount. Often the exact distribution of power among those involved is not known even to the participants. Each has some approximate estimation of the power distribution, but the distribution of power may be only imprecisely defined, and judgments about relative power may differ.

To obtain an understanding of how social choices are made, it is necessary to clarify the role of power in the decision process. Although there have been many interesting, speculative analyses of power in the sociological literature, little of it sheds useful light on the social choice problem [2, 4, 5, 9, 10, 14, 17]. Recently, however, the literature of game theory has produced some insightful notions that bear directly on the processes of social choice. The discussion in this paper will deal with the distribution and the role of power among a group of persons who must effect a social choice. The ideas of Shapley, and Shapley and Shubik will be discussed; their notion of power is termed σ-power here [22, 23]. A notion of power, termed δ-power, will be introduced that will emphasize the participants' perception of their own power to influence the decision process.

Shapley and Shubik have offered a method for evaluating the distribution of power in social choice situations where a specific decision must be made and the voting power of each participant is known. A committee in which each member has a single vote, the Security Council of the United Nations where the major powers have a veto, and a corporation where the power is distributed according to the ownership of stock are examples of such situations.

The notion of power (σ-power) attempts to solve the problem that is raised by the fact that power is not always distributed exactly as votes are distributed. When one man holds 51 percent of the stock in a corporation, for many purposes he holds complete power, and the decision processes of such a group usually reflect this reality; the persons involved usually defer to the power holder. They attempt to influence decisions by influencing the majority stockholder. In the situation in which each person has a single vote the σ-power distribution is identical to the distribution of votes. In a group of four persons, where the votes are distributed 10-5-5-1, the person holding the ten has more than fifty percent of the power, though his votes total to fewer than fifty percent of the total.

Shapley and Shubik offer a definition of power in which the power of each member of a decision-making group depends on the chance he has of being critical to the success of a winning coalition; the chance he has of effecting a winning coalition. Hence, where one man is a winning coalition he has complete power; where each person has a single vote they each have equal σ-power. In situations between these extremes, the power distribution is not so clear and the calculation of σ-power is more subtle.

The Shapley and Shubik definition of power does not take into consideration the many personal, political, and sociological factors that affect any analysis of power in an actual social choice, but as they point out, their scheme is a very useful first approximation of the actual power distribution in a committee or group situation. They explain the general rationale for their definitions of power as follows.

Consider a group of individuals all voting on some issue. They vote in order, and as soon as a majority has voted for a resolution, it is declared passed. The voting order of the members is chosen randomly and it is possible to compute the frequency with which an individual belongs to the group whose votes are used to effect the decisions; and more importantly, it is possible to compute how often the person is *pivotal*. This number, the number of times the person is *pivotal*, yields the index of σ-power. This index yields a measure of the number of times the action of an individual affects the decision, changes the state of affairs of the group. The Shapley and Shubik scheme credits an individual with *1/nth* power where there are *n* persons each holding one vote. If votes are weighted unequally, the resulting power distribution is complicated; generally more votes mean more power, but σ-power does not increase in direct proportion to an increase in votes.

Considering the passage of a bill in our executive-congressional system, the σ-power of the House of Representatives, the Senate, and the president are in the proportion of 5:5:2; and the σ-power indices for a single congressman, single senator, and the president are in the proportion 2:9:350. In the Security Council, which consists of eleven members, five of whom have vetoes, the σ-power measure gives 98.7 percent to the Big Five and 1.3 percent to the six small powers. Each major nation has a power ratio greater than 90 to 1 over a single smaller nation. A share owner in a corporation holding 40 percent of the stock with the remaining 60 percent distributed equally among 600 small shareowners has a power index of 66.6 percent. The 400:1 ratio in share holdings yields a power advantage greater than 1,000 to 1 [23].

It is quite clear that this very precise measure of power in a committee system is only an approximation of the realities of the decision process in social choice situations. As a result, it is necessary to introduce another concept, δ-power, which is designed to describe the power distribution the participants in a decision process actually act upon.

In some committees or social decision situations, where the decision rules and voting weights are explicitly formulated, the σ-power index can serve as an excellent first approximation of the actual distribution of power among the participants. When the appropriate historical, sociological, and psychological analysis is done, it is possible to obtain a realistic picture of the role power plays in effecting the social choice. However, in a large number of social choice situations decision mechanisms are not explicitly defined, and the participants behave on the basis of their own beliefs about, or perceptions of, their power. Understanding these phenomena is essentially the understanding of a set of beliefs, a social-psychological process. Any analysis of a complex social choice process, where the power mechanisms are not explicitly defined, requires this analysis of the δ-power distribution, an analysis of the participants's beliefs about their own power to influence the decision.

The σ-power and δ-power analyses are not unrelated, for in the dictatorship situation and in the situation of equal or near equal distribution of power, the participants ordinarily have reasonably accurate perceptions of their power. In the former situation the persons involved usually attempt to affect the decision by influencing the powerful person; in the latter situation the persons involved are usually aware that their power is *1/nth* of the total. In the situations between these two extremes, where it takes some effort to compute the σ-power distribution even when we know the Shapley formula, the most confusion occurs; and the participants may be confused or uncertain about their power.

In complex organizations, this complex and indefinite power situation is often present. Two, three, ten, or even more people may share the power to determine a decision. A detailed analysis of the facts of the situation and the perceptions and beliefs of the participants is necessary to untangle the threads of the power relations.

The Joint Welfare Function

In the example discussed above, of the husband and wife who had contradictory preference patterns, we saw that the conflict was solved simply and directly. This simple resolution was made possible because the husband perceived that his wife had a strong distaste for alternative B and a strong preference for alternative A, whereas he had only a slight preference for B over A. Difficult social choices may be resolved by taking into account the strengths of preferences of the participants. A decision process that allows a single group member to veto a proposal makes explicit use of the belief that a single, strong, negative preference should be allowed to outweigh all other positive preferences. The veto provisions of the Security Council voting procedures and the ability to veto entrance into membership in college fraternities and adult social clubs are examples of this process.

When this technique is used, when persons involved in the social choice process take into account the strength of preferences of other participants, it becomes clear that some intuitive process involving interpersonal comparison of utility is involved. We may hypothesize that the decision process is one in which some *Joint Welfare Total* is maximized; where a difficult social choice decision is made, we hypothesize that intuitive interpersonal comparisons of utilities are made [11, 12, 13, 16, 21, 24].

If we examine the husband-wife decision to go to the movie—select alternative 1—in these terms, the following analysis may shed light on the decision. We assign the utilities to the situation as shown in Table 2.

TABLE 2

ALTERNATIVE	PAYOFF TO:		JOINT PAYOFF
	H	*W*	*Sum*
1	8	10	18
2	10	−30	−20

If the couple goes to the movie (selects alternative 1), the payoff to the group is 18, whereas if they go to the concert (select alternative 2), the payoff to the group is −20.

It is possible to develop a more sophisticated line of reasoning using a simple algebraic model suggested by Sawyer [19]. We have hypothesized that a group tends to select the outcome that offers the highest Joint Welfare Total (JWT) to it; the JWT may be computed as follows:

Let individuals be designated $A, B, \ldots, Z$.

The payoffs to the individuals are $P_a, P_b, \ldots, P_z$.

The alternatives to be chosen are designated $1, 2, \ldots, n$.

The payoff to the set of individuals for the various alternatives are designed $P_{a1}, P_{a2}, \ldots, P_{zn}$.

A payoff to another person may not have the same value to one's self as an equal payment to one's self. This may be expressed in the model by assuming that a payoff to another person is some fraction or multiple of the payoff to one's self. Then, the parameters that reduce a payment to another to a payment to one's self may be designated

$$x_{ab}, x_{ac}, \ldots, x_{ba}, x_{bc}, \ldots, x_{zx}, x_{zy},$$

where x_{ab} is the fraction that transforms a payment to B to a payment to A.

The members of a group faced with a decision communicate among themselves, and in this process they are able to communicate to each other—in some intuitive or perhaps explicit way—the utilities of the various alternatives to each other. Once these communications are possessed by the members of the group, some intuitive multiperson, interpersonal comparison of utilities process occurs. Discussions, bargaining, clarifications, and the like occur, and then the group choice is made.

We are now in a position to examine how a group of individuals may determine the Joint Welfare Total of the various alternatives from which they must select a group choice. Consider the example of Table 1. The JWTs may be computed once the parameters are hypothesized [19, pp. 3–9]. If, for person A, a payoff to another person is worth one half of a payment to himself, then $x_{ab} = x_{ac} = 0.5$; and if for person B, a payoff to another is worth just as much as a payoff to himself, then $x_{ba} = x_{bc} = 1$; and if for C, a payoff to another is worth only $1/100$ of a payment to himself, then $x_{ca} = x_{cb} = 0.01$. The Joint Welfare Totals can be computed using the following formulae:

$$JWT \ (\text{Alt. } 1) = P_{a1} + (x_{ab} \ P_{b1} + x_{ac} \ P_{c1}) + P_{b1} + (x_{ba} \ P_{a1} \\ + x_{bc} \ P_{c1}) + P_{c1} + (x_{ca} \ P_{a1} + x_{cb} \ P_{b1})$$

$$JWT \ (\text{Alt. } 2) = P_{a2} + (x_{ab} \ P_{b2} + x_{ac} \ P_{c2}) + P_{b2} + (x_{ba} \ P_{a2} \\ + x_{bc} \ P_{c2}) + P_{c2} + (x_{ca} \ P_{a2} + x_{cb} \ P_{b2})$$

$$JWT \ (\text{Alt. } 3) = P_{a3} + (x_{ab} \ P_{b3} + x_{ac} \ P_{c3}) + P_{b3} + (x_{ba} \ P_{a3} \\ + x_{bc} \ P_{c3}) + P_{c3} + (x_{ca} \ P_{a3} + x_{cb} \ P_{b3})$$

Substituting the values of Table 1 and the values of x_{ab}, x_{ac}, . . . , x_{cb} we can compute the value of JWT (Alt. 1):

$$JWT \ (\text{Alt. } 1) = 30 + [.5 \ (10+20)] + 10 + [1 \ (30+20)] \\ + 20 + [.01 \ (30+10)] = 125.4$$

The Joint Welfare Totals of Alternatives 2 and 3 can be computed similarly:

$$JWT \ (\text{Alt. } 2) = 110.5; \ JWT \ (\text{Alt. } 3) = 125.3$$

Since the Joint Welfare Totals of Alternative 1 and Alternative 3 are approximately equal and larger than that of Alternative 2, we hypothesize that it is unlikely that Alternative 2 will be chosen. The probabilities of choosing Alternatives 1 and 3 are approximately equal. However, the arguments concerning the Joint Welfare Total are but one factor of the many that determine a social choice. For the simple example of the husband and wife who had to choose between the concert and the movie, maximization of the Joint Welfare Total appears to be an adequate hypothesis. In other more complex decision situations, the many factors dealt with in this paper may modify the decision. For example, where one person has the power to determine the decision he may select the alternative that maximizes the payoff to himself, though another alternative might have a higher Joint Welfare Total. Some other relevant factors will be discussed below.

Bargaining and Coalition Formation Processes

When persons must combine contradictory preferences into a social choice in situations in which the power distribution does not permit a single individual to determine the outcome, the process is completed successfully usually because the participants are able to bargain, negotiate, form coalitions, compromise, and make side payments among themselves. The usual social choice situation in a realistic setting is complex enough so that the persons involved may effect a satisfactory social choice by producing an outcome that yields some rewards to each participant who holds some power. This procedure of dividing the rewards of the social choice situation is analogous to the payoff function—and the phenomenon of making side payments—of game theory. In fact, in the earlier explication of the Condorcet effect the ordinal statements of the original paradox were transformed into a game-like statement, assuming cardinal measures of the utilities.

Thus, the theory of games of strategy may be seen to be a theory for the production of social choices among individuals with different preference patterns. Payoff functions are the ways of expressing the preference patterns of the persons involved; the person prefers the outcome with the largest payoff to himself, or in the case of the non-zero sum game, the alternative with the highest Joint Welfare Total.

Game theory has been seen to have both descriptive and normative aspects. The entire corpus of solution theory may be seen to be prescriptions for the production of reasonable social choices. Two-person, zero-sum theory prescribes a reasonable value of a game when the parties involved are in direct conflict. In two-person, non-zero sum and n-person theory, solutions, to the extent they are successful, prescribe the social choices the parties should make when there are elements of both conflict and cooperation present.

In a series of papers Thomas Schelling has offered a series of hypotheses concerning bargaining processes and has related them to choices, decisions, and strategies in the conduct of international affairs. Schelling is primarily responsible for an entire reorientation of game theory, from zero-sum, non-zero-sum orientation to one in which social choices are conceived of as being on a continuum from pure coordination, through mixed motive games, to pure conflict games. Schelling has offered a variety of provocative hypotheses about the role of communication, bargaining, threat, promises, and a variety of other behavioral phenomena. Schelling's work too can be interpreted to offer hypotheses about certain social choice problems [20].

Since most social choices can be effected only if coalitions are formed, processes of coalition formation must be understood, if an understanding of social choice mechanisms is to be obtained. Gamson recently reviewed experimental studies of coalition formation and found "an encouraging convergence of theoretical explanations of coalition formation" [8]. He discusses four "theories" of coalition: a minimum resource theory, a minimum power theory, an anticompetitive theory, and an utter confusion theory.

The minimum resource theory "emphasizes the initial resources to effect a decision which the players bring to the situation, rather than their strategic bargaining position." The central hypothesis states that a coalition will form in which the total resources (weights or votes) are as small as possible, while still being sufficient to effect a decision favorable to the coalition that has formed [8, p. 86].

The minimum power theory is a modification of the minimum resource theory. It makes use of the Shapley value and states that all participants will demand a share of the payoff proportional to their pivotal power (σ-power in terms of this paper). This pivotal power hypothesis is again a minimum resource hypothesis, but in this case the power of the winning coalition is defined by the Shapley values, σ-power [8, p. 88].

Gamson describes a hypothesis about the formation of coalitions derived from the work of Vinacke and his associates. Players whose behavior supports the anticompetitive hypothesis are focused on maintaining the social relationships in the group. An anticompetitive norm exists against efforts to strike the most advantageous deal possible. Coalitions will form along the lines of least resistance [8, p. 90].

Gamson offers an "Utter Confusion Theory"; he states: "Many coalition situations are conducted under conditions which are not at all conductive to rational calculation and analysis. It is well known that political conventions, for example, are frequently scenes of bedlam. Thus, according to this theory, coalition formation is best understood as an essentially random choice process. The coalition which forms will be the result of such fortuitous events as a chance encounter or a missed telephone call" [8, p. 92].

Individual Differences

When individuals actually are attempting to merge their preferences into a social choice, undoubtedly characteristics of the individual—certain individual differences—play some role. It is possible to hypothesize that certain cognitive intellective factors such as intelligence, bargaining ability, and persuasiveness do have an effect. Some people may be particularly skillful bargainers, or particularly skillful in the task of persuasion, and they may effect a social choice in their favor. Also, certain personality factors may affect outcomes; a more aggressive person may be more effective in having the outcome be favorable to himself. Even though at this time it is not possible to specify what particular factors or individual characteristics do affect outcomes, there is every reason to believe, a priori, that individual characteristics do affect outcomes. The few studies that have been done that have attempted to examine the effect of individual differences on bargaining and negotiation behavior have been rather disappointing [6, 7]. Undoubtedly, individual differences do affect the outcomes of bargaining processes; however, until now it has been difficult to specify precisely what individual characteristics do affect outcomes in a particular way. This is probably because our studies of individual differences, though there are many of them, have not isolated significant factors that affect bargaining behavior. It may also be that the part that individual differences play may be small and may be masked by the formal, structural properties of the bargaining situations.

Group Processes

The present analysis deals with the summation of individual preferences of members of a small group. The extensive literature of the field of small groups then can be seen to bear upon the present analysis. However, the small group literature is an extensive, uncoordinated body of knowledge with few, if any, general principles that can aid in the understanding of the processes of social choice. There are, however, numerous studies that yield isolated results that are relevant to the present problem. Vinacke and Lieberman, in separate studies, found that in cases of three-person interaction two individuals may unite against a third whom they perceive to be stronger; they will form a coalition and gain rewards from the stronger-appearing person [15, 25]. Schelling, too, has argued that in a bargaining situation the weaker member may gain concessions from the stronger because the two have coordinate interests and the stronger must yield concessions to the weaker [20].

Careful review of the small group literature would undoubtedly reveal other studies that describe phenomena—characteristics of individuals functioning in a group situation—that will shed light on social choice processes. These many phenomena considered together may detail a picture that is not particularly elegant or simple; but then, it is likely that an understanding of the processes of social choice, when we obtain it, will not be elegant or simple either.

Previous Experiences and Future Social Choice Possibilities

One set of processes that undoubtedly have great influence on the social choice problem, but have been virtually unstudied, are the processes involving the effect of past commitments and decisions, and anticipations of the effect of future social choice situation and commitments on the present problem. Difficult social choice situations, where preference patterns are hopelessly contradictory, may be resolved because of the past experience of the group, or because those members of the group who have their preferences satisfied can make commitments about future social choices, making concessions or promises in advance.

The group in an actual social choice situation is usually one with a significant past history, and also the prospect of continued lengthy existence in the future. This feature often enables the participants to make a difficult social choice; but this feature is particularly difficult to study experimentally, and even empirically. However, a thorough treatment of the question of social choice must deal with such questions.

Concluding Discussion

Now that we have examined the normative and descriptive aspects of the social choice question, we are in a better position to understand why our social problems are so difficult to solve, what some genuine contributions to the solution of these problems the behavioral sciences might make, and also what the limitations of these contributions might be. The rigorous study of collective decisions has shown us that conflicting preference patterns can transform a seemingly simple problem into one that is exceedingly difficult to solve. The Condorcet paradox shows us that when only three persons must choose from as few as three alternatives a hopeless situation can arise. It should be no surprise, then, that when many people must choose from many alternatives we will frequently have intractable conflicts.

The behavioral sciences can make a variety of contributions to the solution of social problems. They have made in the past, and they can continue to make in the future, the conventional contribution of generating valid propositions about behavior: they can tell us how we can change attitudes, what the mechanisms of prejudice are, what we have to do to understand and change complex organizations, how we can educate more efficiently, and how we can motivate and reward people to elicit behavior we think desirable.

But valid propositions about behavior do not automatically lead to the adoption of programs designed to solve social problems based on these valid propositions. Our studies of decision-making, including the study of collective decisions, have a number of unique contributions to make to the solution of social problems beyond merely clarifying why we have difficulty in finding such solutions.

Studies of collective decision-making, including game theory, provide the decision-maker with a set of concepts and a way of thinking that can be most valuable. The decision-maker whose analyses of his problems include an explicit consideration of the notions of rational solution, the utilities of the actors involved, bargaining and coalition formation, power, and the fair division of payoffs will have a clearer picture of his problems. In particular, collective decision-making analyses offer very sophisticated notions of a fair or rational solution of a conflict. The naïve decision-maker usually has only vague notions of what a fair or rational solution to his problem is; the student of game theory and social choice can, in some instances, give rather mathematically precise definitions of the notions of rationality and solution. Even where our solution notions are inadequate, our analyses make explicit the precise nature of the inadequacy. The analyses of rationality in the game theory literature accomplish a similar task: they make precise what the criteria of rationality are. Thus, we may know quite precisely in what sense our behavior is, and is not, rational.

The analyses of solutions found in the literature of game theory and Arrow's impossibility theorem tell much about the difficulty of finding convincing, desirable outcomes in difficult conflict situations. The difficulties in finding solutions to n-person games illuminate the reasons for the difficulties of the resolution of conflicts that exist in real life. And Arrow's theorem makes it clear that it is unlikely that a general social welfare function will be found.

These shortcomings and limitations of the normative aspects of the study of collective decision-making helped to stimulate the study of the descriptive aspects of the problem—how people actually do make decisions. Such studies have yielded knowledge of bargaining and negotiation processes, insight into the phenomena of trust and threat, and information about how closely actual behavior conforms to the prescriptions of the rational models. Not all of these studies have something to tell about actual decisions taken in real life, but there have been few attempts to apply the descriptive findings to actual problems. In one attempt, a notion of trust was discovered in a study of behavior in a three-person game that shed light on the processes of coalition formation and trust as they exist in the conduct of international affairs. Until more such work is done it will be difficult to know precisely how useful descriptive work can be.

In conclusion, it can be said that our studies of collective decision-making processes can be of some help to those persons who must make the decisions involved in the solution of social problems, either because our current normative and descriptive work can at present yield benefits, or because we can construct models of decision processes that more closely approximate reality. However, this assertion should not be interpreted to mean that social scientists can proceed in rapid order to solve collective decision problems as, in earlier days, technological problems were solved. However, the juxtaposition of abstract work with the press of reality will make it more likely that studies of collective decisions will contribute to the solution of social problems.

References

1. K. J. Arrow, *Social Choice and Individual Values*, 2d ed. (New York: Wiley, 1963).
2. R. Bierstedt, "Analysis of Social Power," *American Sociological Review* 15 (December, 1950), 730-36.
3. D. Black, *The Theory of Committees and Elections* (Cambridge: Cambridge University Press, 1958).
4. A. Etzioni, *Modern Organizations* (Englewood Cliffs, N.J.: Prentice-Hall, 1964).
5. J. R. P. French, Jr., "A Formal Theory of Social Power," *Psychological Review* 63 (May, 1956), 181-94.
6. L. Fouraker and S. Siegel, *Bargaining Power* (New York: McGraw-Hill, 1963).
7. P. S. Gallo, Jr. and C. G. McClintock, "Cooperative and Competitive Behavior in Mixed-Motive Games," *Journal of Conflict Resolution* 9 (March, 1965), 68-78.
8. W. Gamson, "Experimental Studies of Coalition Formation," *Advances in Experimental Social Psychology*, ed. L. Berkowitz, vol. 1 (New York: Academic Press, 1964).
9. H. Goldhamer and E. Shils, "Types of Power and Status," *American Sociological Review* 45 (September, 1939), 171-82.
10. J. C. Harsanyi, "Measurement of Social Power in n-Person Reciprocal Power Situations," *Behavioral Science* 7:1 (1962), 67-80.
11. ———, "Cardinal Welfare, Individualistic Ethics and Interpersonal Comparisons of Utility," *Journal of Political Economy* 65 (1955), 309-21.
12. ———, "Cardinal Utility in Welfare Economies and in the Theory of Risk-Taking," *Journal of Political Economy* 61 (1953), 434-35.
13. C. Hildreth, "Alternative Conditions for Social Orderings," *Econometrica* 21 (1953), 81-94.

14. H. D. Lasswell and A. Kaplan, *Power and Society* (New Haven, Conn.: Yale University Press, 1950).

15. B. Lieberman, "Experimental Studies of Conflict in Two-Person and Three-Person Games," *Mathematical Models in Small Group Processes,* ed. J. Criswell, H. Solomon, and P. Suppes (Palo Alto, Calif.: Stanford University Press, 1962).

16. R. D. Luce and H. Raiffa, *Games and Decisions* (New York: Wiley, 1957).

17. G. Psathas and S. Stryker, "Bargaining Behavior and Orientations in Coalition Formation," *Sociometry* 28 (June, 1965), 124-44.

18. W. H. Riker, "Voting and the Summation of Preferences," *American Political Science Review* 55 (December, 1961), 900-911.

19. J. Sawyer, "The Altruism Scale: A Measure of Cooperative, Individualistic, and Competitive Interpersonal Orientation," *American Journal of Sociology* 71 (January, 1966), 407-16.

20. T. C. Schelling, *The Strategy of Conflict* (Cambridge: Harvard University Press, 1960).

21. R. Sohlaifer, *Probability and Statistics for Business Decisions* (New York: McGraw-Hill, 1959).

22. L. S. Shapley, "A Value for *n*-Person Games," *Contributions to the Theory of Games,* Vol. II, ed. H. W. Kuhn and A. W. Tucker (Princeton, N.J.: Princeton University Press, 1953).

23. ———, and M. Shubik, "A Method for Evaluating the Distribution of Power in a Committee System," *American Political Science Review* 48 (1952), 787-92.

24. P. Suppes and J. L. Zinnes, "Basic Measurement Theory," *Handbook of Mathematical Psychology,* Vol. I, ed. R. D. Luce, R. Bush, and E. Galanter (New York: Wiley, 1963).

25. W. E. Vinacke and A. Arkoff, "An Experimental Study of Coalitions in the Triad," *American Sociological Review* 22 (August, 1957), 406-14.

part **2**

DECISION-MAKING AIDS

Ronald L. Ernst
Marshall C. Yovits

INFORMATION SCIENCE
AS AN AID TO
DECISION-MAKING

The interconnections between information science and decision-making, as two areas of study and research, are becoming increasingly clear. The discussion that follows seeks to describe these interconnections and relationships through the use of a generalized model of an information system.* The model is believed to have general applicability to a wide variety of real-world decision-making situations and provides opportunities for quantification of aspects of decision processes. The utility of the model may be measured in terms of how well it satisfies these conditions.

Generalized Information Systems

Previously [12, 13], it has been proposed that the flow as well as the science of information may most conveniently be viewed and understood with the use of information systems. Such systems are abstractions of the essential components of command and control systems, management systems, document systems, biological and human information processing systems, and so on. A generalized information system consists of four interconnected components as depicted in Figure 1.

The components are an information source that acquires and

---

*The authors wish to acknowledge the partial support of the National Science Foundation through the Computer and Information Science Research Center at the Ohio State University in the development of the material presented.

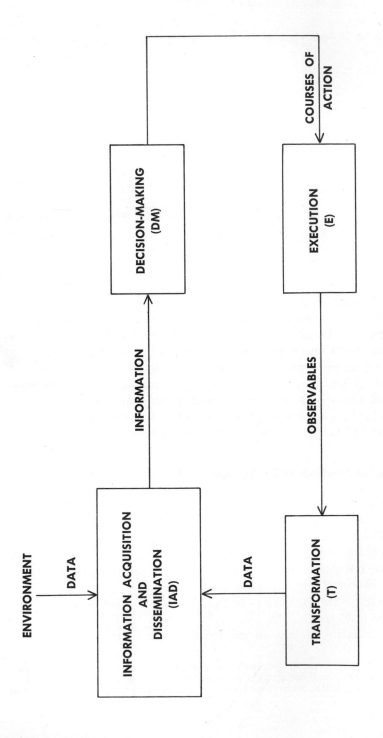

Fig. 1. Generalized information system.

disseminates information (IAD), a decision-maker that accepts the information from the source and disseminates courses of action (DM), an execution function (E) that takes the courses of action and converts them into observables (the resultant of the courses or plan of action), a transformation function (T) that accepts the observables and transforms them into data that are fed to the IAD. Each component thus accepts and disseminates measurable quantities, is capable of performing operations on the quantities, and further has storage or memory capability. With respect to the latter, the IAD contains data obtained from the environment, from the transformation already discussed, and basic reference data; the DM stores information about the system, environment, and as will be noted later, may store information about the system operation; E stores methods of transforming courses of action to observables, and likewise T stores the conversion function of observables to data.

From this brief description it should be obvious that the generalized information system possesses the characteristics originally stated as being desirable. It is an organization that has generality, applicability, utility, reality, and is quantifiable.

In this model the decision-maker plays a dominant role. From the generalized information systems point of view, the decision-maker must satisfy the conditions of accepting, storing, and operating on information to generate courses of action [13]. However, the suggestion that the decision-maker may have stored information about the environment and system operation and the fact that the decision-maker generates courses of action or plans indicates that decision-making is a central and dominant function of information systems, and hence a focal point of information science. The purpose of this paper is to explore some of the implications of decision-making as a major function within information science.

Decision-Making

Decision-making has been approached from at least three distinct points of view. One approach is descriptive: it attempts to describe how a decision is made, not only in terms of the antecedent conditions, but the decision-making process, the state of the decision-maker at the time of the decision, and the consequences of the decision. Another approach is formal and prescriptive or normative in nature. This approach is exemplified by game theory [e.g., 7], statistical decision theory [e.g., 2], and Bayesian decision theory [e.g., 10]. The third approach is somewhat nebulous: it implies that decision-making cannot really be understood.

The first two of these approaches are well known. For this reason, little note will be made of them other than to point out that their impact has been substantial, particularly in management science and in the design of military command and control systems. The third, however, presents an entirely different problem for our approach.

The origin of the problem stems from the feeling that decisions may be influenced by a number of factors, many of which have no apparent bearing on the information provided. That is, for all intents and purposes, an independent observer either sees no directly relevant information or may presume that extraneous information has been used in making a decision. The former case is sometimes called a "shadow" decision. The latter is commonly referred to as an irrational decision. It usually involves political, social, or personal considerations.

Analysis of the problem posed by this approach reveals a relatively simple solution. The analysis is common among all decision-making theories and is resolved in the following way: consider the decision-maker—either man or machine—as a black box receiving information, processing it, and emitting courses of action. Formally, this constitutes a mapping of the courses of action onto the input information. In this approach, this mapping is unknown or little understood. For the other two theories, the mapping is either known or may be calculated.

More formally, the decision-maker may be treated as a machine in an algebraic sense, that is, as a finite state machine. A finite state machine possesses an initial, a transitional, and terminal state [e.g., 3]. For present purposes, the initial state is the information input. There are two major sources of sets of information associated with the initial state. These are from the information source, or IAD, as we have termed it, which includes information about the environment as sampled by the IAD, and whatever is stored in the decision-maker's memory. The terminal state is the courses of action generated. There are three major classifications of terminal states. These are (a) the courses of action either a priori adequate—known to result in a single course of action or set of courses of action given the input state, (b) a posteriori adequate—found to result in a single course of action or set of

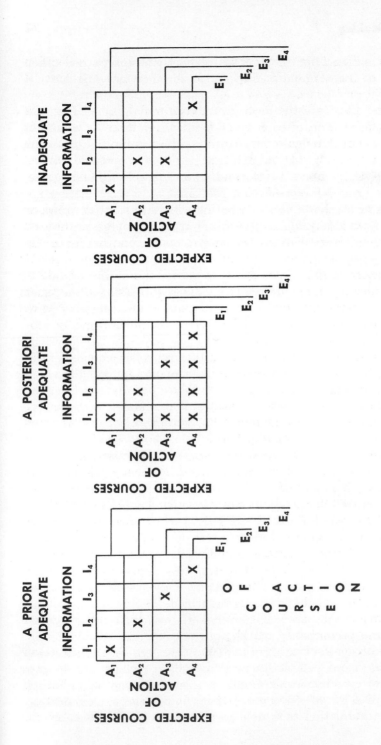

Fig. 2. Examples of decision matrices.

courses of action after the process of decision-making has taken place (c) or indeterminate, that is, no singular mapping may be found.

To better illustrate the nature of the terminal states, Figure 2 shows a typical form of each given a known or fixed information input state. In this figure, an arbitrary information input of four states $(I_i, i=1, \ldots, 4)$, an arbitrary set of four possible courses of action $(A_j, j=1, \ldots, 4)$, and four unique terminal states, $(E_k, k=1, \ldots, 4)$ representing the input to the E function are used. The figure shows how (by noting whether or not the rows or columns are uniquely filled) the initial state I progresses through the transitional state A to the terminal state E, and whether or not E is unique.

The purpose of this discussion is to clarify the nature of a decision. In summary, there are relatively few distinct states that exist in decision-making. Moreover, this discussion also suggests ways of making decisions within the context of the general model proposed at the outset of the paper. That is, how can the decision-maker utilize information from the IAD and select courses of action? The abstract structure provides a means for handling this and related questions.

All of the initial and terminal states of the model, with the exception of one, have been defined. The exception consists of what may be stored in the decision-maker's memory. One possibility includes prior experience (political, economical, social, historical, and so on) related to the decision-maker's frame of reference. Another includes his knowledge of system operation. The latter case is treated in detail, mainly because it may be formalized more rigorously than the former. Essentially, we are proposing that the decision-maker has knoweldge of system operation, how the system should operate, and what should constitute "good" system operation. Although this may be experiential to a large extent, many of the aspects of the decision-maker's knowledge of system operation have been or are capable of being identified.

The point is that the decision-maker must have some overall model of the performance of the total system that results in he generation of some set of observable actions. This model need not be—and for more complex situations will probably not be—an analytical or even explicable model. It need not even be a rational model. It is a frame of reference that the decision-maker uses to relate the information to which he has access to some set of observables. As indicated, this model will probably be heavily influenced by the background, experience, and outlook of the decision-maker. Indeed, when it is sometimes said that a particular type of decision-making is an art, it is meant that the model can be learned only by experience and cannot be described in analytical terms. "Common Sense" would also fall into this category.

When additional information is received by the decision-maker, he then establishes some courses of action that will result in observable actions. Information about these observables is eventually fed back to the decision-maker so that he can decide whether his model and his decisions were accurate and satisfactory. If the information fed back is not the expected information, then the decision-maker can either change his decisions, resulting in new courses of action or he can change his model of the process. These ideas have already been developed in detail [12, 13].

Knowledge of system operation, including environmental factors, may be represented as in Figure 3. In this figure, the decision-making function is represented as the IAD, E, and T functions, each of which, rather than a real entity as in the generalized model, is a perceived or inferred characteristic of system function. The flow, indicated by the numbers 1, 2, and 3, constitute the mapping of A onto I, anticipated observable actions, and anticipated data respectively. That is, it is assumed that the decision-maker is aware of, and effectively uses characteristics of, the environment of the system, and that he has knowledge of environmental factors influencing his own behavior. In the same sense, it is further assumed that he has knowledge of the operation of the IAD—how it collects, stores, disseminates information, and how data from T are returned to it and processed through it—and of pertinent sources of perturbation. The same is held for the other functions—namely E and T. It is assumed that the decision-maker infers how execution is accomplished, what the necessary inputs and probable outputs are, and what factors influence the E function. For T, both observables and data are presumed known as is the processing function and environmental inputs. Quite generally, this is a delineation of what is held in store in the DM, with the additional qualification that the decision-maker may have knowledge of what perturbs or influences his decision and how this influence occurs.

Knowledge of this kind is frequently referred to as "know how," "executive capability," or simply a description of the model of system operation. The internalization of the system is superficially

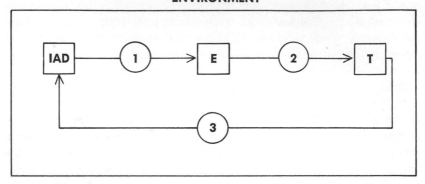

ENVIRONMENT

① Information
② Courses of Action
③ Data

Fig. 3. Representation of stored information in decision-making model.

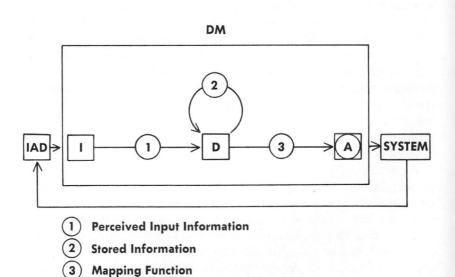

DM

① Perceived Input Information
② Stored Information
③ Mapping Function

Fig. 4. Decision-making subsystem.

similar to a concept proposed by Churchman [4]. This concept is of a world view or Weltanschauung held by the decision-maker relative to the system he is regulating or managing. Our point of view differs to the extent that the world view is a structure internal to the decision-maker, and hence part of his processing capability.

From our point of view, the primary function of the decision-maker is to establish that mapping of information into courses of action which best regulate the system given the constraints of the system already delineated. Since this may be accomplished in a variety of ways depending upon the system constraints, further formalization is profitable. The formalization is realized by returning to the model of the decision-maker as a finite state machine. The underlying assumptions, namely initial, transitional, and terminal states along with several instances of each have already been given. The present discussion is limited to these instances and, in a sense, is a recasting of the problem.

For the recasting, consider the decision-making subsystem outlined in Figure 4. This subsystem consists of the IAD feeding information as the subsystem input. The subsytem output is courses of action to E and T as a combined subsystem. Within this subsystem, the principal components are I, the information input set, D, the decision which includes the internalized total systems model as stored information, and A, the courses of action generated. The behavior of the subsystem is governed by the I, D, and A functions, and these transformations within the subsystem. These transformations may be represented in detail by the arrow-associated numbers 1, 2, and 3, in Figure 4.

Number 1 represents the link of the perceived information to the decision-maker. Number 2 indicates stored information within the decision function. This information can be compared with the input set of information. The result of this comparison is a set of projected courses of action designated by number 3.

Each of these states and their transitions should be thought of in terms of expected values, that is, as anticipated events or occurrences. In this respect they are "hypothetical." Given an information set, however, they are fully capable of being estimated.

The flow and possible routes of flow, denoted by the arrows, generate a number of models of decision-making. For illustrative purposes, four possible types of models are shown in Figure 5.

The model at the top of the figure represents decision-making where there is little a priori uncertainty regarding the execution of

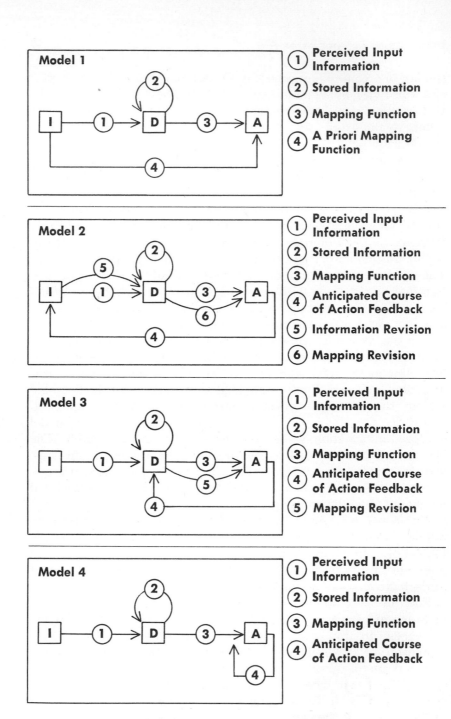

Fig. 5. Four models of decision-making subsystems.

a decision and its influence on system behavior. Each component and numbered arrow flow are identical to that of Figure 4 except that an additional flow, designated by the number 4, is included. This represents the case of a fixed and known decision for one set of input information. This model is appropriate for decision-making systems for which specific, well-understood, unique courses of action are associated with each set of input information. It is analogous to the a priori adequate class of terminal states.

The second model shown is exceedingly more complex. In addition to the components and flow of Figure 4, A feeds back the expected action to the information input for a check on its suitability. (This is indicated by number 4 in the diagram.) In such a situation multiple courses of action that may be generated are considered, and the resulting output data are compared with the input information. Thus, a best course of action may be decided upon through further processing. From the comparison the information must again be inputted to D through 5. This input is a modified information input. A new mapping function indicated by number 6 is produced. This model arises from the necessity of the decision-maker to compare the results or anticipated results of his decision with the original information. In order for courses of action to be generated, the original input information must be revised, re-inputted, and remapped. The model is analogous to one of the a posteriori adequate class; the feedback is required to obtain proper system activity.

A special case of this model is given in the third example. For this model, feedback to D takes place through number 4, and a new mapping function to A through 5 is generated. This model revises a decision on the basis of expected outcomes of courses of action. It is the widely known Bayesian model.

Finally, the fourth example indicates a decision model of a form such that no singular course of action or consistent set of courses of action may be made. This model indicates a situation in which two distinct sets of information and courses of action could result in the same execution or an execution irrelevant to the information. Although this could imply that the information or courses of action were equivalent or redundant, it could also imply that the mapping function could not lead to a unique terminal state A. Such a model could arise under a variety of circumstances. The fourth model represented in Figure 5 illustrates an anticipated course of action that loops back on itself through number 4. The loop obviously could lead to an inconsistent set of courses of action transmitted to the E function, a reserved decision, or no decision at all.

As previously noted, with these simple considerations many models of decision-making could be constructed. They could differ not only in structure and flow but in content. The formal structure, however, is highly significant in that it provides the basic features of decision-making. Moreover, when applied to an actual decision-making situation, the structure is quantifiable. Criterion measures—times, errors, and probabilities, for example—could be substituted for any of the numbered transitions in the flow diagrams. Finally, it should be pointed out that the emphasis throughout has been on anticipation. That is, how does the decision-maker expect his decision to be processed?

Information and Decision-making Aids

We have now established a close relationship between information and decision-making by establishing the role of decision-making within generalized information systems. However, we have spoken of information loosely. At this point it is important to establish a rigorous definition of information.

Information has many distinct meanings. One meaning involves the exchange of a communication with linguistic or semantic content [e.g., 1]. Another meaning is quantitative, involving the measurement of numbers of available choices [e.g., 11] or precision of measurement [e.g., 5, 6]. Yet another meaning refers to printed matter, verbal communications, visual communications, and similar kinds of sources.

Within a generalized framework, each is too restrictive to provide the necessary criteria, utility, and analytical expressions for application to realistic situations, such as may be treated by information science. For this reason, we have chosen to define information as "data of value in decision-making." The definition is not new, having been proposed earlier by McDonough and Garrett [8]. Moreover, Payne [9] has extended the notion by suggesting that the value and use of information is the principal factor for the existence of information systems. The point to be stressed is that information is not raw data or isolated facts but a structure that can be used by the decision-maker in regulating the system. The structure is obviously dependent not only on the particular system but on the decision-maker. To this extent, information is highly "context" sensitive."

Context sensitivity is in part system and environment dependent and in part decision-maker dependent. The extent of context sensitivity can be illustrated by considering what is required of operating information systems.

Operating information systems should have several desirable informational characteristics. A partial listing of such characteristics includes accuracy, relevance, timeliness, sufficiency, lack of bias, and adequacy. Accuracy refers to the "truthfulness" or fidelity of the information. Relevance refers to the bearing the information has on the control or regulation of the system. Timeliness refers to the time of the arrival of the information. Sufficiency is concerned with whether or not the content of the information, though accurate, has distortion. Adequacy refers to the amounts of information that the decision-maker needs; typically he receives too little or too much.

If these criteria are not met, the difficulty of making a decision is compounded greatly. Generally, the decision-maker is forced into a situation of relying on his own judgment or stored information, attempting to make a good guess, delaying his decision, or reserving his decision entirely. From a systems point of view, information generated under these conditions has little value. The consequences for system operation could easily be catastrophic. This follows not only from the desirability of the characteristics but from casual observation. Yet, somehow the system usually seems to survive.

We believe that the model we have proposed suggests not only ways in which these criteria may be achieved but also how, in their absence, the system continues to function. For the former, the issue is resolved by systems design; for the latter, the issue is resolved by systems analysis.

A partial solution can be found within our model by considering what is contained within the information acquisition/dissemination function, the decision-making function, and the interface of the two. Initially, because we have defined information as data of value in decision-making, the IAD must contain data that in part satisfy the criteria listed. Such data may be viewed as a set of elements generally, although in fact the precise content will depend on the system itself. The elements of the data set must be capable of being structured. It is the structuring that exerts a profound influence over decision-making. The form of the data elements is not of great importance: they may be independent, dependent, or, by some rule, implicative of some other element. The structure may be either contained in the data set or inferred from the set by the decision-maker.

Inferences by the decision-maker regarding the processing of the information may be made. The types of inference possible we have previously identified as conversation, reduction, or translation [13]. In conservation the decision-maker preserves the information content as his information input. In reduction he reduces the set of data as his informative input; and in translation he changes the form or the structure of the data as his informative input. The interface, then, must be capable of transmitting the information. Because passive dissemination of information is not likely to possess the degree of desirability of any of the criteria mentioned, it may be more fruitful to allow an interrogative or interactive interface in which the decision-maker may ask questions of his data base.

Reconsideration of the models of decision-making developed here reveals some of the motivation for their application. The models were anticipatory in the sense that the decision-maker was assumed to be expecting the system to behave in a certain way. System feedback, then, is important in the sense that the decision-maker needs to compare the output of the system with his own expectations. It was also for this reason that the models were developed as internalizations of the system. From a systems design point of view, the information acquisition/dissemination function should contain data highly relevant to the decision-maker's needs. He may then, by appropriate interrogation, obtain information about the system behavior before executing a course of action by examining the likely system outputs. Moreover, the actual feedback provides him with a check on both the accuracy and the adequacy of his model or mapping function.

We believe that this systems approach is not only fruitful for the future design of information systems but for the understanding of information science. Information science is the study of information systems of this general form. Information systems may be dichotomized as artificial or natural, depending upon whether or not they were constructed by man. It is also possible to have mixed systems, resulting either from the evolution of an artificial system to a system containing natural properties or the evolution of a natural system to a system containing artificial properties.

The criticality of the decision-making function in information systems has been shown. The future or fruitfulness of our approach remains to be seen, since it relies heavily on the application and potential modification of the generalized information systems model to specific information systems.

For decision-making aids the implications are fairly straightforward. The information contained within the source must serve the needs and uses of the decision-maker. To a large extent it must be capable of responding to intelligent questions asked of it, particularly when the initial set of information is not sufficient to provide the decision-maker with a potential set of courses of action. Thus the source should be interactive with the decision-maker in some degree. Because the information must serve the needs and uses of the decision-maker, it must naturally be system relevant. Without relevance, execution and transformation are impossible. Finally, the entire system, defined by its components, must provide feedback to the decision-maker. It is only in this way that the decision-maker can evaluate the adequacy of his model and subsequent actions. We have indicated that this closure is through the Information Acquisition/Dissemination function. In the absence of the closure, the decision-maker remains in a state of uncertainty. To aid him in the reduction of his uncertainty, feedback through his source is obviously required.

References

1. Y. Bar-Hillel and R. Carnap, "Semantic Information," *British Journal of the Philosophy of Science* 22 (1953), 86-105.
2. D. Blackwell and M. A. Girschick, *Theory of Games and Statistical Decisions* (New York: Wiley, 1954).
3. T. L. Booth, *Sequential Machines and Automata Theory* (New York: Wiley, 1967).
4. C. W. Churchman, "Hegelian Inquiring Systems," Internal Working Paper No. 49, September, 1966, Space Sciences Laboratory, University of California, Berkeley.
5. R. A. Fisher, "Theory of Statistical Estimation," *Proceedings of the Cambridge Philosophical Society* 22 (1925), 700-725.
6. D. A. S. Fraser, "On Information in Statistics," *Annals of Mathematical Statistics* 87 (1966), 890-96.
7. R. D. Luce and H. Raiffa, *Games and Decisions* (New York: Wiley, 1957).

8. A. M. McDonough and L. J. Garrett, *Management Systems: Working Concepts and Practices* (Homewood, Ill.: Irwin, 1965).

9. A. H. Payne, "On Measuring the Value of Information—With Implications for Communications Systems," Institute for Naval Analyses Report No. AS 624 785 (January, 1965), Washington, D. C.

10. H. Raiffa, *Decision Analysis* (Reading, Pa.: Addison-Wesley, 1968).

11. C. E. Shannon, "A Mathematical Theory of Communication," *Bell System Technical Journal* 27 (1948), 623-56.

12. M. C. Yovits, "Generalized Information Systems," *Electronic Handling of Information,* ed. A. Kent et al. (Washington: Thompson, 1967).

13. ———, and R. L. Ernst, "Generalized Information Systems: Some Consequences for Information Transfer," Computer and Information Science Research Center Report No. 1968-1, October, 1968, Ohio State University, Columbus, Ohio.

Charles M. Eastman

TOWARD A THEORY OF
AUTOMATED DESIGN

Ongoing studies at Carnegie-Mellon University and elsewhere are attempting to specify the information-processing mechanisms by which people design. Being studied is how information given in a typical design problem is added to and modified so as to result in a finished design solution. Proposed specifications of design processes are being tested by modeling them on a computer. Specifically, these studies are moving toward the development of computer programs that will accept as input the typical information available to a designer, apply the same or more elaborate considerations and processes, and output a finished design solution. Currently, principal efforts involve architectural design.

One motive behind these efforts is to gain a better understanding of what intuitively seems to be intelligent and "creative" design. Such understanding may allow design to be better taught. This work also leads toward computer aids that may significantly augment human design capabilities. These efforts can be viewed as part of a larger effort concerned with computer augmentation of human intellect.

Human Problem-solving Processes

The psychological foundations of a theory of design have been well developed in the information-processing model of human problem-solving. Design is considered as a specific kind of problem-solving.

The premises of current problem-solving theory may be summarized as follows. It assumes that man's nervous system transforms and integrates information from the environment, from the individual's physiological feedback systems, and from his memory. "Thinking" is considered as the *process* that brings information from these various sources together to produce new information. All results from the processing of information is the product of the information content that is processed, the sequence in which it is brought together, and the means of processing used.

Most generally, human information-processing is a mode of decision-making. But it differs from traditional decision theory models in that the evaluation of individual decisions cannot be made directly. The issue is best understood by considering the classic example of chess. The goal of chess is to capture your opponent's king before he captures yours. Decision theory would require a player to identify and evaluate all move combinations in a decision tree so as to find the combination that leads to the goal. It is estimated that 10^{120} move combinations would require evaluation before any objective decision could be made for the first move. The issue is that no intermediate objective functions exist. Thus evaluation of chess moves according to a decision tree is in reality impossible. Many interesting tasks similarly lack means for direct evaluation. Other forms of decision-making are necessary. Problem-solving theory deals with indirect means for generating and evaluating decisions.

The information-processing approach to studying mental processes leads to several implications. All known modes of processing require the input information to be organized in a specific *representation* or *language* [4]. The *elements* represented in the language (the equivalent of words in verbal language and variables in mathematical languages) can only be combined or transformed according to specific rules, known as the *syntax* of the language. Thus, given some information requiring processing, it seems necessary that a person transform it into some sort of language, then process the information according to appropriate syntactical rules applied to the information elements. A syntax is not deterministic, but only partially puts bounds on how information can be related. Thus, appropriate secondary rules of processing must also be applied to allow the desired information to be efficiently generated.

Two examples of syntactic models of thinking are shown in

SYNTAX:

SENTENCE → NP + VP

NP   → FNP / (DET + N)

VP   → (VI + ADJ) / (V + NP)

FNP   → FN / (FN + ', who' + VP + ',')

ELEMENTS:

DET → 'a(n)' / 'the'

N   → 'store' / 'house' / 'bicycle'

FN   → 'John' / 'Grandfather' / 'Larry'

VI   → 'is'

V   → 'hit' / 'bought' / 'needs'

ADJ → 'old' / 'tired' / 'sorry'

EXAMPLES:

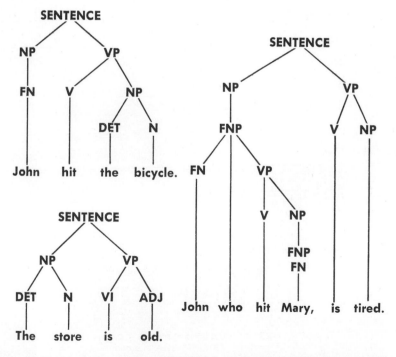

Fig. 1. A subset of the syntax of English is applied to a few of its possible elements. In the syntax and elements a "/" stands for the disjunctive *or* and the elements between quotation marks are literals. In the examples replacements are made from the top down. Lines from a node define the specific replacements made.

Figures 1 and 2. Figure 1 presents a very limited and simplified subset of the syntax for English and a few of its elements. Some of the sentences that can be generated with this system are presented. Notice in Figure 1 that some syntactic rules are *recursive*—they indirectly call themselves. Specifically, a noun phrase (NP) may be replaced by a formal noun phrase (FNP), which may be replaced by a verb phrase (VP). The verb phrase may consist of a verb and a noun phrase. Thus, a noun phrase may be a component of its own replacement. Recursive systems are theoretically capable of generating an infinite number of legal

SYNTAX:

Formula $\rightarrow$ f = f

R1 f = f $\rightarrow$ c + f = c + f

R2 f = f $\rightarrow$ c − c = c − f

R3 f = f $\rightarrow$ c ÷ f = c ÷ f

R4 f = f $\rightarrow$ c × f = c × f

R5 f + f $\rightarrow$ add operation

R6 f − f $\rightarrow$ subtract operation

R7 f ÷ f $\rightarrow$ divide operation

R8 f × f $\rightarrow$ multiply operation

ELEMENTS:

c $\rightarrow$ any numerical constant

f $\rightarrow$ any numerical function

EXAMPLE:

"If a certain number is multiplied by six and the product increased by forty-four, the result is sixty-eight. Find the number."

R3 $\rightarrow$ X × 6 + 44 − 44 = 68 − 44

X × 6 + 44 = 68

R8 $\rightarrow$ X × 6 = 24

R2 $\rightarrow$ X × 6 ÷ 6 = 24 ÷ 6

R6 $\rightarrow$ X = 4

Fig. 2. The syntax of arithmetic and its application to a simple problem. In school, each of us spends a good amount of time memorizing R4, R6, R7, and R8.

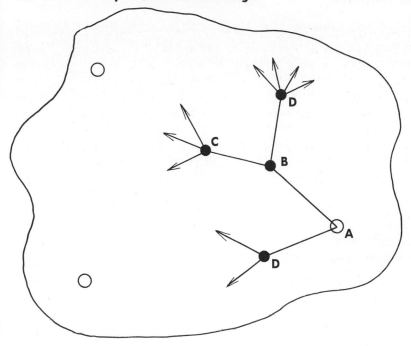

GIVEN:

    1. An initial information state A;
    2. A set of operators;
    3. A set of goals X.

FIND:

    An information state that satisfies X.

Fig. 3. Problem-solving may be conceptualized as a problem space, a set of operators, and a goal specification.

statements. Thus, finite processing rules can generate infinitely varied statements. Figure 2 shows the elements and syntax for a sheet of arithmetic. In this case, an initial input is provided. The task is to determine the appropriate syntactic rules to apply and their sequence in order to reach the desired result [see 9, 10, 20].

An alternative but functionally equivalent formulation of the syntactic model of information-processing is that of a *problem space* (Fig. 3). A problem space is defined by the given *problem state* and all permutations of operations that can transform this state into new states. Thus, the problem space is the set of all states possibly generated by a given formulation to a well-defined problem. Productive thinking involves the application of operators to knowledge states so as to achieve a state that meets given criteria [29]. In this formulation, a solution space is equivalent to a representation; operators are equivalent to syntactic rules.

In both formulations, secondary rules are needed to generate the desired information state. The conceptual attractiveness of the second formulation of problem-solving has encouraged the use of the terms *search* (of the problem space) and *search strategies* as the name for these secondary rules. Problem-solving studies have been especially interested in search strategies of large and complex problem spaces.

An issue only beginning to be studied is the means by which a task statement is translated into a workable problem specification. In most real problems, all the information needed is not given. The representation in which to solve the problem, the information elements operated on, the operators that can be utilized, or the goals to be achieved through processing—one or more may be missing. A subtask of problem-solving is the organization, expansion, and translation of the information given about the problem into a complete problem statement allowing processing. Figure 2 provides an example of the translating of the word problem into its arithmetic form.

This task recently has been formulated in an information retrieval paradigm where information from a problem-solver's experience and learning is accessed and translated into a language that facilitates processing [17]. A few programs have been written that automatically carry out this translation. For instance, Bobrow has written a program that translates a verbal description of a problem into its algebraic formulation [8]. Another program has been written that translates between English and geometric figures [12].

In summary, problem-solving processes seem to be made up of two classes of activities. One is a retrieval process that takes as input general information about a problem, organizes it, and augments it with information from a large storage bank. This process specifies the problem. The other is the search for an appropriate knowledge state within a particular problem formulation and language.

The usual means for studying problem-solving is to give a subject a complex task to solve. By carefully recording the external manifestations of changes in his knowledge state, much can be learned about the information brought to bear on any decision, the sequence of operators applied, the representations used, and his general strategy of problem-solving. All behavior—verbal, written, sketched, facial expressions, and so on—is recorded in a protocol. By analyzing the protocol, it is possible to determine the sequence of operations applied and the corresponding changes in the problem state. By analyzing the structure of different problem-solving protocols, and exploring the implications of alternative processing sequences, the theory of problem-solving is being elaborated [see 29, and 33, 26].

The Design Process

Generally, when the term *design* is used, it refers to the spatial arranging of physical entities. Although structural, mechanical, visual, and other forms of analyses are certainly a component of design, its central and integrating aspect seems to be the search for a physically realizable configuration that, when analyzed, satisfies the goals identified for the situation. Thus, design can be defined as the selection and arrangement of physical components in a two- or three-dimensional space subject to constraints and/or evaluation criteria. The constraints and evaluation criteria are derived from performance and qualitative requirements that the element being designed must satisfy [17].

Design clearly is an example of problem-solving. It is initiated when a task, normally explicated as the generation of construction specifications for some type of physical entity, is assigned. The entity to be produced must be realizable within a specific environmental and economic context. It also may be required to perform in a particular fashion or to possess particular attributes. Thus, there are acceptability or goal criteria. The specification required to complete the task assignment is not initially known. Information-processing must be initiated to determine its specific form.

Over thirty detailed protocols dealing with design problem-solving have been collected and analyzed by researchers at Carnegie-Mellon University. Some of these have involved realistic, though small, architectural, product, or engineering design problems. Others were abstract exercises whose purpose was to elaborate different aspects of the total design process. Several of these studies have already been presented in the literature [14, 17].

It is not possible to cover in detail here all of the insights and hypotheses that have come from these studies. Thus, only an overview is presented of what currently seems to be the necessary aspects of an intelligent and creative design process. The overview consists of insights gained both from theoretical work that applies information-processing theories of problem-solving to the task of design and from empirical studies of collected protocols of intuitive design.

PROBLEM SPECIFICATION

Upon receiving a design problem, a designer must interpret it according to available information. The relevant information may be available in his own memory and/or from external sources.

In memory, the general class of problems being considered seems to have associated with it a wide variety of information that has been relevant in the past. A set of physical elements that are the intrinsic components of the thing being designed is one kind of information associated with most problem classes. In architecture, these may include room types, attributes of those rooms, mechanical, structural site, and all the other types of physical elements normally available for consideration. In the Carnegie-Mellon University studies these components have been called Design Units (DUs). Also associated with the problem class are a variety of constraints and goals that usually seem to be necessary for the successful performance of the class of element being designed. Some of this information is directly associated with the problem class and is immediately retrieved. It is directly available to consciousness once the problem has been described. But other information is only indirectly associated and may require extensive processing before it can be accessed.

This general view of human memory is based on assumptions that information is both directly stored and regenerated from its elements. Its specific form is only a secondary issue. But to enable regeneration or retrieval from memory, cues must be provided that distinguish the desired information from all other that is potentially available or is to be uniquely regenerated. These cues seem to be *associative* in nature. That is, if the name of an object is provided, we can directly retrieve its attributes and function.

Conversely, if a list of attributes or functions are available, we may be able to directly retrieve the object. Information is stored according to content relationships. Associations relate verbal, visual, tactual, and all other kinds of information [see 13, 32].

Retrieval does not take place entirely at the outset of the problem. The initial problem inputs simply do not offer enough of the necessary access cues to distinguish all the information required to completely define the problem space. Instead, the designer utilizes the information immediately retrievable to begin searching his incomplete problem space. That is, he generates and evaluates possible solutions or aspects of solutions. In doing so, he generates new arrangement and spatial information that can be used as cues for new accesses to memory. These new cues allow further information to be retrieved about the problem. Designers are found to cycle between retrieval and search processes. The inference-making capabilities of this dual strategy seem extremely powerful. The detail strategies that are applied to identify when search or retrieval is appropriate have not yet been studied. The details of the control process directing this cycling may eventually explain many of the strengths and the weakness of human design capabilities [17].

REPRESENTATIONS IN DESIGN

Evidence suggests that man, like other information processors, is limited by the processing languages he has available. Each language extends his processing capabilities to new types of information and transformations. Thus, mathematics allows processing and information generation that is not possible without it. Orthographic projection allows spatial relations to be considered in more detail than would be possible otherwise [see 6].

In order to gain significant implications from or to integrate diverse information, it must be put into a form allowing processing. The processing languages that designers have been found to rely on include orthographic projection, algebra and calculus, and syllogistic logic. Processing sequentially takes place in these and other representations in order to deal with the diverse information retrieved. For example, a mathematical representation may be used to carry out structural analysis, a non-directed graph used to analyze circulation layouts, perspectives used for spatial massing, and vertical and horizontal sections used for acoustic considerations. The implications derived from one representation are translated into another for further processing.

Within this sequential use of different representations, a general direction of development is also evident. Scale grows smaller, detail greater. Initially, only large aggregations of DUs are manipulated and only major constraints are applied to the information states that are generated. Later, these are subdivided into more detailed DUs. For instance, an office building may be initially considered with its mechanical tower as a single entity. Later, the elements of the tower are identified, e.g., stairs, elevators, restrooms, and so on, and each given general dimensions. Later, each of these components is fully developed. At each change of detail, the representation may change. As detail changes, constraints and goals are also redefined in more detailed form.

Thus a total design problem, with its many thousands of detailed DUs, is hardly ever processed as a single problem. Rather, it is broken down into subproblems that can be independently treated. Each subproblem is first considered in isolation, then later integrated with other subproblems. Successful integration of subproblems usually requires some of them to be iteratively solved.

Minsky in his review of artificial intelligence [27] pointed out the value of subdividing any large search problem into multiple subproblems. If a problem requires the selection of ten elements, where each element has ten possible alternatives and constraints delimit the acceptable combinations to only one, the number of possible combinations of elements is 10^{10}. This is the size of the problem space that must be searched. But if this problem is subdivided into only two subproblems of equal size (each with five elements), then the size of each subproblem space is only 5^{10} or about 10^7. Two subproblems thus involve only 2 by 10^7, a 1,500-fold decrease over the original problem size. The saving is gained from the assumption that each subproblem is independent. But even if complete independence does not exist, iterations of the subproblems are practical. In fact, anything less than 1,500 iterations is still a saving. Each subproblem is defined by its own elements and problem space, and its own subgoals.

Alexander has criticized the assumptions designers make as to what are relevant subproblems in the design of a complex system [1]. He argues that reliance on traditional problem subdivisions eliminates from the solution space many valuable alternatives that are worthy of exploration. Evidence from our studies suggests that the different subproblems utilized by a designer are in large part determined circumstantially by what has been retrieved from memory. It also seems true that the style of many designers is an outgrowth of the subproblems they identify and the sequence in which they are processed. Thus, if a structural module is chosen as a subproblem for early resolution, its influence in the final result often is readily perceived. If patterns of activities are abstractly considered early in the process and fairly directly translated into a solution, then this too has a direct stylistic result.

SEARCH

The processing strategies applied to generate new information states in any problem-solving representation have been found to be essentially similar [30]. Detailing of these strategies as they are used in design is only beginning to be explored. One simple strategy that has been expressed in design protocols is shown in Figure 4. It consists of a depth-first exhaustive search and utilizes stacked DUs and operators. That is, DUs and operators are sequenced in successful operations in one direction. When failures are encouraged, backtracking takes the opposite sequence. This strategy has been given the name *generate-and-test*.

Another strategy used by designers is *heuristic search*. It is best understood, in terms of its application to design, by following through the process shown in the schematic flow chart of Figure 5. As applied to a space planning, the basic operation in heuristic search is the application of a DU and an operator to an existing problem state. That is, a DU is selected and an operator is chosen to locate it or move it. If the location chosen by the operator can hold the DU, it is tested in that location against the relevant problem constraints. If it does not satisfy the constraints, then the failure is evaluated. If any information is available that outlines a course of action that often works in the existing "failed" situation, it is utilized to determine another location or to select another DU; otherwise, a more general selection procedure is used to select another location. If no location for a particular DU is currently

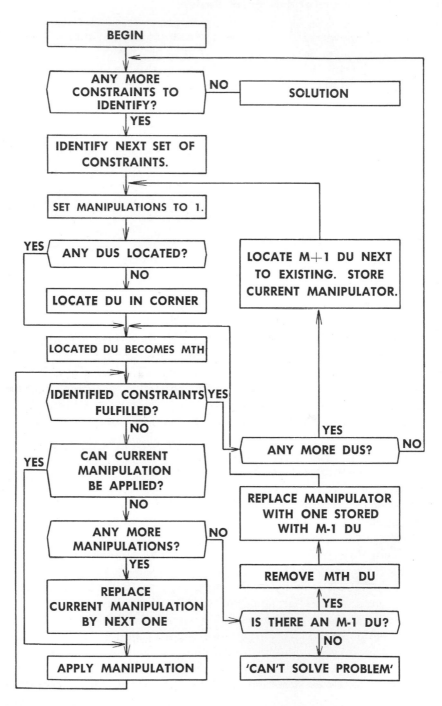

Fig. 4.   Flow chart of heuristic search procedure.

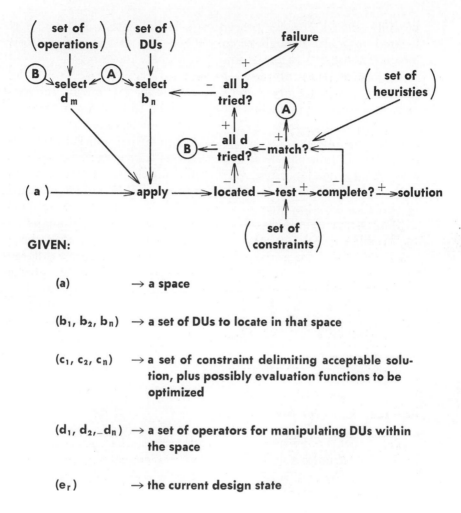

GIVEN:

(a) → a space

(b_1, b_2, b_n) → a set of DUs to locate in that space

(c_1, c_2, c_n) → a set of constraint delimiting acceptable solution, plus possibly evaluation functions to be optimized

$(d_1, d_2, -d_n)$ → a set of operators for manipulating DUs within the space

(e_r) → the current design state

FIND:

a set of operators of the form
$(e_r, b_n, d_p) \rightarrow e_r + 1$

that will generate a state e_s such that it fulfills
(c_1, c_2, c_n) .

Fig. 5. A heuristic search formulation of the space-planning problem.

possible, then a backup procedure selects another DU to be relocated to make enough room. When one DU is satisfactorily located, another is selected and the process repeated.

Various analyses are used to select DUs for processing. For instance, one commonly found rule is that the DU having the most constraints or goals attached between it and those already arranged should be located next. Size also may be considered a constraint and may be one parameter of a polynomial used in selecting the next DU. Details of selection procedures vary greatly between individual designers. They vary from simple stacks to complex polynomials and sequential decision processes. Detail examination of three search strategies used in design is made elsewhere [19].

Many other details certainly exist in the processes humans use to "creatively" solve design problems. It may be possible that a few individuals have evolved design processes significantly different from those described here. If so, it is expected that future studies will enable us to identify them. From our studies thus far, individual differences have been shown to come not from different processes than those we have described but from variations in the details of the processes of information retrieval, search, and problem decomposition. Design processes seem to be specifiable in these terms.

Progress in Automated Design

The previous discussion has considered what is now known about the structure and content of problem-solving processes in design. Let us now turn to a short review of current capabilities in modeling aspects of design problem-solving on a computer.

SPACEPLANNING REPRESENTATIONS

Any extensive application of computers to augment design requires machine data structures that are operationally isomorphic with the natural problem-solving languages used in design. Perspectives, syllogistic logic, plans, elevations and sections, and mathematics all seem needed. Many of these capabilities already are available, but significantly lacking currently are computer languages capable of handling *space planning*. By a space-planning language is meant all forms of orthographic projection, of which plans, sections, and elevations are examples. To the outsider, it would seem that the existence of computer graphics and the ability to draw figures on a compueter-driven "scope" would be sufficient for handling space-planning tasks. But the lack is not one of hardware—the apropriate computer machinery—but software. Current computer graphic languages generally have been found deficient for handling space planning in at least three ways:

1. Only objects are represented in the data structure; the voids between objects are not. Determining if enough empty space exists to hold a new object now requires that the total representation be processed in order to compute the size of an empty space. Major processing inefficiencies are the result.

2. Each element in the data structure is ordered according to a programmer-defined topological relation. This is needed for analyzing circuits and other kinds of flow. Yet needed for space planning is an ordering by spatial adjacency. Only this allows the dimensions of adjacent spatial domains to be directly processed for determination of distances. Otherwise, complex analyses are required.

3. In existing computer graphics, the boundaries of each filled space are now defined by a closed set of line segments. In order to check for overlaps of domains, intersections between all line combinations must be searched for. This is an expensive operation for one that will be used often. Other methods for checking line overlaps need to be developed [see 18].

Though computer graphics do not facilitate space planning, other representations do. The simplest representation useful for space planning, and the only one used to any extent currently, is the array (Fig. 6). Essentially, space in this representation is subdivided into a grid. The state of each domain in the grid is defined by the value of the corresponding array variable. The location of any domain is identified by its subscripted variable. Adjacent domains are identified through the sequential numbering of the subscripts. Empty space and filled space are both represented. Several significant space-planning programs have been written that utilize arrays for representing space [5, 24].

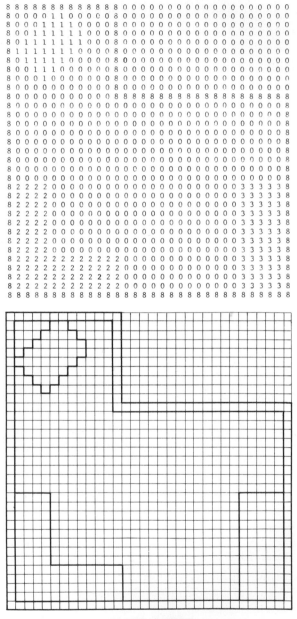

PLAIN ARRAY

six inch grid
1089 domains
maximum error = 8.5 inches

Fig. 6. Array representation of spaces.

Array representations of space are simple to use and are easily implemented in general-purpose programming languages. But they make highly inefficient use of computer memory and processing times if details must be represented. Big, homogeneous spaces consume as much memory as intricate details.

Alternative representations have been developed that resolve many of the problems inherent in the array. Two of them are shown in Figures 7 and 8. The first representation is used by the Stanford Research Institute to model space in their robot project [31, 34]. It consists of a modified array that begins with a space being subdivided into four equally sized domains. If there are details in a domain, it is subdivided into four more equivalent domains. Subdividing can be applied recursively until the desired detail is achieved. In this way large homogeneous spaces are represented by large domains, details by small domains.

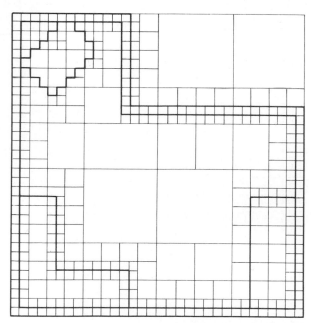

HIERARCHICAL ARRAY

six inch minimum grid
411 domains
maximum error = 8.5 inches

Fig. 7. Domain representation of spaces.

```
 .5  (6.5W,10.0E)
 .5  (.5W,2.1E,1E,.5A,2.9E.5W,10.0E)
 .5  (.5W,1.6E,1.4A,2.5E,.5W,10.0E)
 .5  (5.W,1.1E,2.3A,2.1E,.5W,10.0E)
 .5  (.5W,.6E,3.1A,1.8E,.5W,10.0E)
 .5  (.5W,.3E,3.1A,2.1E,.5W,10.0E)
 .5  (.5W,.5E,2.4A,2.6E,.5E,.5W,10.0E)
 .5  (.5W,1.1E,1.3A,3.1E,.5W,10.0E)
1.0  (.5W,5.5E,.5W,10.0E)
 .5  (.5W,5.5E,10.5W)
4.5  (.5W,15.5E,.5W)
4.3  (.5W,1.8B,11.2E,2.5C,.5W)
1.2  (.5W,6.0B,7.0E,2.5C,.5W)
 .5  (16.5W)
```

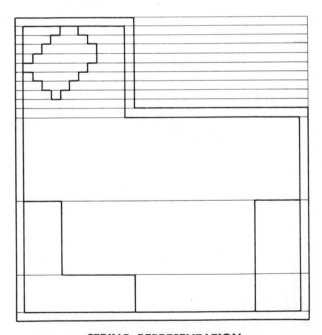

STRING REPRESENTATION

six inch minimum horizonal grid
65 domains
maximum error = 4.2 inches

Fig. 8. Row-domain representation of spaces.

Figure 8 shows an alternative way of subdividing space. It groups space into horizontal rows, scanning a figure horizontally much like a television camera. Similar types of spaces within a horizontal scan are grouped into single domains, then all like rows are grouped. This representation allows more detail to be expressed in less memory than any other representation yet conceived. It has been implemented in the SNOBOL 4 programming language [23] and used by the author for limited exploration of various search strategies. Operating on this representation is more complex than the others. Scanning a wall horizontally requires a different operation than scanning one vertically. The resulting complexity of processing negates some of its other efficiencies.

Several other representations have been implemented that successfully allow space planning. Like those above, they all only approximate irregular shapes [see 18]. Work is now proceeding at Carnegie-Mellon University on the programming of a representation that should accurately represent any regular geometric shape. Thus radii and skewed figures should be accurately handled. The cost of gaining this extra detail seems to be a highly complex representation and large memory requirements.

All of the representations described here allow object manipulation, easy checking of overlaps, and easy calculation of the distance between objects. Each also allows the appending of other non-spatial and attribute information to any of the represented objects. Thus, they should prove useful for many space-planning applications.

The space-planning representations described above allow evaluation of specific arrangements in as much detail as desired. But protocols show that more general representations are used in the early stages of design to explore the feasibility of different general classes of arrangements. These representations have traditionally been called schematics, pattern studies, or "bubble diagrams." A significant study now being completed by Grason formalizes a set of general goals often considered in schematics. Grason used a dual graph representation and theorems from graph theory to determine the realizability of adjacency and access relations prior to committing any parts of the design to actual locations. This appears to be the first time that theorem-proving techniques have been used to abstractly evaluate spatial constraints [see 21].

SEARCH

Only simple search strategies for space planning have thus far been explored in implemented programs. An algorithm for generating a spatial arrangement using the degree of interaction between elements as the major evaluation criterion has been programmed; it employs the array of circulation costs between spaces using the given exterior bounds and planarity as constraints [5]. It also uses the array. Only one known operational program includes a generalized search strategy and can incorporate any kind of spatial constraint [15]. It utilizes the generate-and-test search strategy shown in Figure 5, an array representation, and was programmed in ALGOL on Carnegie-Mellon's G-20 computer. It showed itself capable of space planning and solved simple arrangement problems. But its exhaustive search approach made it too slow for all but the simplest of practical problems. It was several times slower than a human being.

Two projects are now underway at CMU that will explore more complex search techniques. One is an implementation of the heuristic search process shown in Figure 6. The inclusion of decomposition procedures are planned for both studies.

If an automated design system is to allocate its processing capabilities to subproblems at different levels within a hierarchical decomposition, then a control procedure must be available to determine when search should proceed with the current subproblem and when other subproblems at other levels in the hierarchy should be reexamined. The issue is an important one, affecting both the style and quality of the solution and the efficiency of search. Manheim [25] has proposed and programmed one method of sequencing search among alternative subproblems. His method is based on an evaluation of the likelihood of each course of action achieving different values of the problem's evaluation criterion and is applied to a transportation example. Though his program has the weakness of requiring the designer to manually input a set of probabilities for each alternative solution, it is an important first exploration of the control structure of a hierarchical automated design system.

It is too early to tell how elaborate search procedures must be before they begin to compete with humans in finding satisfactory design solutions. In search, efficiency is clearly the major problem. Only by continuing to hypothesize and experiment, both with designers and computers, will we be able to eventually identify the search processes necessary to efficiently solve complex design problems.

INFORMATION RETRIEVAL SYSTEMS

All the space-planning programs written thus far take as input a well-specified set of conjunctive DUs (some subsets may be disjunctive) and a set of constraints and attempt to find an arrangement of those DUs that satisfies the constraints. A large data set is required to set up any problem. But it is our interest eventually to write programs that take as input not a well-defined problem specification but only a crude statement of a problem class with a short list of special considerations. We wish to implement programs that take as input the information usually given to a human designer. Such a program would include a large information retrieval system that would retrieve a set of means to deal with a specific example of a problem class through logical inferences made on a large store of information. The search program would explore the feasibility of different possible elements and constraints generated by the information retrieval system.

Significant efforts are now under way at several institutions to develop large associatively structured memories that allow general information to be stored and retrieved. For instance, Quillian has programmed a semantic memory allowing derivation of the contextual meaning of most words or sentences [32]. Another effort is being undertaken by Greane and Rafael at Stanford Research Institute [22]. Their program aims at storing any kind of relational or attribute information and allowing retrieval of all significant inferences. Other significant efforts are underway at Stanford University [7, 11].

These efforts in large-store associative memories begin to model human long-term memory. They set the groundwork for future attempts to tie an information retrieval system to a search system for use in design. Those interested in an important first effort at making this union should refer to a paper by Moran [28].

PROBLEM SPECIFICATION

An important effort obviously needed to realize automated design is the explication of constraints and objectives for different classes of design problems. Given the most sophisticated of processes, a design solution is still only as good as the content of the problem specification. The information to be stored in an associative memory and retrieved for different problem classes must be identified. The specific criteria that allow satisfaction of general cost and performance criteria must be determined.

Alexander and his group at Berkeley have initiated an important set of studies that attempt to explicate and validate the criteria that should be satisfied in solving different classes of design problems [1, 35]. These represent an important improvement of the more traditional building type studies published by F. W. Dodge and Rheinhold. Expansion of this sort of effort is a necessity if design is to become more objective, whether it is carried out by man or machines.

REMAINING AUTOMATED DESIGN STUDIES

Four different aspects of a theory of design have been reviewed: representations, search, hierarchical decomposition, and information retrieval. The current state of design research in each has been outlined. But many other issues wait to be studied; a few are:

1. The system integration of search and information retrieval processes is required so that both gain inputs from each other. The significance of a dual process has been explicated in our protocols. But we know little of how they work or the control mechanism that directs them together.

2. Space-planning search processes must be integrated eventually with more complex evaluations such as discrete flow simulations or total-heat-gain analyses. Current evaluation criteria are simplistic approximations of these kinds of evaluations. The value of automated design should be in facilitating these kinds of complex analyses.

3. The extension must be made of machine representations to other domains, such as color, texture, and light reflectance. The sophistication of automated design will depend on our ability to include these kinds of considerations and to generate and evaluate combinations of these attributes.

Herbert Simon, in a more general review of design methodology, adds to this list several more significant theoretical issues that are basic to a science of design [36].

The Future of Automated Design

In a more speculative vein, this review can be completed by suggesting where these current efforts may lead. If the processes now being studied are sufficient to allow reasonably economical generation of competent design solutions, then the future holds the possibility that prototypical design problems may be more efficiently solved by a computer than by man. Also, control of the quality of the resulting design will be greater than in current manual processes. As a result, it may be that there will begin to appear automated design programs applied to at least two areas of building design. The first is in those well-defined aspects of design problems where major innovation is not usually demanded. Many aspects of building design are currently solved routinely. They include mechanical systems, power distribution systems, restrooms, fire stairways, mechanical cores, and often structural systems. If prefabricated home-building ever catches on, it might be expected that computer-generated custom design of housing would provide a middle ground between monotonous tracts and the exorbitance of a handcraft building and design process.

The second application of automated design is likely to be in those areas of space planning where functional performance is critical. Most architects already rely on research studies and prototypical solutions to design radiology and other kinds of laboratories and operating and intensive care suites in hospitals. In the future, instead of providing a set of design standards for these types of facilities, governmental agencies could provide computer programs that will design alternative solutions for these aspects of facilities. The solutions generated will fit within the space and material constraints imposed by the designer, but will always produce arrangements that provide the required performance.

KNOWLEDGE TRANSFER IN THE DESIGN PROFESSIONS

Automated design is fundamentally different from traditional design in at least one respect. The traditional mode of design is intuitive. Each person who designs learns primarily from his own experience. Whether it is from case studies in school or professional experience, most insight in design is currently gained from direct contact with problems. The implication is that the knowledge that others have gained is largely untransferable. Each generation must first gain for itself what the previous one knew about design, then possibly take a small forward step. Obviously, within this process of knowledge transmission the potential for growth is weak.

Science currently offers one method for more productively transferring knowledge. By making ideas explicit, they are not only available for testing and refinement but also for direct transmission throughout the world. Today, a person can pick up a book and come to understand ideas that scientists in the past may have spent their whole lives developing.

But the recorded word has until recently limited science to explicating information content. The explicating of process was limited to a few branches of mathematics. With the advent of the computer, processes too are explicated. Thus, not only the content of thought—a particular information state—but also the process of generation can be recorded and disseminated.

This new situation offers a whole new mode of knowledge transmission. By explicating the experience of a problem-solver in the form of a computer program that models his own capabilities, both the unique content and the power of his processes are available for correction and improvement by others. The knowledge of one designer is also directly available to another. Furthermore, that knowledge is in a form allowing it to be utilized anywhere, solving problems on any computer on which it is run. Thus, the expertise of one problem-solver is multiplied as required.

If current assumptions concerning the practicality and feasibility of automated design are valid, then at some time in the future, one would expect designers not to compete at all with the competency of a computer. An automated design program will incorporate the combined expertise of hundreds of individuals and will surpass human design in all respects except idiosyncrasy. Once a program is completed, its use will be available anywhere it is desired. Designers may still be concerned with nonprototypical design problems, but these will become increasingly rare as the competence of automated design systems develops.

At this point, the role of design becomes totally innovative. A designer's contribution is the improvement in a search strategy, in generating new constraints or goals to be applied to design problems, or a new retrieval technique. These are what produce real innovation even today. As innovations are made, they will be programmed so that all of society may benefit. If this is possible, it certainly is the maximum of knowledge amplification. Optimistically, it is within the potential of automated design.

References

1. C. Alexander, *Notes on the Synthesis of Form* (Cambridge: Harvard University Press, 1964).
2. ————, S. Ishiwaka, and M. Silverstein, " A Pattern Language Which Generates Multi-Service Centers," Report by the Center for Environmental Structure, Berkeley, California, 1968.
3. S. Amarel, "On the Mechanization of Creative Processes," *IEEE Spectrum* 3:4 (1966), 112-14.
4. ————, "On the Representation of Problems and Goal-Directed Procedures for Computers," *Purposive Systems: Proceedings of the First Annual Symposium of the American Society for Cybernetics* (New York: Spartan, 1968).
5. G. C. Armour and E. Buffa, "A Heuristic Algorithm and Simulation Approach to Relative Location of Facilities," *Management Science* 9:2 (January, 1963), 294-309.
6. J. Ballay, "Visual Information Processing," *Proceedings of the Environmental Design Research Association Conference* (Chapel Hill, N.C.: School of Design, North Carolina State University; in press).
7. J. Becker, "The Modeling of Simple Analogic and Inductive Processes in a Semantic Memory System," *Proceedings of the International Joint Conference on Artificial Intelligence* (New York: Association for Computing Machinery, 1969).
8. D. Bobrow, "Natural Language Input for a Computer Problem Solving System," Massachusetts Institute of Technology, Ph.D. thesis, Project MAC Technical Report MAC-TR-2, 1964.
9. N. Chomsky, *Syntactic Structures* (The Hague: Mouton, 1957).
10. ————, and G. A. Miller, "Introduction to the Formal Analysis of Natural Languages," *Handbook of Mathematical Psychology,* ed. R. D. Luce, R. R. Bush, and E. Galanter (New York: Wiley, 1962), II, chap. 11.
11. K. Colby, L. Tesler, and H. Enea, "Experiments with a Search Algorithm for the Data Base of a Human Belief System," *Proceedings of the International Joint Conference on Artificial Intelligence* (New York: Association for Computing Machinery, 1969).
12. L. S. Coles, "Syntax Directed Interpretation of Natural Language," Ph.D. dissertation, Carnegie Institute of Technology, 1967).
13. J. Deese, *The Structure of Associations in Language and Thought* (Baltimore, Md.: Johns Hopkins University Press, 1965).
14. C. Eastman, "Explorations of the Cognitive Processes in Design," ARPA Report, Department of Computer Science, Carnegie-Mellon University, DDC Number 671-158, February, 1968.
15. ————, "LAYOUT: An Algorithm for Finding a Non-Over-lapping Arrangement of Two-Dimensional Objects within a Bounded Space and Meeting a Variety of Constraints," internal working paper, Department of Computer Science, Carnegie-Mellon University, April, 1968.

16. ———, "On the Analysis of Intuitive Design Processes," *Emerging Methods of Environmental Design and Planning,* ed. G. Moore (Cambridge: M.I.T. Press, 1970).

17. ———, "Cognitive Processes and Ill-Defined Problems: A Case Study from Design," *Proceedings of the International Joint Conference on Artificial Intelligence* (New York: Association for Computing Machinery, 1969).

18. ———, "Representations for Space Planning," internal working paper, Department of Computer Science, Carnegie-Mellon University, March, 1969.

19. ———, "Problem Solving Strategies in Design," *Proceedings of the Environmental Design Research Association Conference* (Chapel Hill, N.C.: School of Design, North Carolina State University; in press).

20. J. Feder, "The Linguistic Approach to Pattern Analysis: A Literature," Technical Report 400-133, Department of Electrical Engineering, New York University, Bronx, February, 1966.

21. J. Garson "A Dual Linear Graph Representation for Space Filling Location Problems of the Floorplan Type," *Emerging Methods in Environmental Design and Planning* (Cambridge: M.I.T. Press, 1970).

22. C. C. Greane and B. Rafael, "Research on Intelligent Question Answering," Scientific Report No. 1, SRC Project 6001, Stanford Research Institute, Menlo Park, Calif., 1967.

23. R. Griswold, I. Poage, and I. Polansky, *The SNOBOL 4 Programming Language* (Englewood Cliffs, N.J.: Prentice-Hall, 1969).

24. R. B. Lee and J. M. Moore, "CORELAP-Computerized Relationship Layout Planning," *Journal of Industrial Engineering* 18:3 (March, 1967).

25. M. Manheim, *Hierarchical Structures A Model of Design and Planning Processes* (Cambridge: M.I.T. Press, 1966).

26. G. A. Miller, E. Galenter, and K. H Pribram, *Plans and the Structure of Behavior* (New York: Henry Holt, 1960)

27. M. Minsky, "Steps toward Artificial Intelligence," *Proceedings of the Institute of Radio Engineers, IRE* (March, 1961), March, 1961, HFE-2:39-55.

28. T. Moran, "A Model of a Multi-Lingual Designer," *Emerging Methods in Environmental Design and Planning,* ed. G. Moore (Cambridge: M.I.T. Press, 1970).

29. A. Newell, "On the Analysis of Human Problem Solving Protocols," *Calcul et Formalisation dans les Sciences de l'Homme,* ed. J. Gardin and B. Janlin (Paris: Presses Universitaires de France, 1968).

30. ———, "Heuristic Programming: Ill-Structured Problems," *Progress in Operations Research,* ed. P. Aronofsky (New York: Wiley, 1969), Vol. III.

31. N. Nilsson, "A Mobile Automation: An Application of Artificial Intelligence Techniques," *Proceedings of the Joint International Conference on Artificial Intelligence* (New York: Association for Computing Machinery, 1969).

32. M. R. Quillan, "Semantic Memory," Bolt, Berenek, and Newman DDC Report AD 641-671, October 1966.

33. W. Reitman, *Cognition and Thought* (New York: Wiley, 1965).

34. C. A. Rosen and N. Nilsson ,"Application of Intelligent Automata to Reconnaissance," Third Interim Report, Rome Air Development Center, Stanford Research Institute Project 5953, December, 1967.

35. C. Rusch et al., "School for the Visually Handicapped" (ditto, Department of Architecture, University of California, Berkeley, 1966).

36. H. Simon, *The Sciences of the Artificial* (Cambridge: M.I.T. Press, 1969).

Florencio G. Asenjo

THE GENERATION OF FORM
BY GEOMETRIC METHODS

Mathematics is the great systematizer. It is the language of physics —the most scientific of sciences—and the primary model for exact thinking. For this very reason artists often shun it in their formal equipment, art theoretically being the realm of vague boundaries, deliberate imprecision, and whim. But since mathematics and art are both human creations, it is inevitable that they should reflect aspects of that same reality from which they each evolve. Indeed, even abstract mathematics and abstract art share a common wealth of perceptions, conceptualizations, and imagery that spring from the same sources; therefore, there is much in mathematics that the artist can use. Mathematics can help him to differentiate confused categories, to articulate vague ideas about form, to recombine and create from newly gained points of view. With this theme as the dominant note, this paper will consider three contrasting families of geometric ideas and outline their aesthetic applications, keeping design especially in mind. These three families—symmetry, polarity, and association—are essential for any systematic analysis of form, whatever its domain. Each of the three adds an entirely new look—really a new dimension—to the others, and a judicious and controlled use of the three together can often determine the principal formal features of an artistic style. However, although the subjects selected are fundamental ones, they by no means exhaust the treasury of concepts that mathematics holds in store for the artist in search of new solutions to the eternal problems of aesthetic composition.

Symmetry

When people speak of symmetry, they usually have bilateral symmetry in mind; that is, the kind of symmetry produced by mirror reflection in which the mirror surface lies at the halfway point between an object and its reflection. In early Greek architecture, for example, bilateral symmetry ruled supreme, and a facade with a left half that was not the exact mirror image of the right half would have been considered a wanton artistic sin. Bilateral symmetry has provided artists of all periods with an especial sense of satisfaction, judging from its extensive use throughout the history of art. A typical sonata movement begins with a theme, A, continues with a second theme, B, and an elaboration of both, and ends with a repetition of A. When theme A is repeated, it is, of course, not a mirror image of its first presentation; however, the over-all ABA form of the sonata has bilateral symmetry. The fugue, although it lacks bilateral symmetry as a whole, often contains themes reflected both vertically or horizontally—that is, either with respect to a given pitch or a given instant. Nature, too, seems to revel in bilateral symmetry. Man's body shows this, as do the bodies of most living creatures, which explains why bilateral symmetry appears in art forms as far back as prehistoric times. Although symmetry is in itself static, nevertheless it appears in dynamic situations, i.e., situations in which some distribution of forces is involved; electric charges are positive or negative, magnetic forces are directed to either north or south, and recent research supports the existence of matter and antimatter. Some laws of atomic physics rely heavily on bilateral symmetry, and we find it again in chromosomes and spermatozoa. Clearly, the contrast of left and right pervades both nature and art.

But bilateral symmetry is only one of the forms of mathematical symmetry, a fact not generally known by nonspecialists. Translation along a straight line—either in space or in time—and rotation around a fixed point generate translatory and rotational types of symmetry. An ornamental band, a line of equidistant columns, or any pattern in which the same figure is repeated side by side one-dimensionally an indefinite number of times are examples of translatory symmetry. Rotational symmetry, in turn, is the symmetry of a cell, a dome, a column, an octopus. Whereas bilateral and rotational symmetries are both finite in the sense that they achieve completion in a limited portion of either space or time, translatory symmetry is infinitistic in principle. An ornamental band and a line of columns are physically limited but suggest an unlimited continuation. On the other hand, since a circle can be divided variously into several equal parts, each possible division generates a different kind of rotational symmetry—pentagonal, hexagonal, and so on.

Some figures possess more than one kind of symmetry. A daisy possesses it both bilaterally and rotationally. A leaf with bilateral symmetry can be translated indefinitely along a frieze. A band of stars displays in one single example all three of the symmetries referred to so far. But these combinations of symmetries can be produced in a more intimately related fashion. Consider a point in a plane that keeps translating away from a fixed point and rotating around it simultaneously. The composition of these two movements generates a spiral, a centrifugal infinitistic figure whose occurrence in nature is fairly widespread; snails and nebulae are spiral-shaped, for example. Then think of a helix, the result of rotation and translation on the surface of a cylinder; this is exemplified in architecture by the circular staircase. A well-known staircase of this type is in the Vatican Museum and is presumably the one from which Frank Lloyd Wright got his idea for the central ramp in the Guggenheim Museum, another famous example of a helix.

Two- or three-dimensional translatory patterns open new symmetric possibilities. Consider a honeycomb, in which a rotational figure, a hexagon, is translated horizontally and vertically. Consider, too, the modern prismatic buildings—those crystal, three-dimensional rectangular honeycombs. Le Corbusier maintained that the rectangular prism is architecturally superior to the pyramidal model in vogue in the nineteen twenties—the Empire State Building, the Chrysler Building, and such. In this preference Le Corbusier was yielding to the pleasures of regularity and uninterrupted symmetry rather than exposing himself to the uneasiness and uncertainties of improvisation. However, it is improvisation added to symmetry that creates one of the greatest charms of Romanesque architecture. Remember all the capricious little figures, never repeated, carved on the capitals and friezes of Romanesque churches, figures that mock at the rigorous symmetry of the buildings, providing a departure from strict order that in the end emphasizes that order through delightful contrast.

Two- and three-dimensional translatory symmetries are also decidedly infinitistic, which is perhaps why they did not appeal to the ancient Greeks, overwhelmingly finitistic in their conception of the world. Not so other civilizations. When one visits the mosque in Córdoba, Spain, one cannot avoid a dizzy feeling of infinity while standing in the midst of that symmetrical sea of columns and arches that spreads in every direction as far as the eye can reach. A similar impression comes from the highly refined patterns on the walls and ceilings of the Alhambra in Granada, patterns that extend in seemingly endless succession from room to room.

An ornamental pattern that is generated by translation of a given figure along two dimensions is in mathematics sometimes called a lattice. Lattices belong predominantly to the plastic arts, having little to do with literature and music. When the idea of a lattice is transferred to three dimensions (as in the example of the prismatic buildings mentioned earlier), we enter into an entirely new category of psychological effects. Crystals, molecular structures, the stairs of a pyramid, all show that although from the standpoint of mathematics the addition of one dimension does not generally change the structure, this is not entirely the case in the eyes of the beholder. In general, two-dimensional forms seem lifeless, so that a painting's effectiveness depends on the illusion of three-dimensionality it can create, a fact that even the abstractionist Piet Mondrian knew very well. But then, the space in which the human body grows, moves, and feels is three-dimensional, the reason that an artist strives for three-dimensional effects to gain impact.

Identifying the above symmetries opens the door to new systematic combinations of them; through these, discovery becomes the by-product of careful planning rather than the result of an accident. All the kinds of symmetry discussed are variations of a single algebraic idea, the concept of group. With this mathematical concept one can see that these symmetries belong together in a single form-generating category despite their disparate superficial appearance.

Polarity

Theoretically, pure symmetry has no connection with force; therefore, in order to bring in the idea of force, we shall use the word "polarity" as a comprehensive term to cover all the phenomena of attraction or repulsion of entities. These phenomena occur both in art and nature, and have their mathematical expression in the ideas of vector, vector space, and field of forces. We have already mentioned the polarity of electric charges. Other examples of polarity are the contrast between masculine and feminine or between a tall building and a flat one. These last two use gravitational forces differently, one defying them and the other completely yielding. The dynamically neutral distinction between left and right easily acquires polar connotations by making a few additions

Fig. 1. Here, literally, is a face with two looks. Notice the intense and dizzying effect produced by a concentration of polarity; then make a mental comparison with the expressionless face of a blind man.

—stained glass and gargoyles to a Gothic cathedral, a Calder-type mobile to the center ceiling of a perfectly regular hall. Clearly, it is not difficult to add polarity to a static structure.

A vector is a directed magnitude representing the intensity and

direction of a local attraction or repulsion. The vector assigned to a point in a given space indicates the polar effect of all the attractions and repulsions to which the neighborhood of that point is subjected. Each vector measures the potential change of position of a reacting entity when placed at that point. The factors that make an entity susceptible are, of course, the nature of the entity and the field of forces in which it is imbedded; an electrically charged body responds to an electric field, a piece of iron is susceptible to a magnetic field, a heavy mass is affected by the gravitational field, and a man and woman are susceptible to the biologically charged field of human society.

In the arts, including literature and music, the importance of polarity cannot be exaggerated. For example, when we talk about the "central" character of a drama, we are actually referring to a vector characteristic, as is the case when we speak of the "penetrating" look of a portrait or when we describe dissonance in music as "hurting." In all these cases the polarity of the work awakens a dynamic subjective response through a process of induced resonance. From this subjective viewpoint polarity originates in anything capable of moving us, be it toward or away from the object in question, i.e., by appeal or aversion. Obviously, romantic art leans heavily on polarity, whereas classic art depends more on symmetry.

The concept of vector space as an abstract representation of an aesthetic field of forces can help the artist, writer, or composer to gain awareness of the relative strength of relationships between the parts of an artistic whole, relationships that he senses but of which he may not be fully conscious except in their local effects. But it is characteristic of a field of forces that every entity in the field has an ubiquitous influence, its presence being felt throughout the entire field. These distant influences are sometimes fatal to an artistic intention, but they can be either subdued or put to good use as long as their existence is known. The difficulty here is a little like the one of becoming aware of the air we breathe. The artist, then, would do well to systematically analyze with some kind of vector representation each of the many attractions and repulsions that woven together constitute the dynamic structure of his work. Undoubtedly the artist already does this in an incomplete and often subconscious way; by making the operation explicit, all of the poles or centers of a work are exposed. These poles may be of two kinds: (1) they may function as sources for the field of forces, spreading outgoing influence and causing various local attractions and repulsions to take place in near or even remote neighborhoods; or (2) they may function as "sinks" (a nonpejorative expression), that is, as centers of ingoing polarities whose tendency is to dominate the field and simplify its polar structure to the lowest possible level of complexity. A hen that moves about surrounded by her chicks presents a quasi-stationary situation in which the hen is the source of polarity. A big fish that swallows the little ones keeps restoring balance by a steady elimination of competitive forces: it is a sink. The structure of T. S. Eliot's *Family Reunion* is based essentially on the second kind of polarization. The central character of the play is so dominant that the rest of the cast remains in shadow despite the author's valiant attempts to bring them out. But at the same time the central character is also submerged in a polar situation exclusively his own, for he cannot resist the attraction of an enigma that fascinates him. The articulation of these two systems of forces is the polar backbone of Eliot's drama, and when the enigma is solved and the attraction turns into repulsion, the character escapes and the play ends with dissolution of the vector structure that sustained it. This net of forces is behind the dramatic significance of every situation in the play, giving tension and direction to each of them.

Poles are not necessarily obvious in a work, and there can even be fields of force whose poles are entirely external: these are the so-called solenoidal fields. For example, a painting depicting a prayer has its center literally removed to infinity, although the painting still may contain several additional sources or sinks. In a Greek tragedy fate is always a major force, everywhere and yet nowhere—precisely as in a solenoidal field—so that the general effect is one of an invisible deus ex machina, a puppeteer who leads men to their destruction regardless of the strength of their character and the nature of their conflicts. Further, it is possible to have a vector composition resolved locally into an irreducible rotating pair of forces whose effect is that of a whirling center. There are, then, (1) spaces of rest; (2) spaces of pure translation (not in the sense of symmetry, of course, but in the sense of actual or potential motion); (3) spaces of pure rotation (Rodin's "The Kiss," Rubens' "The Abduction of the Sabines"); and (4) combinations of them all. (Applications of polarity to musical aesthetics, in particular, have been discussed separately in the article "Polarity and Atonalism" listed in the bibliography.)

Association

The word "association" refers to the coordinated relationships of the parts in a whole, its unity. Often a work is criticized because it is disconnected, because it lacks unity, because it is fragmentary and without strong associative ties. This idea of association is by far the most basic of the three we are discussing. It is useful to remember, then, that in topology connection and inclusion are two of the discipline's most fundamental ideas.

In a topological space one is not concerned with distances, areas, volumes, angles, or any other metric properties, but rather with the relationships of inclusion, overlapping, and disconnection between regions. A region is any set of points in a space such that any two of the points can be connected by a continuous curve without intersections that is totally contained within the region (Fig. 2a). Another important idea in topology is the order of connection. A region may have other regions within it whose points do not belong to the first one; regions, one may say, with "holes," the number of which plus one, by definition, is the order of connection of the region. Thus, whereas the area in Figure 2a is simply connected, the one in Figure 2b is doubly connected. In the region in Figure 2b it is impossible to take the two marked lines that connect two points and make them coincide through a process of continuous deformation without moving out of the shaded area. A doughnut and a ring are doubly connected three-dimensional regions. In these and similar cases it is important to emphasize that from the viewpoint of topology the shape of the region is irrelevant, so that figures of the most disparate outside appearance can be considered topologically identical if it is possible to shape one into coincidence with the other through a continuous transformation in which no tearings or penetrations take place, a transformation that preserves the order of connection as well as the relationships of inclusion or exclusion between corresponding regions of the figures.

There is still another topological distinction that we must mention, the one between limited and unlimited regions. The whole of a three-dimensional space is an unlimited region, but the inside of a ring is limited by the surface of the ring, which is the boundary of the region. If the boundaries of a limited region belong to the region, the region is called closed (otherwise, it would be called open). The interior of a region is what remains after having taken away its boundaries.

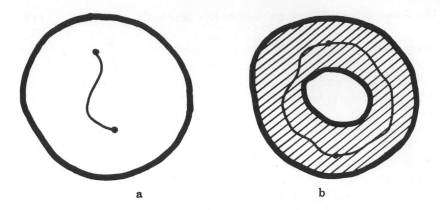

a   b

Fig. 2. (a) Simply connected topological region. (b) Doubly connected topological region.

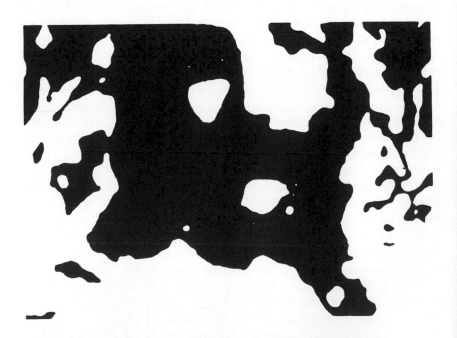

Fig. 3. Although it does not seem so at first sight, this is a figure of Christ, centered and facing us. It is a notable example of the degree to which the perception of a topological association necessarily precedes the understanding of a work. The figure helps us to become aware of the existence of two phases—the grouping of regions and the subsequent aesthetic appreciation—by interpolating a lapse between them.

In man's perception, life and art seem pervaded by countless topological associations and relationships of inclusion, overlapping, and disconnection, all of which we take for granted without much reflection. The story of a dream is a doubly connected aesthetic region because the dream is seen from the outside, that is, from the region of the awakened state. Without being aware of it, we perceive the presence of an ideal boundary between the regions of wakefulness and sleep. A painting of a landscape, although physically limited by its frame, is perceived as an unlimited, simply connected region unless it also depicts a house, a mill, a castle—or several of them. To each different topological structure the mind reacts readily with a new subjective response, the perception of boundaries being a key factor in our conception and articulation of life and art. In this regard, plurally connected spaces have a quality of richness that derives from a singular feeling of novelty (and, in a sense, achievement) that comes from simply crossing a boundary and entering a new region—a new vantage point from which to view the world.

The *Arabian Nights* is a single tale interrupted by innumerable subsidiary tales. Similarly, if we accept the current interpretation that Kafka's novels are not unfinished but purposely left with gaps in the middle to allow room for unlimited interpolations, then we have examples of regions whose order of connection is virtually infinite. In Kafka's novels a multitude of obstacles and boundaries are interposed between the chief character and his objective to give a feeling of unbounded frustration (in *America, The Castle,* and *The Trial* the protagonist is obsessively driven by some vital objective). In mathematics, the topological structure of Kafka's novels would be called a "nested sequence of intervals," and it is this formal characteristic that gives Kafka's style its peculiar quality, so apt for describing the nightmarish, anguished atmosphere of our increasingly bureaucratic environment.

When dealing with a system of associations, one can always superimpose symmetries and polarities, which so increases the number of potential combinations that it becomes impossible to catalog them. It is the artist's creativity that must separate the various formal aspects of his art in order to choose fresh combinations of them from an entirely new viewpoint. This century has rejected the romantic prejudice that warned against the rational, and especially the mathematical, analysis of art because it would smother the irrational sources of inspiration. In spite of this rejection in principle, not very much has been done toward a systematic application of mathematical concepts to the formal analysis of aesthetic effects. Nevertheless, to close a region or to leave it open, to make a hole in it or not, to include A in B or to keep them separate, all these geometric decisions affect the impression that a work of art finally makes upon the mind. Artists would do well to glance at the catalog of topological configurations, not with mathematical detachment but with the eagerness prompted by their aesthetic appetites. Such a glance would reveal a reservoir of formal combinations awaiting the happy discoverer who has the knowledge to use them. This knowledge requires training oneself to see diversity in unity as well as unity in diversity—the first, in order to distinguish new categories from uniform phenomena (different kinds of symmetry, polarity, and association, for example); the second, to become aware of what is common to seemingly diverse entities (a man and a facade, wrestling and whirlpools, a cup and a ring). This twofold training would solve the riddle of apparently identical situations that produce diverse subjective reactions, as well as that of apparently diverse situations that strike us as similar. Such an approach is the road to understanding the formal origins of aesthetic effects.

Final Remarks

There are many other concepts that mathematics can lend to art to pave the way for new aesthetic combinations, among them threads, one-sided surfaces, and coloring maps, all topological topics of considerable interest to design. (Nowadays Möbius strips are seen in museums as pieces of abstract sculpture, and Henry Moore's style is certainly inspired by topological forms.) Also interesting for the arts is the study of pathological curves and surfaces, important in that they set new boundaries for intuitive concepts whose limits are usually taken for granted. There are curves (Peano) that can fill a plane—a one-dimensional line covering a two-dimensional space; continuous curves (Weierstrass) that have no tangent; curves (Sierpinski) that intersect themselves at each of their points, consisting therefore of points of intersection exclusively, and so on. These examples are not offered merely as interesting curiosities; they are geometric constructions full of heuristic value for an artistically receptive mind.

Mathematics is precise and decisive, but reality seems intrinsically unpredictable and confused—in man's view, at least. Perhaps it is impossible ever to completely develop the thesis outlined here, either because reality possesses totally amorphous streaks that no kind of systematization can shape or because reality's complexity is beyond our intellectual and sensory limitations. But in any case, no theoretical approach can be fully congruent with real events. Without question mathematics can indeed enlarge the artist's conception, but art will always be unpredictable and blissfully confusing, as proved beyond doubt by the enormous variety of aesthetic interpretations. This granted, the lesson to draw is not to indulge in any kind of free irrationalism, but rather to learn to be satisfied with limited growth in the articulation of reason and fact. Fortunately, there will always be room for perfection, which will keep the way open for a limitless number of departures, variations, and artistic and intellectual adventures. This, indeed, is in the nature of life, and we must rejoice that it is so, for it is only thus that we escape the dullness of a world in which all events are deduced from premises.

References

1. F. G. Asenjo, *El Todo y las Partes* (Madrid: Editorial Martínez de Murguía, 1962), especially chap. 22.

2. ———, "Polarity and Atonalism," *Journal of Aesthetics and Art Criticism* 25:1 (1966), 47-52.

3. H. Eves, *A Survey of Geometry*, 2 vols. (Boston: Allyn & Beacon, 1965).

4. D. Hilbert and S. Cohn-Vossen, *Geometry and the Imagination,* trans. P. Nemenyi (New York: Chelsea Publishing Co., 1952).

5. K. Lewin, *Principles of Topological Psychology,* trans. F. and G. Heider (New York: McGraw-Hill, 1936).

6. W. Lietzmann, *Visual Topology,* trans. M. Bruckheimer (London: Chatto & Windus, 1965).

7. H. Weyl, *Symmetry* (Princeton, N.J.: Princeton University Press, 1952).

part **3**

DECISION-AID APPLICATIONS

Thomas E. Hoover

DECISION AIDS FOR THE PLANNING AND DEVELOPMENT OF UNIVERSITY FACILITIES

The decision-making process with respect to the development of university facilities is one that must consider a large number of detailed and varying requirements in the formulation of priorities and alternative development strategies relative to satisfying an uncertain future market for university services. It is a class of problem that seeks to relate and allocate limited capital funds to a large number of programs highly variable in their activities and space needs, in anticipation of funding and partly unknown future teaching and research activities. As such, it is not unlike the capital budgeting problem encountered by large industrial organizations and by government.

Increasing demand for the services of higher education during the past two decades, manifesting itself in terms of increased student enrollments as well as increased interest in postgraduate education, has created a situation in which it has become critically important that limited capital funds be allocated effectively so as to provide well for future needs. In view of the complexity of the problem, and in view of the difficulty of measuring effectiveness, a great deal of work has been undertaken recently for developing systems that will be of use to decision-makers for selecting reasonably optimum development strategies and programs. One such system for the Ohio State University is described below.

The organization of universities and the distribution of decision-making responsibilities at various levels has an influence on the design of the system and how it is used. Each department of the university has the responsibility for providing the special facilities for its instruction and research programs. They must carry out this responsibility often without full knowledge of what enrollments will be and what the fast-changing world of research will require in the way of supporting facilities. In addition, decision-makers at the departmental level have few, if any, space resources of their own to reallocate, and they have no real way to directly create new floor space and facilities. Decision-makers at the college level are in a much more flexible position to reallocate facilities, although they have frequently refrained from doing so. They too, however, are limited in what floor space and facilities they can cause to be created.

The decision-maker at the university level is in a better position to reallocate space. Although this authority is not exercised frequently, he can, to a limited extent, create floor space by remodeling and by using internal funds for capital construction. However, in making these decisions, he is faced with the same uncertainties regarding future needs as are decision-makers at the departmental and college levels. In addition, he faces more directly three other conditions: (1) the long lead times necessary for obtaining funds and for programming, designing, and constructing facilities; (2) the almost total dependence on state and federal sources of capital funds; and (3) the small amount of discretion allowed him in the allocation of such funds among projects because state and federal sources usually earmark funds for particular projects.

At the state level, all university proposals, often from a number of campuses, are in competition. Decision-makers at this level must choose, on some basis relative to statewide needs and the limited resources available, between instructional and research programs and the facilities required to support them and the locations at which these investments are to be made.

At many state universities, over-all population growth in the state and open-ended admissions policies have caused great unfilled needs for space. The growing graduate enrollment, previously mentioned, has a dual effect: not only does it increase the number enrolled but it also increases the length of time students are at the institution.

There also has been a great deal of confusion and conflict over the relative worth of capital dollars versus operating dollars to the university. Regardless of the confusion, there always has been great competition to obtain capital dollars. For the purpose of estimating the cost of an academic program, $1.00 per net assignable square foot (NASF) has been used as an estimate of the annual capital cost of floor space. With the increase in the cost of construction, it may not be too long before $2.00 per NASF becomes more realistic. Thus, a program utilizing 50,000 NASF with operating costs amounting to $300,000 could be considered as a $400,000-per-year operation if the cost of space is included. Since 70 to 80 percent of the operating dollars are personnel-related, and since people are the primary generators of the need for space, it may be useful for decision-makers to consider possible trade-offs within and among programs between capital and operating expenditures. A critical, unsolved problem that prevents some trade-off analyses is the general lack of measures of effectiveness in academic programs. Without these, cost-effectiveness analysis is greatly hampered.

Interest in development of a rational basis for planning and allocating of space started at the university level, has spread to the state level, and now is even finding its way into the federal level (in terms of interest in grant allocations for construction).

Initially, methods of planning were largely project-oriented, providing basic laboratories and offices to house departments. In a period of largely stable enrollment, staff, and population, and little sponsored research, this project-oriented approach was adequate. Little quantitative analysis was undertaken regarding utilization, capacities, and space needed to meet future growth.

The next level of sophistication involved some quantitative guidelines of total space needed per full-time equivalent student. The guidelines varied greatly depending upon the size and complexity of the institution. A guideline provided a good after-the-fact analysis of existing space and a good long-range total university space projection, if the right size and complexity range was picked.

Currently used methods recognize differing needs by general room types, levels of study, and program. The system to be described is really the next step in the evolution of a system to provide a basis for rational decision-making in the capital funds allocation process.

The system is composed of four phases of activity. The first phase involves the use of a simulation model for estimating and evaluating space requirements by academic program and year. Exogenously prepared population forecasts and participation rates are used to provide inputs to the model in terms of enrollments and other space-using populations. Student enrollment by academic program and by year are projected. Teaching staff and other staff are estimated directly as a function of student enrollment or are set independently by quantifying decision-makers' policies. The projections and estimates take into consideration the patterns of part-time enrollments and part-time staff, differences in the degree of theoretical and empirical research between programs, and other factors that affect the way in which floor space is used.

The second phase involves the use of the output of the first phase by facility-planners and decision-makers to develop building projects that satisfy the space needs and to construct capital budgets that will fund the proposed projects. The third phase requires the construction of a project network to reflect known restrictions, time relationships, and precedence relationships for the projects proposed in the second phase. The fourth phase is the adjustment and evaluation phase. Adjustments can be made in the proposed projects and in the proposed schedule, and the simulation model can be used to evaluate the effects of the adjustments.

The space requirement simulation model consists of a number of linear functions with which space-needs estimates are generated. The various classes of space found at the university are represented in the model. Constants are used in the functions that represent the NASF per activity unit for that class of space. For example, the need for research laboratory space for a given program may be represented in the following way:

$$RLS = S_o + M_r(R_t - R_o) \text{ for } R_t > R_o, \text{ otherwise, } R_t - R_o = 0$$

where

$RLS = NASF$ of research laboratory and service space

$S_o = NASF$ of RLS required for base-level operations

$R_t =$ Projected full-time equivalent (FTE) research space users for year, t.

$R_o = FTE$ research space users for base-level operations

$M_r =$ Representation of the "ideal" space module: $NASF$ per FTE research space user

A simple version of the general space needs model is as follows:

$$N_{ij} = \frac{\sum_{k=1}^{K} [S_{ik} + M_{ik}(A_{ijk} - A_{ik})]}{(1 - F_i)} \text{ for } A_{ijk} > A_{ik}, \text{ otherwise,}$$

$$A_{ijk} - A_{ik} = 0$$

where

N_{ij} = Total *NASF* for program i in period j

S_{ik} = *NASF* of space type k required for base-level operations in program i

M_{ik} = Representation of the "ideal" space module (*NASF* per activity unit [A]) for type k in program i

A_{ijk} = Projected activity units for period j associated with type k in program i

A_{ik} = Activity units associated with the base-level space, S_{ik}, for type k in program i

F_i = A general allowance for storage and miscellaneous space for program i

The activity unit for a given type of space is fixed, e.g., FTE staff is a common activity measure for office space. Student contact hours (SCH) and/or section hours are example measures of activity for scheduled instructional space categories.

Inputs to the simulation in addition to the student population, the load it generates, and the staff required for the student load are the present inventory and the net changes that will take place in it between the base year and the target planning year. The net changes include new construction (in-process and/or planned) and space to be removed by razing buildings.

Outputs from the simulation include the space projections (gross and net needs) by program, by year, and a measure of space utilization that is a measure of effectiveness. The space utilization measure requires some explanation. As noted, space is projected using linear equations with the constants representing ideal modular units of space. However, the supply of space is elastic for a given level of demand. For example, classrooms may be planned using a factor of 1.00 NASF/SCH, but the need for classroom space in that program will not be critical until utilization reaches 0.67 NASF/SCH. Thus for each type of space there is a range of acceptable utilization between the ideal and the near-saturation point that represents maximum possible use of space. A measure exceeding the ideal presents no problem, but a measure below the minimum indicates a critical shortage.

The simulation model is used to make forecasts of space requirements for several years and for a few alternative population forecasts. The output showing space needs and utilization by program and year can be used to develop maximum and minimum conditions to which planners and decision-makers can respond.

The number of years in the planning period for the institutions varies with the source of funding, normal lead time for a facility from its authorization until it is ready for occupancy, and the availability of data on which to base long range forecasts.

Given the space needs data, the facilities-planners and decision-makers must develop a set of building projects that will satisfy the space needs and propose a capital budget that will fund the projects. The system becomes quite open-ended at this point, constrained only by the space needs data, physical development plan (if available), and natural affinities of academic programs.

Facility-planners and decision-makers must choose programs or combinations of programs that have projected deficits in space that will enable a building project to house them to be created within the constraints associated with physical development plans (including land-use criteria) and natural program affinities.

They must also choose between building for long or short planning periods and between building general-use or specific-use facilities. They must weigh the several advantages and disadvantages of each. For example, building specific-use facilities using a long planning period may be cheaper (in today's dollars) and provide adequate expansion space; but in turn it may divert badly needed future dollars to a program that, if it does not grow as expected, may leave unoccupied space to be converted to other uses at a high cost.

Trying to satisfy the needs of many programs and still provide long-run expansion for each is a difficult task. One possible solution is to select projects that will satisfy space needs for groups of similar programs for the years in question. The assumption behind this is that the flow of future funds will be such that the secondary programs occupying space in a facility built for a primary program will get new facilities and the space they vacate can be used for expansion of the primary program in the facility.

Another problem facing the facilities-planner is the detail to which a proposed project is planned. The detail employed is a function of the type of funding support an institution gets. If only specific projects are supported, then very detailed plans and estimates must be made. If only general appropriations are involved, then fewer details are required. The latter approach does not imply that accuracy can be relaxed. The latter approach permits a more flexible response to the changing conditions facing an institution.

Depending upon the type of funding, capital budgets representing gross totals or complete documentation of specific projects are developed for each year. Initially, the budgets are expressed in base-year dollars and later updated to future-year dollars when scheduled starting dates are determined.

Any particular plan cannot possibly provide for all contingencies. There are some alternative courses of action that decision-makers can employ in the event of change. When a plan results in under-building because of lack of funding or faster-than-expected growth in the population and enrollment, the expansion of certain programs may be curtailed. The space-needs models can be used to compute program capacities where restrictions are required.

If an overbuilt condition should occur, faster growth rates in some programs may be encouraged or conversion of space for other uses may be considered. Again, the space-needs model can be used to calculate capacities and to help estimate growth rates.

Implementation of program growth may be hampered by the failure to acquire resources when they are needed. The space-needs models enable the data to be calculated that may be used to ensure that space will be coordinated with the other resources.

Individual projects have their own chain of events (from the development of architectural programs of requirements, through the design stage, to actual completion of construction) that varies in time duration depending upon the size and complexity of the project.

Putting all the projects and project events into a network requires attention to several factors from which precedence relationships can be derived. First, priorities must be established for projects based upon space deficits and the importance of the program to decision-makers. Second, location preferences resulting from physical development plans may imply certain precedence relationships. For example, if a development plan calls for a building housing a high-priority program to be located on a site that contains an obsolete building housing a program, then space for that program, regardless of its priority, must be found before the site can be vacated for the new building. Where location and priority provide a mutually conflicting situation, then one or the other must be changed. Third, fund flow per year and/or the number of projects that can be managed at any one time may force projects to be advanced or deferred over others.

Once all the precedence relationships (real and implied) are resolved, the preliminary project network can be derived. The starting year can be fixed tentatively and base-year project costs can be updated. If funding restrictions are violated as a result, appropriate adjustments can be made.

The preliminary project network is tested using the simulation to see if the proposed projects will produce the required space and yield acceptable space utilization profiles. The results of the run should yield data to indicate if any adjustment in the projects and/or the network are required.

The simulation model may be run in a sensitivity analysis in which the effects of various contingencies such as faster-than-expected growth in population may be tested. Some adjustments may be suggested as a hedge against these contingencies. Slack in the network may also serve as a hedge against contingencies.

Before adjustment and reevaluation can be considered complete, the degree to which the projects solve the space needs by discipline group for the years under study must be checked to ensure that this is under control.

Changing time and events demand that the system be responsive to change. The planning period must be extended at the end of each year, and the project plans must be adjusted in response to unexpected changes in the population, delays in planning and construction, and delays and/or losses in funding.

After each period, the plan is updated for both the project planning period and the forecasting period. The method used to extend the plan depends upon the degree to which projects are fixed in the initial period. For example, an institution may be working with a six-year capital plan (which is funded two years at a time) and a forecasting period of from ten to twelve years.

Every two years, the project plan may be extended for six years and the forecast may be extended for a period of from ten to twelve years.

The stability of the solution is potentially a great problem. If reevaluated every two years, there is a chance that at least a part of any six-year plan will be found invalid. The response is to retain what cannot be changed and alter the balance of the plan in the time remaining in the planning period. If the population and policy elements are stable, then changes probably will be minimized. The long-range-forecast data also help produce stability, providing, of course, that they are reasonably accurate.

The space-use models have been used in several phases of planning at the Ohio State University. Most of the current capital plan project estimates were developed using the space-needs estimates as a basis. Two professional college expansion programs were developed using the model.

The reaction of individual departments and colleges is mixed. Representing small maturing programs adequately and handling the special facilities with low utilization seem to be the major problems. Reaction is also mixed depending upon the planning period. The longer the period, the more acceptable the results are. The shorter the period, the more real the need is, and thus there is greater sensitivity to the results.

Elaboration of the system as a decision aid for development planning and budgeting is continuing. If its utility as a decision aid is demonstrated, it will be installed as an ongoing part of university operations. State-level planners have expressed an interest in the use of such a system to aid them. The statewide system will include not only the space-requirement model but other components as well. The system could be adapted for such use because a uniform information system encompassing all resources and student enrollments exists to support it.

The system described is just one that may be used in facilities planning. Much more experience is needed with all elements of the system to say that it will perform well in the face of the many adverse conditions that may be encountered. The key to the general success of the approach rests to a great degree on the success of program budgeting in universities. Without a commitment to rational resource allocation and to coordination in the process of their allocation, the utility of the system to decision-makers is weakened.

Many components of the system need further investigation both in a specific and a general context. The whole area of student population and load forecasting needs analysis. The trade-off between the degree of detail of forecasts in a given year and the number of years in the forecast needs to be studied. Space-needs models can be improved by further analysis.

The alternatives available to facilities-planners and decision-makers can be better quantified. Such questions as the following need to be answered: (1) What is an economical size for a building project? (2) What is an optimal planning horizon for a facility? (3) What are the factors and their cost implications for choosing to build facilities for specific or general uses?

The problem of what are meaningful measures of program effectiveness remains unsolved. However, the solution to this problem is as much a job of soul-searching for university faculty and administrators in higher education as it is a job of research.

In conclusion, there is an important task remaining that is as much political as it is analytical. Controlling agencies need to be convinced that continuing flows of funds are needed and that the type of funding should allow flexibility in choice of projects within reasonable bounds. Perhaps this and other planning systems can be used to help convince controlling agencies that there is a rational basis for requests for funds.

References

1. H. D. Bareither and J. L. Schillinger, *University Space Planning* (Urbana: University of Illinois Press, 1968).
2. R. I. Levin and C. A. Kirkpatrick, *Planning and Control with PERT/CPM* (New York: McGraw-Hill, 1966).

Richard L. Francis

ANALYTIC APPROACHES TO FACILITY LAYOUT AND DESIGN

The purpose of this paper is to present a largely nontechnical review of the use of two analytical models as decision aids in solving facility layout and design problems. The models are referred to as the linear assignment model and the quadratic assignment model; both models are examples of mathematical programming models. The discussion emphasizes the application of the models rather than the mathematics involved.

By way of introduction, consider Figure 1. Imagine that the grid squares of Figure 1 represent 160 seats in a theater, and that the black square represents some focus of interest, such as a speaker at a lectern. Suppose further that there are to be 104 customers in the theater; the following "theater design" problem may now be posed: Given that each customer would like to be as close to the focus of interest as possible, but that at most one customer can occupy any seat, which seats would the customers choose? Hopefully, the solution to the problem is highly intuitive; the customers would be arranged in an approximately semicircular pattern about the focus of interest, as is shown in Figure 2. Such patterns are well known, of course; examples include semicircular Greek theaters designed as early as the second century B.C. The discussion of early Greek theaters by Bieber [3] suggests that their designers recognized the fact that a semicircular design would permit members of the audience to be as close as possible to the focus of interest.

An alternative wording of the theater design problem might be

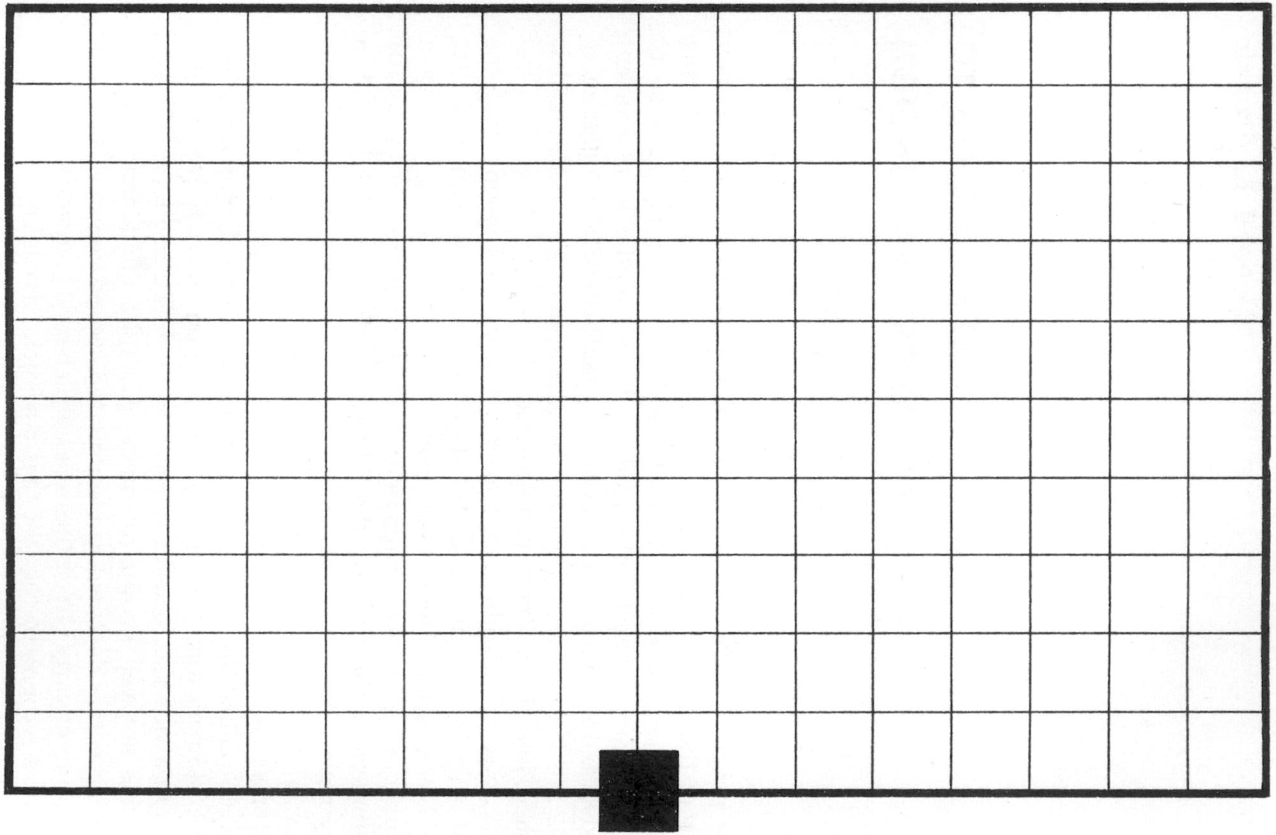

Fig. 1. Grid representation of theater seats.

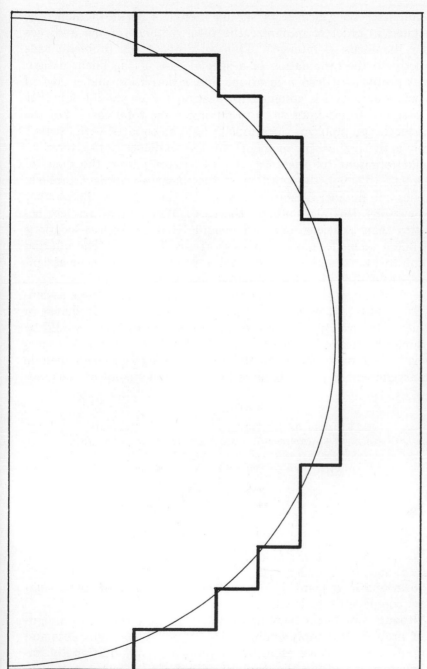

Fig. 2. Closest seating of theater patrons to a focus of interest.

as follows: To which seats should members of the audience be assigned in order to minimize the total distance of the audience from the focus of interest? This wording of the problem leads directly to the formulation of a special case of the linear assignment problem: Given n locations and n activities, and a cost of c_{ij} when activity i is assigned to location j, how should activities be assigned to locations so as to minimize the total cost? For the theater design problem, "locations" would be equated with "seats," and "activities" with "members of the audience"; the term c_{ij} would represent the distance of grid square j from the focus of interest. (Though the wording of the linear assignment problem implies the number of activities must be the same as the number of locations, this need not be the case. When there are less activities than locations, one can imagine that the excess locations are taken up by "dummy activities" at a cost $c_{ij} = 0$.) The solution of the theater design problem when formulated as a linear assignment problem is identical with that shown in Figure 2.

A simply hypothetical numerical example of the linear assignment problem, as well as two possible assignments, is shown in Table 1; the example is for the case $n = 3$; the terms c_{ij} would be obtained by relabeling locations A, B, and C as 1, 2, and 3 respectively. Examples related to the theater design problem include the assignment of plants to sites [13], the assignment of machines

TABLE 1

AN EXAMPLE OF THE LINEAR ASSIGNMENT PROBLEM:
COSTS, c_{ij}, FOR ACTIVITIES 1, 2, AND 3 AT LOCATIONS A, B, AND C

Activities	Locations		
	A	B	C
1	1	2	3
2	3	2	1
3	2	3	1

Possible Assignments	Costs Incurred
1 to C, 2 to A, 3 to B	3+3+3=9
1 to B, 2 to C, 3 to A	2+1+2=5

to locations in a plant [16], and the assignment of instrument panel components to locations [10].

Although one might be tempted to try to solve the linear assignment problem by simply enumerating all possible assignments and computing the cost for each, this approach is computationally unsatisfactory for all but the smallest values of n. Given n activities and n locations, there are n factorial different assignments; for 10 activities and locations, there are 3,628,800 different assignments.

Fortunately, there is a solution procedure for the linear assignment problem that is highly satisfactory; the formulation of the problem as a linear assignment model, which may be stated mathematically as follows:

Subject to the following conditions,

$$x_{ij} = \begin{cases} 1 \text{ if activity } i \text{ is assigned to location } j \\ 0 \text{ if not} \end{cases}$$

$$\sum_{i=1}^{n} x_{ij} = 1, j = 1, \ldots, n$$

(assign some activity to location j)

$$\sum_{j=1}^{n} x_{ij} = 1, j = 1, \ldots, n$$

(assign activity i to some location)

minimize the objective function, (total cost):

$$\sum_{i=1}^{n} \sum_{j=1}^{n} c_{ij} \, x_{ij} .$$

The economists Koopmans and Beckman [13] appear to have been the first to recognize that the linear assignment model could be applied to location problems. (It should be noted in passing that the linear assignment model is usually referred to simply as the assignment model, and has many other applications than those mentioned above.) A number of algorithms [2, 7, and 14], which are computationally quite efficient, have been developed for solving the linear assignment model; introductory discussions of the best known of the algorithms may be found in [5] and [18]. All of the algorithms involve establishing an initial assignment and then determining a sequence of additional assignments, each of which has a cost no greater than the previous one; as each new assignment is determined, a simple criterion establishes whether a least cost assignment has been found. For any large-scale use of an algorithm a digital computer would be employed. A self-contained discussion of the use of the linear assignment model for locating machines in a plant layout may be found in the paper by Moore [16]; the paper may possibly also serve as an introduction to the best known algorithmic procedure for solving the linear assignment problem. Some problems related to these types of problems are considered by Francis [8, 9].

Although the applications of the linear assignment model to location and layout problems are interesting, there are many such problems to which the model is not applicable, such as those having "interactions" among activities. Table 2 gives a simple hypothetical example of a problem having interactions. Three plants are to be assigned to three locations; there are shipments between

TABLE 2

AN EXAMPLE OF THE QUADRATIC ASSIGNMENT
PROBLEM: INTERACTIONS IN A PLANT LOCATION CONTEXT

Plant 1 *Location*	*Plant 2* *Location*			*Plant 1* *Location*	*Plant 3* *Location*			*Plant 2* *Location*	*Plant 3* *Location*		
	A	B	C		A	B	C		A	B	C
A	–	4	6	A	–	1	8	A	–	5	6
B	4	–	2	B	1	–	7	B	5	–	3
C	6	2	–	C	8	7	–	C	6	3	–

Possible Assignments	*Quadratic (or Shipment) Cost*	*Linear Cost*	*Total Cost*
1 to C, 2 to A, 3 to B	6+7+5=18	9	27
1 to B, 2 to C, 3 to A	2+1+6=9	5	4

plants, and the shipment costs depend upon the relative locations of the plants. For example, if plant 1 is at location A and plant 2 is at location B, then the shipment cost between the two plants is 4; if plant 2 is at location C, the shipment cost between the two plants is 6. Total shipment costs (also called quadratic costs for a reason to become clear shortly) are given for two possible assignments; the linear costs were obtained from Table 1 assuming that the costs in that example are also applicable for this example. Numerous other examples of interactions exist. In a plant layout context, the interaction might represent the cost of the flow of materials between departments [1]; in an office layout context, the cost of paper flow and personnel travel between departments [20]; in an instrument panel layout context, the total amount of eye travel [10]; in a wiring board context, the cost of connecting wire [19].

The example of Table 2 is one illustration of what is referred to in the mathematical programming literature as the quadratic assignment problem; the formulation of this problem is again due to Koopmans and Beckman [13]. In passing, it should be pointed out that, outside of the mathematical programming literature, applications of the quadratic assignment model to layout and/or location problems are usually not referred to as such; the use of terms such as "relative location of facilities" or "assignment of facilities to locations" is more common. The total enumeration approach is even less feasible for solving the quadratic assignment problem than for solving the linear assignment problem; for a quadratic assignment problem involving the assignment of 12 activities to locations, it has been estimated that the computation time involved in enumerating and computing the cost of all assignments would be approximately ten years on the GE 265 computer, and three years on the IBM 7090 computer [17].

As with the linear assignment problem, the quadratic assignment problem may be formulated in precise mathematical terms as follows:

Data: c_{ij} = cost when activity i is at location j

d_{ijpq} = "interaction cost" when activity i is at location j and activity p is at location q

minimize:

$$\sum_{i=1}^{n} \sum_{j=1}^{n} c_{ij} x_{ij} + \sum_{i=1}^{n} \sum_{j=1}^{n} \sum_{p=1}^{n} \sum_{q=1}^{n} x_{ij} d_{ijpq} x_{pq}$$

subject to

$x_{ij} = 0$ or 1 for all i and j

$$\sum_{i=1}^{n} x_{ij} = 1, \ j = 1, \ldots, n$$

$$\sum_{j=1}^{n} x_{ij} = 1, \ i = 1, \ldots, n.$$

When all the terms d_{ijpq} in the quadratic assignment model are zero, a comparison with the linear assignment model demonstrates that the two models are identical. It is the terms involving the d_{ijpq} that distinguish the two problems; notice that when $x_{ij} = 1$ and $x_{pq} = 1$, then activity i is in location j and activity p is in location q, so that the cost $x_{ij} d_{ijpq} x_{pq} = d_{ijpq}$ makes a contribution to the total cost. If either $x_{ij} = 0$ or $x_{pq} = 0$, then activity i is not in location j or activity p is not in location q, so that the term

$x_{ij}\ d_{ijpq}\ x_{pq}=0$ and makes no contribution to the total cost. The shipment costs of Table 2 provide examples of the terms d_{ijpq} on relabeling locations A, B, and C as 1, 2, and 3 respectively.

Just as for the linear assignment model, there are algorithms for finding minimum cost solutions to the quadratic assignment model; the algorithms of Gilmore [11] and Lawler [15] are the best-known; a substantially complete list of references on the quadratic assignment model may be found in the paper by Hillier and Connors [12]. However, it is unfortunately the case that the quadratic assignment problem, which has many more facility layout applications than the linear assignment problem, is substantially more difficult to solve; computational results for the algorithm are discouraging [12, 17]. Partly because finding minimum cost assignments in a computationally efficient manner is at present so difficult, there has developed a substantial interest in heuristic solution methods, which may be characterized briefly as methods that find "good" solutions, but do not always find a best solution. Enough different heuristic approaches have now been developed for solving the quadratic assignment problem that a comparison of the various approaches is of considerable interest; such a comparison may be found in the recent and quite readable paper by Nugent et al. [17].

As representative of two heuristic approaches for solving the quadratic assignment problems, the works of Armour and Buffa [1] and of Vollmann, Nugent, and Zartler [20], will be examined briefly. The work of Armour and Buffa is commonly referred to by the acronym CRAFT (Computerized Relative Location of Facilities Technique); the most complete set of references on CRAFT may be found in [4], together with an introductory discussion. Briefly, the CRAFT approach is as follows; given an initial assignment of facilities (which may be of different sizes and shapes) to locations, among all pairwise interchanges of facilities that are feasible, that interchange is made which results in the greatest decrease in the total cost. The pairwise interchange procedure continues until the total cost cannot be further decreased. The procedure is feasible for problems of reasonable size only when a digital computer is used, of course; the CRAFT computer program is available through the IBM SHARE library [6]. The CRAFT procedure is among those compared by Nugent et al. [17].

A heuristic procedure similar to the CRAFT procedure is employed by Vollman et al. [20], whose work is of particular interest in that it is one of the few instances in which experience is reported on real applications of a heuristic procedure for solving the quadratic assignment problem, and in that it deals with problems of office layout, as opposed to job shop layout or plant layout. One is happy to be able to report that the experience is quite favorable; a study carried out involving the office layout of a large oil company determined that significant cost reductions could be achieved through use of the procedure. The study is also of particular interest in that intangible aspects the procedure could not deal with were taken into account by using the procedure as a design aid for an architect. Both the oil company and the architect found the procedure to be of considerable value.

References

1. G. C. Armour and E. S. Buffa, "A Heuristic Algorithm and Simulation Approach to Relative Location of Facilities," *Management Science* 9:2 (1963), 294-309.

2. M. L. Balinski and R. E. Gomory, "A Primal Method for the Assignment and Transportation Problems," *Management Science* 10:3 (1964), 578-93.

3. M. Bieber, *The History of the Greek and Roman Theater* (Princeton, N.J.: Princeton University Press, 1961).

4. E. S. Buffa, "Facilities Design for Intermittent Systems," *Production-Inventory Systems: Planning and Control* (Homewood, Ill.: R. D. Irwin, 1968), chap. 10.

5. C. W. Churchman, R. L. Ackoff, and E. L. Arnoff, *Introduction to Operations Research* (New York: Wiley, 1957).

6. CRAFT Computer Program, SHARE Library No. SDA 3391, The I.B.M. Corporation.

7. L. R. Ford, Jr., and D. R. Fulkerson, *Flows in Networks* (Princeton, N.J.: Princeton University Press, 1962).

8. R. L. Francis, "Sufficient Conditions for Some Optimum-Property Facility Designs," *Operations Research* 15:3 (1967), 448-66.

9. ———, "On Some Problems of Rectangular Warehouse Design and Layout," *Journal of Industrial Engineering* 18:10 (1967), 595-604.

10. L. E. Freund and T. L. Sadosky, "Linear Programming Applied to Optimization of Instrument Panel and Workplace Layout," *Human Factors* 9:4 (1967).

11. P. C. Gilmore, "Optimal and Suboptimal Algorithms for the Quadratic Assignment Problem," *Journal of the Society for Industrial and Applied Mathematics* 10:2 (1962), 305-13.

12. F. S. Hillier and M. M. Connors, "Quadratic Assignment Problem Algorithms and the Location of Indivisible Facilities," *Management Science* 13:1 (1966), 42-57.

13. T. C. Koopmans and M. Beckman, "Assignment Problems and the Location of Economic Activities," *Econometrics* 25:1 (1957), 53-76.

14. H. W. Kuhn, "The Hungarian Method for Solving the Assignment Problem," *Naval Research Logistics Quarterly* 2 (1955), 83-97.

15. E. L. Lawler, "The Quadratic Assignment Problem," *Management Science* 9:4 (1963), 586-99.

16. J. M. Moore, "Optimal Location for Multiple Machines," *Journal of Industrial Engineering* 12:5 (1961), 307-13.

17. C. E. Nugent, T. E. Vollmann, and J. Ruml, "An Experimental Comparison of Techniques for the Assignment of Facilities to Locations," *Operations Research* 16:1 (1968), 150-73.

18. M. Sasieni, A. Yaspan, and L. Friedman, *Operations Research: Methods and Problems* (New York: Wiley, 1959).

19. L. Steinberg, "The Backboard Wiring Problem: A Placement Algorithm," *Society of Industrial and Applied Mathematics Review* 3:1 (1961), 37-50.

20. T. E. Vollmann, C. E. Nugent, and R. L. Zartler, "A Computerized Model for Office Layout," *Journal of Indstrial Engineering* 19:7 (1968), 321-27.

Francis Hendricks

DEVELOPMENT ACTION SEQUENCING UNDER HIGHLY CONSTRAINED CONDITIONS

An interesting class of problem for which decision aids have proven useful is the one having a large number of units of two types for which a sequence network is to be formulated where units of each type exercise a condition or constraint that must be satisfied over units of the other type. Such network formulation problems, particularly when the number of units or elements is even moderately large in number, challenge the human mind's information-processing capacity to reach a solution efficiently and easily. Such problems are widely encountered in management, planning, and design; and where the network formulation process can be stated explicitly, the solution methodology can be established as an algorithm for repeated routine use, often in conjunction with computer systems.

A typical manifestation of this class of problem is in remodeling, construction, and redevelopment, where changes and improvements are to be created while on-going operations and services cannot be interrupted and where a variety of contingencies can occur to disrupt sequencing and scheduling. Rebuilding an airport while maintaining it in full operation, remodeling a building while tenants continue to use it, the construction of a subway or freeway system, and the renewal of a military installation or portion of a city are but a few familiar cases where existing conditions exercise a constraint over proposed changes and improvements, and vice versa, and where progress schedules may be disrupted by changes in priorities and projects, supply and availability problems, accidental destruction of space and other resources, and the like.

A description follows of a general methodology for constructing action sequence chains or networks for this class of problem. The description, presented in illustrative form, including the means for dealing with a number of common contingencies, considers the case where existing buildings are replaced by new buildings while their functions remain in operation during the process. It is believed that the description may be generalized to cover a variety of different situations having essentially the same problem structure.

Assume a rectangular district subdivided into twelve subareas that may represent blocks or development parcels. Figure 1 indicates the locations of existing buildings and the subareas within which the proposed buildings are to be located.

The information sets shown in Table 1 indicate which of the existing buildings are to be replaced by new buildings and into which new building the functions located in existing buildings are to be relocated.

TABLE 1

REPLACEMENT OF BUILDINGS AND RELOCATION OF FUNCTIONS

New Buildings to Replace Existing Buildings		Functions to be Relocated from Existing to New Buildings	
New	*Existing*	*Existing*	*New*
a	–	P	f
b	Q	Q	g
c	R	R	i
d	S	S	c
e	T	T	b
f	U	U	h
g	–	V	d
h	W	W	a
i	X	X	e
j	Y	Y	j
–	P		
–	V		

It will be noted that two subareas are currently vacant and that they are to be the subareas within which new buildings a and g are to be located. In general, a development action sequence chain is begun with a new building that is to be located in a vacant subarea. Such buildings can be built immediately since no demolitions are required, no activities are involved that need to be relocated, and no interruption of any necessary function will occur.

The next element in the development action sequence chain con-

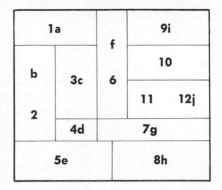

Fig. 1.   Diagram of subareas showing the locations of existing (upper-case letters) and proposed (lower-case letters) buildings.

cerns the existing buildings housing those functions that will be moved into the new building. When the new building is completed, the functions will be moved, the existing buildings demolished, the site cleared, and the process repeated until all new buildings have been constructed and all functions are relocated.

To make more convenient the use and manipulation of the data contained in the two information sets shown in Figure 1, it will be useful to present them in the form of binary matrices as shown in Figure 2. Both matrices are formed by placing a zero at the intersections of the rows and columns except at those intersections where the column and row designation coincide with the data presented in each of the rows of Table 1. Thus, Table 1 indicates that the new building b is to replace the existing building Q; the number one is placed at the intersection of column b and row Q.

For situations of the complexity of this demonstration, development action sequence chains can readily be formulated from the matrices set forth in Figure 2. However, for the highly complex situations for which this methodology is most valuable, it would not be convenient to assemble the development action sequence chains manually. In highly complex situations involving many existing and new buildings, the methodology should be programmed for a computer.

Manually, the development action sequence chains are formulated as follows. Examine the Building Replacement Matrix (BRM) to identify the columns that contain all zeros. The new

BUILDING REPLACEMENT MATRIX

New Buildings to Replace
Existing Buildings

	a	b	c	d	e	f	g	h	i	j
P	0	0	0	0	0	0	0	0	0	0
Q	0	1	0	0	0	0	0	0	0	0
R	0	0	1	0	0	0	0	0	0	0
S	0	0	0	1	0	0	0	0	0	0
T	0	0	0	0	1	0	0	0	0	0
U	0	0	0	0	0	1	0	0	0	0
V	0	0	0	0	0	0	0	0	0	0
W	0	0	0	0	0	0	0	1	0	0
X	0	0	0	0	0	0	0	0	1	0
Y	0	0	0	0	0	0	0	0	0	1

FUNCTION RELOCATION MATRIX

Functions to be Relocated From
Existing to New Buildings

	a	b	c	d	e	f	g	h	i	j
P	0	0	0	0	0	1	0	0	0	0
Q	0	0	0	0	0	0	1	0	0	0
R	0	0	0	0	0	0	0	0	1	0
S	0	0	1	0	0	0	0	0	0	0
T	0	1	0	0	0	0	0	0	0	0
U	0	0	0	0	0	0	0	1	0	0
V	0	0	0	1	0	0	0	0	0	0
W	1	0	0	0	0	0	0	0	0	0
X	0	0	0	0	1	0	0	0	0	0
Y	0	0	0	0	0	0	0	0	0	1

Fig. 2.   Data in figure 1 presented in matrix form.

buildings designated by the headings of those columns are the ones to be constructed within vacant subareas; chains are begun with this type of project. From the BRM, it can be seen that two new buildings, a and g, satisfy this condition.

Next, examine the Function Relocation Matrix (FRM) to identify the existing buildings whose functions will be relocated in new buildings a and g. The FRM indicates that the functions in building W will be relocated in new building a and the functions in building Q will be relocated in new building g. Thus, the vacating and demolition of buildings W and Q are the next elements in their respective chains.

The process consists of alternately inspecting the BRM and the

FRM for the identification of the next element in the chain until identification is made of the last new building in the chain, BRM, along with the existing building to be demolished from which functions are to be relocated within the new building. This procedure will produce two development action sequence chains:

a-W-h-U-f-P   and   g-Q-b-T-e-X-i-R-c-S-d-V.

It will be noted also that there is a one in the diagonal of the FRM. This means that the functions located in existing building Y are to be relocated within the same subarea in new building j. When this condition occurs, the functions in existing building Y will have to be temporarily relocated in an empty building—in this case either existing buildings P or V—during the demolition of Y and the construction of j.

To handle the temporary relocation of the functions in existing building Y within existing building P using the original matrices, it is necessary to add an additional column and row to both the BRM and the FRM. The additional row may be identified as P', reflecting the use of the existing building P for temporary relocation purposes. This is an extra step in the development process and, hence, an extra link in the development action sequence chain. Correspondingly, an additional column is added to the BRM and the FRM as a pseudo-project representing the temporary relocation of the functions in existing building Y that are destined to be relocated ultimately in new building j. Let the pseudo-project be designated at j'. Thus, the augmented original matrices will appear as shown in Figure 3.

The final development action sequence chains for the demonstration are:

a-W-h-U-f-P'-j'-Y-j-P   and   g-Q-b-T-e-X-i-R-c-S-d-V.

The basic methodology described above for the formulation of development action sequence chains will always produce a logical order of development actions with the fewest number of temporary relocations of functions, although that order may not involve the shortest amount of time relative to other possible ordering involving additional numbers of temporary relocations of functions. In addition to the straightforward formulation of development action sequence chains, the methodology may be augmented for the pur-

BUILDING REPLACEMENT MATRIX

	a	b	c	d	e	f	g	h	i	j	j'
P	0	0	0	0	0	0	0	0	0	0	0
P'	0	0	0	0	0	0	0	0	0	0	1
Q	0	1	0	0	0	0	0	0	0	0	0
R	0	0	1	0	0	0	0	0	0	0	0
S	0	0	0	1	0	0	0	0	0	0	0
T	0	0	0	0	1	0	0	0	0	0	0
U	0	0	0	0	0	1	0	0	0	0	0
V	0	0	0	0	0	0	0	0	0	0	0
W	0	0	0	0	0	0	0	1	0	0	0
X	0	0	0	0	0	0	0	0	1	0	0
Y	0	0	0	0	0	0	0	0	0	1	0

FUNCTION RELOCATION MATRIX

	a	b	c	d	e	f	g	h	i	j	j'
P	0	0	0	0	0	0	0	0	0	1	0
P'	0	0	0	0	0	1	0	0	0	0	0
Q	0	0	0	0	0	0	1	0	0	0	0
R	0	0	0	0	0	0	0	0	1	0	0
S	0	0	1	0	0	0	0	0	0	0	0
T	0	1	0	0	0	0	0	0	0	0	0
U	0	0	0	0	0	0	0	1	0	0	0
V	0	0	0	1	0	0	0	0	0	0	0
W	1	0	0	0	0	0	0	0	0	0	0
X	0	0	0	0	1	0	0	0	0	0	0
Y	0	0	0	0	0	0	0	0	0	0	1

Fig. 3.   Augmented BRM and FRM to reflect interim relocations.

pose of handling a number of influences that might arise to change the construction program. The following are among the most common:

1. Interim relocations of activities to allow construction of high priority buildings at an earlier date

2. Accidental destruction of an existing building

3. Change in the site of a planned building

4. Elimination or addition of a new building due to a change in requirements

If a new building, which is to be located on the site of an existing building, is to be constructed earlier than projected, it will be necessary to arrange for the temporary relocation of the functions housed within the the existing building that is to be demolished in order to provide a site for the new building. If the temporary relocation is to be to one of the existing buildings, the procedure for handling this case utilizing the matrices set forth in Figure 3 is similar to the ones described above for the temporary relocation of functions which are to be housed in a new building within the same subarea.

An illustration of the procedure follows. Assume that new building i is to be constructed immediately following new building a. This change in sequence requires that existing building X be vacated and demolished to provide a clear site for the construction of building i. It means also that the functions in existing building X must be temporarily relocated. Assume also that existing build-

ABRM

	a	b	c	d	e	f	g	h	i	i'	j	j'
P	0	0	0	0	0	0	0	0	0	0	0	0
P'	0	0	0	0	0	0	0	0	0	0	0	1
Q	0	1	0	0	0	0	0	0	0	0	0	0
R	0	0	1	0	0	0	0	0	0	0	0	0
S	0	0	0	1	0	0	0	0	0	0	0	0
T	0	0	0	0	1	0	0	0	0	0	0	0
U	0	0	0	0	0	1	0	0	0	0	0	0
V	0	0	0	0	0	0	0	0	0	0	0	0
W	0	0	0	0	0	0	0	1	0	0	0	0
W'	0	0	0	0	0	0	0	0	0	1	0	0
X	0	0	0	0	0	0	0	0	1	0	0	0
Y	0	0	0	0	0	0	0	0	0	0	1	0

AFRM

	a	b	c	d	e	f	g	h	i	i'	j	j'
P	0	0	0	0	0	0	0	0	0	0	1	0
P'	0	0	0	0	0	1	0	0	0	0	0	0
Q	0	0	0	0	0	0	1	0	0	0	0	0
R	0	0	0	0	0	0	0	0	1	0	0	0
S	0	0	1	0	0	0	0	0	0	0	0	0
T	0	1	0	0	0	0	0	0	0	0	0	0
U	0	0	0	0	0	0	0	1	0	0	0	0
V	0	0	0	1	0	0	0	0	0	0	0	0
W	0	0	0	0	1	0	0	0	0	0	0	0
W'	1	0	0	0	0	0	0	0	0	0	0	0
X	0	0	0	0	0	0	0	0	0	1	0	0
Y	0	0	0	0	0	0	0	0	0	0	0	1

Fig. 4. New ABRM and AFRM.

ing W, which will be vacated due to the construction of new building a, is suitable for the functions in existing building X and that they may be relocated there temporarily. As in the temporary relocation illustration above, an additional column and row must be added to the augmented BRM (ABRM) and the augmented FRM (AFRM). The additional row may be identified as W', reflecting the use of existing building W for temporary relocation purposes. Similarly, let the additional column be designated i', reflecting the pseudo-project of temporarily relocating the functions in existing building X. The new ABRM and AFRM are shown in Figure 4. The reader can verify for himself that the amended development action sequence chains are:

a-W'-i'-X-i-R-c-S-d-V   and   g-Q-b-T-e-W-h-U-f-P'-j'-Y-j-P.

The accidental destruction of an existing building for any reason may be considered as tantamount to the clearing of the subarea in which it is located for the construction of a new building. The effect of this circumstance may be demonstrated by assuming that existing building U has been destroyed and its functions have been relocated in extra, unused space in existing building R. To reflect this, the ABRM and the AFRM may be modified, as shown in Figure 5, adding an additional row to both matrices—designated R'— by placing zeroes in all cells in row U in both matrices, and by placing the number one in row N' in the AFRM at column h. The creation of a new row permits showing that existing building f can be built immediately, i.e., all zeroes in column f of the ABRM. That the functions formerly located in existing building U are now located in R' is shown by the number one in row R' and column h in the AFRM. The deletion of the number one from row U in both matrices indicates that building U does not exist and that its functions are not located there. The resulting three development sequence chains are:

a-W'-i'-X-i-R-c-S-d-V, f-P'-j'-Y-j-P,   and   g-Q-b-T-e-W-h-R'.

A change in the subarea in which a new building is to be constructed without a change in the functions to be relocated in it affects only the BRM. The BRM can be changed easily by moving the number one in the column representing the new building in question from the row representing the existing building in the

ABRM

	a	b	c	d	e	f	g	h	i	i'	j	j'
P	0	0	0	0	0	0	0	0	0	0	0	0
P'	0	0	0	0	0	0	0	0	0	0	0	1
Q	0	1	0	0	0	0	0	0	0	0	0	0
R	0	0	1	0	0	0	0	0	0	0	0	0
R'	0	0	0	0	0	0	0	0	0	0	0	0
S	0	0	0	1	0	0	0	0	0	0	0	0
T	0	0	0	0	1	0	0	0	0	0	0	0
U	0	0	0	0	0	0	0	0	0	0	0	0
V	0	0	0	0	0	0	0	0	0	0	0	0
W	0	0	0	0	0	0	0	1	0	0	0	0
W'	0	0	0	0	0	0	0	0	0	1	0	0
X	0	0	0	0	0	0	0	0	1	0	0	0
Y	0	0	0	0	0	0	0	0	0	0	1	0

AFRM

	a	b	c	d	e	f	g	h	i	i'	j	j'
P	0	0	0	0	0	0	0	0	0	0	1	0
P'	0	0	0	0	0	1	0	0	0	0	0	0
Q	0	0	0	0	0	0	1	0	0	0	0	0
R	0	0	0	0	0	0	0	0	1	0	0	0
R'	0	0	0	0	0	0	0	1	0	0	0	0
S	0	0	1	0	0	0	0	0	0	0	0	0
T	0	1	0	0	0	0	0	0	0	0	0	0
U	0	0	0	0	0	0	0	0	0	0	0	0
V	0	0	0	1	0	0	0	0	0	0	0	0
W	0	0	0	0	1	0	0	0	0	0	0	0
W'	1	0	0	0	0	0	0	0	0	0	0	0
X	0	0	0	0	0	0	0	0	0	1	0	0
Y	0	0	0	0	0	0	0	0	0	0	0	1

Fig. 5. Modified ABRM and AFRM to reflect the destruction of existing building U.

subarea in which it was to be located (placing a zero there instead) to the row representing the existing building in the subarea where it is to be located. Where new buildings are added to, or eliminated from, the development program, it will be necessary to either add or delete a column from the matrices. Such a change is a change in the basic data for the development program. It can be reflected in the matrices by using the same processes as are used to establish them originally.

It should be noted also that once the BRM and the FRM have been created, they can be multiplied, using standard matrix multiplication techniques, to produce a new matrix that describes the sequences directly and thereby eliminates the necessity of alternating between the BRM and the FRM to identify the construction and demolition sequences. In addition, though no application involving more than two constraints has been attempted as yet, it appears that the two-constraint methodology could readily be adapted to handle three or more constraints represented in matrix form.

The methodology for formulating development sequence action chains as described above is most valuable for problems involving large numbers of existing and old units of development whether they be buildings, portions of municipal service systems, or whatever. While the methodology provides for the orderly arrangement of data for manual use, its convenient use and reuse with highly complex programs for generating the information on development action sequence alternatives as a base for further analysis with respect to timing, resource requirements, costs, and so on, will require that it be programmed for a computer. Computer programs of the methodology developed and used by the authors have proved to be useful as decision-making aids for generating alternative chains for evaluating according to criteria exogenous to the method.

References

1. R. G. Busaker and T. L. Saaty, *Finite Graphs and Networks* (New York: McGraw-Hill, 1965), chaps. 6, 9, 10.
2. J. D. Foulkes "Directed Graphs and Assembly Schedules," *Proc. Sympos. Appl. Math.* 10 (1960), 281-89.
3. A. Kaufman and R. Faure, "Introduction to Operations Research," *Mathematics in Science and Engineering,* vol. 47 (New York: Academic Press, 1968), chap. 16.
4. *Master Development Plan Programming System for the Redevelopment of Naval Installations.* Ruth & Krushkhov, consultants to the Western Division of the Naval Facilities Engineering Command, San Bruno, California, November, 1966.

John W. Dickey

ADAPTIVE DIAGNOSIS
OF PROBLEMS

Anyone who has the opportunity to be involved in the education of both architects and engineers faces an interesting and enlightening experience, especially with respect to the significantly different approaches that the two professional groups take in solving problems. Although it is dangerous to generalize, it usually can be said that engineers are extremely adept at analyzing the potentiality of a solution once it has been proposed, but are hard-pressed to deliver a possible solution, especially in an unstructured situation. Architects, on the other hand, can create possibilities for new solutions at an extremely rapid rate, yet appear unable to rigorously analyze the suitability of the ideas. The difference between the two professions is that one appears to rely more on intuition and subconscious "feelings" whereas the other relies more on "systematic" analytical tools.

In viewing this difference in approaches, the observer can only feel that there must be some way in which the two approaches can be brought together to synthesize a technique (or techniques) that would take advantage of the strong points of each—the use of intuition and experience on the one hand and of logic and precision on the other. If such a technique could be found, it obviously would be of immense value to those professionals who are concerned with solving problems inherent in our environment.

NOTE. The author expresses appreciation to Mr. Michael Beachy, graduate student in the Environmental Systems Program of the College of Architecture at Virginia Polytechnic Institute for his assistance in developing some of the thinking for this paper.

A General Approach

The evolving field of operations research offers some potential for finding such a technique. In particular, the early (1763) work of Bayes [1] in dealing with subjectively established probabilities recently has been rediscovered and incorporated in sophisticated mathematical models. This approach appears to be providing some interesting insights into several old problems [3, 6] while at the same time leading to new situations that heretofore have never been explored [4]. The present purpose is to demonstrate, with an example, a Bayesian-related approach.

Perhaps the most vivid example of the use of a Bayesian approach to a problem would be its use as a tool in the problem identification process itself. Almost every architect, engineer, or planner agrees that problem identification is one of the most difficult, nebulous, and yet most important stages in the design or planning process, requiring the greatest expertise on the part of the professional. Thus, if a Bayesian-related technique is of value in problem identification, then it may well be of equal or greater value in some of the other, more tangible stages of the design process, such as identifying solution strategies.

To understand the technique, one must begin by hypothesizing on the general manner in which a problem (or set of problems) is identified. At the beginning, the designer would have only a vague idea of what the actual problem or malfunction may be, and this vague idea most likely would have been derived by noticing certain symptoms that seem to prevail. In an office building during the summer months, for example, the designer may notice that people are working in a rather lackadaisical manner, that some are perspiring, and that most have dressed in their lightest clothing. From these observations, the designer would have a premonition that there was a problem with, say, the air conditioning system or possibly the "heat absorbing" glass used in the windows.

In either case, the designer would not be willing to make any physical changes until he was more confident as to the actual malfunction causing the problem. Consequently, he probably would conduct some tests or experiments to reaffirm or change his present feelings as to the actual malfunction. For instance, in the situation described above, the designer may decide to experiment by lowering to its lowest point the setting on the thermostat controlling the air-conditioner to determine whether that causes a change in the situation. He might also place screens in front of the windows to keep out the sun's rays and observe the outcome of that experiment. He might decide to perform both experiments, depending upon the outcome of the first experiment he conducts and the costs involved. However, regardless of the experiments he chooses to conduct and the sequence in which they are performed, the designer will gain information from them, and he will become more confident about the nature of the problem.

If the problem identification process typified by this example is representative of what happens in most real world situations, then that process might be described as being composed of eight elements:

1. Possible *malfunctions* (problems), m

2. Designer-specified *chances* (probabilities), $P(m)$, that the actual malfunction is of type m

3. Existing *symptoms*, s, that imply different malfunctions

4. Possible *experiments*, e, that can be performed

5. *Costs*, $c(e)$, associated with each experiment

6. Certain outcomes or *responses*, $r(s)$, from an experiment measured by the intensity of the symptom observed

7. Designer-specified *chances* (probabilities), $P[r(s)|m,e]$, that response on symptom s of magnitude $r(s)$ would occur if malfunction m did exist and experiment e were performed

8. *Utilities*, $u[P(m),r(s),e]$, associated with malfunction probabilities corresponding to each possible response on experiment e

These elements would be related as follows. Viewing the various *symptoms* that exist, the designer, based upon his experience and intuition, guesses at the *chance* that a certain *malfunction* may exist. Not feeling overly confident about his guess, he strives to make it more realistic by performing an *experiment* selected on the basis of a *utility* whose value is found by considering the magnitude of the malfunction probabilities (the greater the variation from equal, the greater the utility) and the probable experiment *re-*

sponse and *cost*. He then notes the *response* in terms of changes in the symptoms and revises his estimates of the malfunction probabilities accordingly. This procedure is repeated until the utility becomes great enough for him to feel that he now can move on to the next stage in the design process, that of finding a cure (solution) for the identified malfunction.

As presented thus far, the problem identification process can be seen to rely heavily on subjective probability estimates based on many of those intangible yet significant factors, such as experience, background, and training, that provide the designer with the ability to make "good" guesses. Yet it is possible for the designer to become logically inconsistent with himself when making these guesses, and this obviously would be undesirable. For instance, he may estimate initially that the probability of the malfunction being in the air-conditioning system, in the previous example, as 0.50; and then, after having noted the continuing presence of perspiration after the "turn down thermostat" experiment, he may revise this figure to 0.70. This value, as will be seen later, is logically incorrect and might lead to some mistaken identities that, in turn, might hinder attempts to solve the problem. Thus, it is now possible to begin to see the interplay between the use of experience and intuition and logical manipulation.

The actual mechanics of the logical manipulation to be used in the problem identification procedure are, as intimated above, incorporated in an equation developed by Bayes that can be set forth, as

$$P[m|r(s),e] = \frac{P(m) \cdot P[r(s)|m,e]}{\sum\limits_{m} P(m) \cdot P[r(s)|m,e]}, \tag{1}$$

where

$P[m|r(s),e]$ = the (posterior) probability that the malfunction will be type m given that response $r(s)$ of symptom s has been observed in experiment e;

$P(m)$ = the (prior) probability that the malfunction is of type m; and

$P[r(s)|m,e]$ = the probability that response $r(s)$ on symptom s would be observed if malfunction m did exist and experiment e were performed.

This equation, developed under strict mathematical rules, can be interpreted loosely as follows: the new (posterior) estimate of the chance that malfunction m exists is a relative function of the old (prior) estimate weighted by the chance that certain responses will be found from experiment e.

For present purposes two other equations must be generated, one for determining the over-all probability of getting a given response, $r(s)$, from an experiment, and the other for calculating the "utility" of a given response from a certain experiment. In the first case, the equation is:

$$P[r(s)|e] = \sum_m P(m) \cdot P[r(s)|m,e] , \qquad (2)$$

where $P[r(s)|e]$ is the probability of getting response $r(s)$ to experiment e. This response, of course, depends on what malfunctions actually exist, and this feature is portrayed in the equation.

A measure of utility, like most measures, is difficult to specify. If it is assumed, without detracting from the general applicability of the subsequent discussion, that (1) only one of two possible malfunctions can exist, (2) there is only one symptom, and (3) the response related to the symptom is either positive, meaning the symptom exists, or negative, meaning that it does not exist, then the utility function can be simplified. Logically, it would be desirable to have the chance of one malfunction or the other existing to be as close to zero or one as possible, or, in other words, as far away from the undiscerning 50-50 case as possible. The quantity

$$u[P(m),r,e] = |P(1) - 0.50| + |P(2) - 0.50|, \qquad (3)$$

might be of use in this regard. Since $u[P(m),r,e]$ is the utility derived from obtaining response r (on the one symptom being observed) from experiment e and $P(1)$ and $P(2)$ are the probabilities of having malfunctions one and two respectively, calculated from equation 1 based upon original estimates of the probabilities, $u[P(m),r,e]$ can be seen to give a value of 0.00 for the 50-50 case and 1.00 for the 1-0 or 0-1 case. Thus, a high value for $u[P(m),r,e]$ would indicate that a great amount of confidence could be placed in the assumption that the highly probable malfunction actually existed. A low value would imply that it would be difficult to tell which malfunction was present.

Quite naturally, it would be expected that $u[P(m),r,e]$ would increase as more experiments are performed since the effect of more experimentation would be to provide more information about the malfunction. However, this increase in information must be weighed against (1) the probability of actually achieving it (obtaining certain responses from particular experiments) and (2) the cost of the experiments. This line of thinking would lead to a utility function for a set of experiments as noted in the equation

$$U = \frac{\sum_r P[r|e] \cdot u[P(m),r,e]}{C}, \tag{4}$$

where C is the cost of all of the experiments in the set and e is the last experiment performed. The goal would be to choose, in a sequential manner, those experiments that would lead to the greatest value of U. These would be the ones that would provide a refined ability to identify the malfunction and at the same time keep the costs of experiments low.

A Detailed Example

The hypothetical situation referred to earlier will be used to illustrate the methodology. For the illustration one symptom, people perspiring, and two possible malfunctions, the air-conditioning system and the heat-absorbing glass, will be considered. It will be assumed that both malfunctions have an equal probability of occurring.

Two experiments are feasible—one in which the thermostat is set at the lowest temperature and the other in which a sun shield is placed next to the heat-absorbing glass window. These experiments will cost \$10 and \$20 respectively. It is estimated by the designer that if the air-conditioning system is not functioning (malfunction m_1) and the thermostat is turned down (experiment e_1), the probability of the problem continuing would be 0.80 and of the malfunction being identified, 0.20. He also specified probabilities for the other combinations of possible malfunctions and experiments as shown in the lower portion of Table 1. A complete detailing of the major aspects of the situation is included in the table.

The questions to be answered are those concerning the nature of the actual malfunction and the experiments to be conducted to determine the malfunction, assuming that there is actually only one malfunction. Should experiment e_1 or e_2 be conducted, both or

TABLE 1

CONDITIONS FOR DETAILED EXAMPLE

Symptom
s_1 = Workers in a building are perspiring.

Possible Malfunctions
m_1 = Air conditioning system does not work.
m_2 = "Heat absorbing" glass not absorbing heat from sun.

Possible Experiments
e_1 = Turn down thermostat to lowest temperature setting.
e_2 = Put up screen to shield sun.

Responses
r_1 = Perspiration (Positive)
r_2 = No perspiration (Negative)

Initial Estimates of Malfunctions	*Costs of Experiments*
$P(m_1) = 0.50$	$c(e_1) = \$10$
$P(m_2) = 0.50$	$c(e_2) = \$20$

Probabilities of getting responses if a given malfunction does exist *and* a certain experiment is performed		m_1 e_1	m_2 e_1	m_1 e_2	m_2 e_2
	r_1	0.80	0.10	0.70	0.15
	r_2	0.20	0.90	0.30	0.85

neither? The answer lies in the sequence of experiments that produces the greatest utility.

To begin the procedure, a decision tree is constructed as shown in Figure 1. Each experiment as well as each possible response represents a branch of the tree. The alternate experiments and their responses compose branches from the first set of branches. For example, the performance of experiment e_1 with a positive (continued perspiration) response followed by experiment e_2 with a positive response comprises the complete lefthand branch in Figure 1.

Since the initial chance of the malfunction being either the air-conditioning system or the heat-absorbing glass is 50-50, at least one experiment must be conducted in order to obtain a better estimate of the malfunction. If experiment e_1 were attempted, at a cost of \$10, the probability of obtaining a positive or negative outcome could be calculated by using equation 2. Thus:

$$P[r_1|e_1] = 0.50(0.80) + 0.50(0.10) = 0.45 .$$

Similarly, the probability of a negative response on experiment e_1 is:

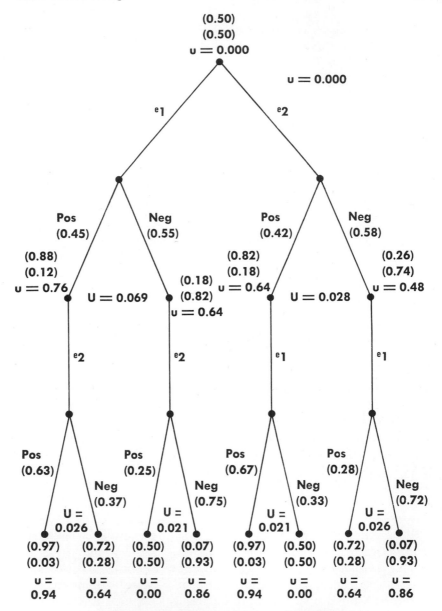

Fig. 1. Decision tree for example problem.

$$P[r_2|e_1] = 0.50(0.20) + 0.50(0.90 = 0.55.$$

Bayes rule (equation 1) then can be used to determine the probabilities of having various malfunctions given a certain response to a given experiment. Considering the first experiment, for instance, the probability that the first malfunction is causing the problem can be calculated as

$$P[m_1|r_1,e_1] = \frac{0.50(0.80)}{0.50(0.80) + 0.50(0.10)} = 0.88 \ .$$

For the second malfunction under the same conditions the probability is:

$$P[m_2|r_1,e_1] = \frac{0.50(0.10)}{0.50(0.80) + 0.50(0.10)} = 0.12 \ .$$

The numbers given in parentheses on the upper left hand branch of Figure 1 are obtained in this manner.

It should be noted that earlier the same example situation was used to demonstrate the possible inconsistency involved in estimating $P[m_1|r_1,e_1]$ directly. At that point, the guess was 0.70, but as can be seen above the actual value obtained from the Bayes equation is 0.88. It can be seen, therefore, that intuitive guesswork should be tempered by logical considerations.

Continuing, the utility $u[P(m),r_1,e_1]$ of obtaining a positive response r_1 from experiment one can be calculated by using Equation 3. It should be anticipated that the response utility should be fairly high, that is, close to 1.00, since the probability of having one malfunction is great $[P(m_1) = 0.88]$. This turns out to be the case since

$$u[P(m),r_1,e_1] = |0.88 - 0.50| + |0.12 - 0.50| = 0.76 \ .$$

The corresponding utility for the negative response is 0.64.

At this point in the process, the designer should consider the utility for the experiment as a whole since he is trying to decide which, if either, of the two experiments to perform. To calculate this utility he should weigh the utility of each response by its chance of occurring. This procedure would prevent him from giving great emphasis to the utility value of a response which will not be likely to occur. Moreover, it would also be desirable at this time to consider the cost of the experiment so that he can balance the possible returns against the expense involved. Taking these two factors of probable response and cost into account, utilizing equation 4, the following is obtained:

$$U(e_1) = \frac{0.45(0.76) + 0.55(0.64)}{\$10} = 0.069 \ .$$

Similarly, for experiment two, it is found that

$$U(e_2) = \frac{0.42(0.64) + 0.58(0.48)}{\$20} = 0.028 \ .$$

Since $U(e_1)$ is greater than both $U(e_2)$ and the utility for doing no experiment, the designer would conclude that it would be desirable to do at least one experiment, and that one should be e_1 (turn down thermostat).

Now that it has been established that e_1 is the first experiment to do, the question must be asked as to whether to do experiment e_2 also. The answer to this question depends on two factors—first, the actual outcome (response) to experiment e_1 and, second, the possibility of an increased utility resulting from performing e_2. Suppose, for example, that e_1 is performed and the people continue perspiring, that is, response r_1 occurs. Knowing this result, the designer can adapt his decision-making process to this particular response and use Bayes equation and equation 2 to calculate new probabilities of different malfunctions existing if certain responses to experiment e_2 are observed. The probability of having a positive response in experiment e_2 is

$$P(r_1|e_2) = 0.88(0.70) + 0.12(0.15) = 0.63 \ ,$$

whereas that for a negative response is

$$P(r_2|e_2) = 0.88(0.30) + 0.12(0.85) = 0.37 \ .$$

Notice that the procedure proposed herein is truly adaptive in that these probabilities are changed from those seen in the upper righthand branches of Figure 1. The cause of this change is the new information about the probabilities of having various malfunctions that is obtained by conducting experiment e_1 (turn down thermostat) and noting response r_1 (continued perspiration). The malfunction probabilities also are altered since, from equation 1, it can be seen that

$$P(m_1|r_1,e_2) = \frac{0.88(0.70)}{0.88(0.70) + (0.12)(0.15)} = 0.97 \ ,$$

and

$$P(m_2|r_1,e_2) = \frac{0.12(0.15)}{0.88(0.70)+0.12(0.15)} = 0.03 .$$

As a consequence of these calculations, it is found that the designer can be more confident than ever that the air-conditioning system is at fault (m_1) if continued perspiration (response r_1) occurs after the sun shield is installed (experiment e_2). The magnitude of the response utility value adds to the strength of this conclusion since

$$u[P(m),r_1,e_2] = |0.97-0.50| + |0.03-0.50| = 0.94 ,$$

and this figure is close to the maximum possible of 1.00.

Once again, however, he must weigh the importance of this utility by the chance that the corresponding response may actually occur. The total cost of experiments up to this point also must be considered. Subsequently, the utility for the *experiment* becomes

$$U(e_1e_2) = \frac{0.63 \ (0.94)+0.37 \ (0.64)}{\$10+\$20} = 0.026 .$$

The conclusion to be drawn at this stage is that although it might be possible that an increased ability to identify the malfunction will result from running the "sun shield" experiment (e_2), say, from 0.88 to 0.97 for malfunction m_1, the extra confidence derived is not enough to overcome the extra cost involved. The result is that the overall utility for performing *both* e_1 and e_2 is diminished over performing e_1 alone, so that e_2 should not be undertaken. This conclusion would imply the end to the process and indicate that the malfunction probabilities are 0.88 for the air-conditioning system and 0.12 for the heat-absorbing glass.

For instructive purposes, it may be best to return to Figure 1 to see what would have happened if experiment e_1 had been performed and a negative (no perspiration) response had been observed. In that case the possibility of conducting the sun shield experiment, (e_2), would still be under consideration, but there would be different probabilities associated with m_1 and m_2. The new utility associated with running experiment e_2, calculated in a manner similar to that in the previous case, would be 0.021. This value would be lower than the 0.069 figure, again implying that experiment e_2 should not be performed after e_1.

Recapitulation

The procedure described above appears to have some interesting possibilities. It is complex even for a simple illustrative situation, yet, when the basics are understood, it becomes easier to use and apply to more complex problems. What is important, however, is that characteristic stressed at the beginning: the ability to provide a mechanism for integrating the intangible perceptive capabilities of the designer with the logic and consistency of mathematics and statistics. The designer has the opportunity to use any skill or experience he has at hand to estimate the chances that certain problems exist. Thereafter, he is guided by logical precepts in choosing experiments to be run and conclusions to be drawn.

This characteristic that allows for the integration of the "qualitative" and "quantitative" aspects of problem identification (and thus of design) is rarely encountered. Most techniques involve either one approach or the other; they emphasize complete reliance either on intuition (as is often the case in architectual education) or on prefabricated logic (as often in engineering education). Both of these approaches have their limitations. The time has come to strive toward combining the advantages of each to synthesize what hopefully will be a valuable technique. The procedure described here is an initial attempt in this direction.

References

1. T. Bayes, "An Essay towards Solving a Problem in the Doctrine of Chances," *Phil. Trans. Roy. Soc.,* London, 53 (1763).
2. W. W. Chu, "Adaptive Diagnosis of Faculty Systems," *Operations Research* 16:5 (1968)
3. A. S. Ginsberg and F. L. Offensend, "An Application of Decision Theory to a Medical Diagnosis-Treatment Problem," *IEEE Trans. System Science and Cybernetics* 4:3 (1968).
4. R. A. Howard, "Bayesian Decision Models for System Engineering," *IEEE Trans. System Science and Cybernetics* 1 (November, 1965).
5. R. D. Luce and H. Raiffa, *Games and Decisions: Introduction and Critical Survey* (New York: Wiley, 1957).

6. M. L. Manheim, *Highway Route Location as a Hierarchically-Structured Sequential Decision Process* (Cambridge: MIT Press, 1966).

7. A. J. Miller, "A Computer Control System for Traffic Networks," *Proceedings of the Second International Symposium on the Theory of Traffic Flow,* ed. J. Almond (Paris: Organization for Economic Cooperation and Development, 1965).

8. H. Raiffa and R. Schlaifer, *Applied Statistical Decision Theory* (Cambridge: Harvard University Press, 1961).

9. L. J. Savage, "Bayesian Statistics," *Recent Developments in Information and Decision Processes,* ed. R. E. Machol and P. Gray (New York: Macmillan, 1963), pp 161-94.

part **4**

HUMAN CREATIVITY AND JUDGMENT

Hoyt L. Sherman

MANAGING VISUAL INFORMATION

Notwithstanding the fact that a large number of highly interesting efforts have been initiated to model the managing of visual information, the present state of the art still suggests that human beings, as compared with other animate and inanimate systems, are most facile at his task. The increasing level of multidisciplinary interest and research oriented toward simulating this highly intricate process suggests that some day, probably not too far off, there will not only be a significantly greater understanding of the process but also that there will be developed systems, algorithms, and other pseudo-processes with which it may be simulated.

The discussion of managing visual information very much involves the matter of relationships. No particular visual element or stimulus can be managed apart from its relationships to other proximate visual elements and to the states of the system with which these elements are interacting. The notion of "relationship" used here relates well to those used by Asenjo and by Ernst and Yovits. Of particular interest are Asenjo's discussion of topology, with its concern for the nature of the connection or relationship between elements, and Ernst and Yovits's discussion of the information relationships and transformations in decision processes. There appears to be a great deal of potential for better understanding and for modeling the process by which human decision-makers manage and utilize visual information with information science theory and methods.

Visual information contains important cues for identifying the apparent relationships among visual elements in space. These apparent relationships are the aesthetic properties of an arrangement or composition as well as the spacial properties. The choice of the word *apparent* is deliberate. It suggests that a particular set of relationships relative to their spacial and aesthetic properties will be perceived differently by a system depending upon the states of the system. In the case of human beings, for example, no two people will attribute the same aesthetic and spacial properties to a set of relationships because the neural states of their minds, based upon their past learning and experience, are different. Thus, a discussion of the subject must consider both the states of the system of relationships perceived and the states of the perceiving system.

As Gestalt psychology defines the visual field as a field of stress among relationships, designing the visual field might be defined as resolving that stress. Such a notion would apply equally well to architecture, sculpture, painting, and the other visual arts. If one is to design the visual field and successfully resolve stress, it is important to understand the visual cues used to identify relations. In this sense the resolution of stress should require the meaningful and purposeful ordering of cues. A successful ordering of cues would be achieved if they revealed to the perceiving system sets of relations that are non-random but structured in terms of recognizably significant and meaningful, in terms of the states of the perceiving system, coherent or unified patterns.

A notion of this type that considers not only the character of the visual field but also the character of the perceiving system that it is interacting with provides a basis for understanding why an environment or a painting is not interpreted in the same way nor is it equally liked or disliked by any two particular people. With respect to visual fields a number of illustrations follow that focus upon two classes of relationships, the relationships between elements in the visual field and their relationship to the perceiving system, while cataloging some of the important and interesting human capabilities about which we have, essentially, only descriptive knowledge.

The first illustration is the familiar figure-ground phenomenon, where there is an apparent alteration between the two confronting faces and the vase in the center shown in Figure 1. If the perceiving system's attention is given to either the faces or the vase, the remaining pattern becomes ground. With the vase as figure, the

Fig. 1.   Face-vase; the interchangeability of figure and ground.

black rectangle becomes ground; and with the confronting faces as figure, the white rectangle becomes ground. The dynamics of this relationship, the whole versus the part, are present in all visual fields. Figure 1 illustrates how the ground forms the figure. It illustrates a mode of perception that is not typical of perceptual habits, which are principally concerned with objects, isolated elements and not relationships.

Position is the first consideration in the understanding of a relationship. It is of primary significance in the limited hierarchy of visual cues by which a perceiving system relates to space. This hierarchy consists, in order of significance, of position, size, and brightness. Two or more positions may take on relational significance in terms of proximity. This phenomenon is illustrated in Figures 2 and 3. Figure 2 consists of a number of spots arranged

Fig. 2.   Random arrangement.

Fig. 3.   Ordered arrangement.

Fig. 4. Brasilia's legislative buildings.

in a random order. Randomly arranged, it is difficult to identify the number of spots if viewed for only a fraction of a second. Figure 3 consists of the same number of spots grouped proximally in three clusters. Here, under the same viewing conditions, the number of spots is immediately identified as fifteen. Proximity has facilitated this immediate sensing of the correct number of spots. The phenomenon is automatic; the viewer is unaware of making that decision. Ordering by grouping is an important means for achieving apparent unity. Brasilia's legislative building, shown in Figure 4, is an excellent application of proximity. A different aspect of proximity is shown in the medieval hill town of San Gimignano in Figure 5.

Proximity and position often indicate direction. Apparent direction is one of the most common aspects of the visual field, and

Fig. 5. San Gimignano.

it is critical to aesthetic order. Direction is best known as perspective with its orthogonals converging at the vanishing point. The vanishing point is frequently the focal point of the composition.

In the limited hierarchy of space cues, size is next in importance. It is obviously the critical aspect of mass and scale. Variation in size, as ordered apparent diminution, is the controlling factor in perspective. Apparent diminution of size as mediated by perspective is not as easy to judge as it would seem. Figure 6 depicts two light poles and a row of traffic guards in perspective. It is hard to believe that the apparent size of the distant pole and traffic guards are really as small as they are when compared with the near elements. This simple photograph attests the persistence of the phenomenon of size constancy. We assume that the distant pole is of the same order as the near pole, and this assumption modifies our perception. However, it is accuracy in controlling apparent size that is critical to effectiveness in design.

It should be noted that the marked in-depth perspective tends to dissipate the space enclosure or form in its focusing attention on

Fig. 6.   Light poles.

the vanishing point unless certain elements or patterns are so disposed as to interrupt this dissipation. At the opposite pole, a too shallow perspective fails to provide a commodious space unless certain architectural or decorative elements are used to apparently enhance the actual space.

Brightness tends to be the most unreliable space cue of the three in this space cue trinity. Constant change in illumination produces a wide variety of brightness levels in the lights and darks of the architectural masses. This constant change makes brightness an unreliable space cue. In spite of the relative spatial unreliability of the brightness cue and its transitory nature, we must cite the role of light and dark as an important factor in mediating solids and voids. Light and shade are somewhat more reliable than shadow in mediating change in plane. In general, the fundamental function of light and dark is to mediate volume, thickness, and substance, whereas the fundamental function of color is to differentiate the visual field.

These two functions are given in the variety of value-color

intrinsic to the materials employed and the change in plane in a given environment. The integrate of the value-color of materials and the transitory nature of light and shade should not only function to display hierarchically the mass, plane change, trim, and detail, but also should become an aesthetic override. In this integration of value-color of materials and the transitory nature of light and shade, we have an aesthetic that is fixed in the relationship of elements and materials but is continuously changing because of the variation of light and shade. Apparent variety within fixed limits—an ideal aesthetic! Suffice it to say, the designed variety generally dominates variety created by light and shade.

Value and color as functioning in the display and aesthetics of form obviously should be an integral part of the designer's vocabulary. At the student level this capacity should be initially developed in a drawing-color-3D class, where form invention is appropriately displayed by value and color contrast. Color is intentionally omitted in this discussion for the basic reason that the perception of color has yet to be understood.

Efforts at describing color harmony by the use of the color wheel and the color solid are relatively superficial. The various systems do not, and cannot, include all of the variables that are requisite to color organization. Knowledge of color harmony is best gained through direct experience.

Having touched on the limited group of the space cues and their role in the aesthetic, let us now examine a cue that is better than

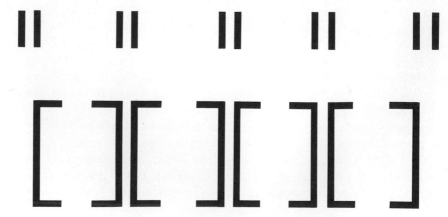

Fig. 7.   Closure.

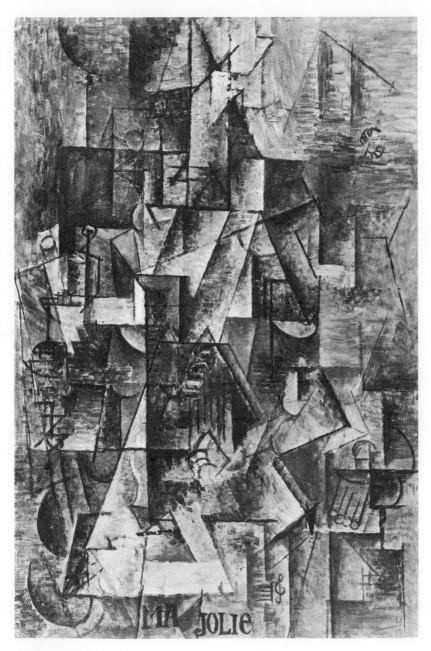

Fig. 8. "Ma Jolie (Woman with a Guitar)," by Pablo Picasso.

proximity in effecting organization. This is the cue of closure, which supersedes proximity. Figure 7 shows the unitary function of closure. Here we see that the apparent units created by proximity (top line) are no longer viable when the proximal patterns are modified to represent closure. The apparent units now are the areas between the proximal patterns; the proximal units are no longer apparent. Closure is not limited to the planar; it is also three dimensional—distant elements may close with frontal elements. In addition, and most important, a given closure may close with other closures to create a field of more inclusive closures. The more inclusive closure can be shown by the early cubist painting in Figure 8. The inclusive closure has an organizing property. Through inclusive closure parts are related to a whole. Attention to closure as an expression of the whole-part relationship is an effective means for determining proportion of the elements.

There are three other unifying elements in addition to closure involved in cubist painting that are also critical to organization. Coincidence of edge is one. Its presence has been in use for centuries as an integral part of the decorative note—in patterned wall, floor, and so on. Coincidence of edge creates pattern integration. It functions as a pattern integrator by having an edge of one element common to the edge of another element. It is most typically seen in the mortar, tile, and siding joint. The integrating characteristics of coincidence of edge is strikingly seen in the Ohio State University's Visual Demonstration Center, where the demonstration of this phenomenon consists of a vertical white cardboard plane approximately 6 × 24 inches, with a playing card hanging three feet in front of this plane, all surrounded by a black void. The observer visually aligns the edge of the playing card with an edge of the white cardboard plane. This creates a coincidence of edge; immediately the hanging playing card is seen as integral with the white plane. The two elements are seen at the same distance.

Continuity, or good continuity, is another unifying phenomenon seen in the cubist pattern. Continuity here, however, is seen as a broken continuity, but its unifying function is not disrupted. The principal applies equally well to architecture. The continuous wall surface and linear elements, such as cornice play a simple but basic role in providing apparent unity to the architectural ensemble. Wright's Robie House, shown in Figure 9, is a superb example of continuity. Texture is an important adjunct property of surfaces in that texture of any kind establishes the position and the existence of surface as a visual and tangible fact.

Fig. 9. Robie house. Frank Lloyd Wright.

Fig. 10.   High Court, Chandigarh.   Le Corbusier.

Most common to all arts is repetition. Repetition is in one sense a form of continuity. It not only establishes a rhythm to pattern and mass but by repetition of the element, identity becomes unity.

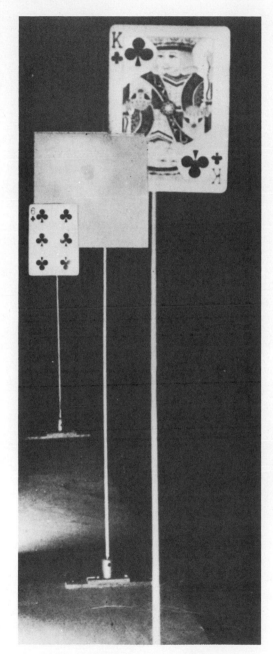

Fig. 11. Overlay demonstration.

Fig. 12. Temple of Luxor.

Still another cue that possesses some degree of integration is the space cue of overlay. This cue not only plays a role of integration but it is also the most effective of the space cues. As integrator, the overlapped portion of a given element is common to the overlapping element. This commonality affords a degree of integration. Furthermore, greater apparent space is experienced with a stimulus that presents overlay than one without overlay. For example, Mr. Wright's architecture, in general, was replete with the cue of overlay. Corbusier's building at Chandigarh (Fig. 10) contains a classical example of overlay. The vertical members at the principal entrance clearly display the role of this cue. Figure 11 further clarifies the significant role of overlay in the visual field.

The overlay cue is ever present in the environment. However, if the cue, which is essentially planar, is to be present, it must be planned for. The significance of this necessity can be understood through comparisons with the massive columns of the temple at Luxor (Fig. 12), which appear to overlap but which are read as colonnades of volume, not overlay.

Similarity, another integrating cue, is potentially possible from ridge line to base line. Similar shapes are given at the primary level in cornice, fenestration, and base course. At the secondary level, similarity may be given in the shape of materials, detail, and trim. Similarity achieves its unity because we assume that similar things are identical. An additional variety of similarity is given by perspective; deformation created by perspective produces this variety.

Mass, the primacy of architecture, must be reaffirmed by roof planes and facade elements. These elements must function not only to enrich facade but also to enhance critical changes in plane; above all, facade elements must play their role in displaying the salient and/or reentrant intersections of enclosing walls that, taken together, tend to establish form and position.

Base line is not only a cue that contributes to the description of the major masses of a given structure but is also most important in relating one structure to another. With planting, the base line is not only further emphasized but the planting serves as a textural value-color transition from the facade to the earth plane. Definition is maintained, but the edge is softened by the planting to provide greater environmental integration.

Pregnanz, another category of unity, is characterized by emphatic form. In one sense, Pregnanz may be related to the word *pregnant*. A common example would be the Rock of Gibralter, from the familiar "Prudential" side. Architecturally, Corbusier's Ronchamp (Figure 13), with its battered walls accented by its nun headdress-like roof, tower, pulpit, and *de stijl* fenestration, speaks positively of Pregnanz; its form tends to be sculptural. The sculptural form does not readily lend itself to analysis as does the familiar rectilinear structure. Ronchamp, however, is derived from cubist patterns.

Circulation as an approach should present principal masses, entrances, and supporting detail. Interior circulation should, hierarchically, appear to lead the individual to all critical visual cues. In addition to the interior visual cues, a properly placed decorative cue may not only contribute to apparent facility in circulation but it may also add interest to the environment.

Fig. 13.   Ronchamp.   Le Corbusier.

Decorative cues provide convenient points for fixation. Involuntary and voluntary eye movement is continually fixating points in the visual field.

The spiral disk demonstration, again from the Visual Demonstration Center, will help to partially sum up the apparent influence of the various phenomena on the part-whole relationship. This demonstration serves to further show the influence of ground on figure. First we observe the disk in motion. The apparent depth is equivalent to a pipe two feet in diameter and 100 feet long, observed at eye level at a distance of twenty feet. At a given cue we shift our attention to a small white target. Immediately the small target appears to expand in size and to come forward. We will not undertake to explain the phenomenon in detail; suffice it to say it belongs to the family of after-image effects.

Important to our thesis is the fact that the visual system is seeking equilibrium. By analogy, this equilibrium is seen as the designed form-organized elements in the environmental complex. Equilibrium is indicated in the drive to effect an internal balance by the immediate appearance of the opposite phenomenon. Excitation, generated by the spiral disk, creates a dynamic field in the visual system to increase the apparent size of the small target. The apparent increase in the size of the target fills the area of the spiral disk.

It is the demonstration of the field dynamics that is most important to design, and to aesthetics in general. It is because of the apparent interrelationship of elements in the visual field that these elements can be so organized as to create an apparent unity of the whole: the parts in relationship to the whole. Wolfgang Kohler's theory of perception adds further evidence to the structure of perception as design: ". . . . A theory of perception must be a *field theory*. By this we mean that the neural functions and processes with which the perceptual facts are associated in each case are located in a continuous medium; and that the events in one part of this medium influence the events in other regions in a way that depends directly on the properties of both in their relation to each other."

References

1. F. P. Kilpatrick, ed., *Human Behavior from the Transactional Point of View* (Princeton, N.J.: Princeton University Press). Prepared under contract with the Office of Naval Research for the Neuropsychiatric Branch of the Bureau of Medicine and Surgery, Department of the Navy, Washington, D.C. This volume contains a complete description of the Ames Visual Demonstrations.
2. W. Kohler, *Dynamics in Psychology* (New York: Liveright, 1940).
3. M. Wertheimer, "Laws of Organization in Perceptual Forms," *Gestalt Psychology*, ed. W. E. Ellis (New York: Humanities Press, 1950).

William T. Morris

MATCHING DECISION AIDS
WITH INTUITIVE STYLES

Discussions of decision-aiding lead one naturally to the subject of mathematical models and digital computers, which have been associated with many of the interesting developments of the past twenty years. In this discussion, however, we set out to explore a somewhat different hypothesis: that the very success of models and computers may have distracted our attention from some of the basic realities of the work of making decisions. It is well known that the benefits of analysis and computation are not to be had unless at least two basic conditions can be realized. To be the subject of analysis, a decision must be anticipated so that the sometimes extensive process of modeling it can be carried out in sufficient time for the results to be of some use in the actual context of affairs. In addition, one must have the skill to take an ill-defined decision situation and translate it into a well-defined research problem so that the concepts involved are operational and the crucial steps of mathematical representation and measurement become possible. Those whose chief professional activity is the making of decisions need not be reminded that these conditions are not readily met, for they are constantly aware of the difficulty of achieving them. Analysts who study and support professional decision-makers might profit from the reminder that, first, in the world of authority and responsibility not all important decision situations can be usefully foreseen and must be regarded as "decisions of encounter" rather than "programmed decisions" [14]. Further, analysts might well explore the possibility of

viewing the decision-maker's all too frequent unwillingness or inability to be explicit about the decision situation as a datum rather
than an annoyance. In other words, instead of concentrating on
the decision-maker's difficulty in communicating to others the
values and predictions he is accustomed to handling implicity,
one might ask what can be usefully done without the need for
explicitness.

These "facts of life," the inability to anticipate and the inability
to be explicit, suggest that a good deal of professional deciding lies
beyond the present frontier of decision analysis [9]. One can
simply accept this as a fundamental limitation, or one can turn
to the world of unanticipated decisions and implicit decision
processes, asking if there is a contribution that science might make
in this world. Can one develop decision-aiding methods that enhance the effective intuitive skills built up by professionals through
years of ill-organized experience? Do the methods of science
preclude it from contributing to those decisions of encounter that
must be made under the pressure and pace of daily affairs? [See
13.] A decision of encounter, an unanticipated decision, is one
that precludes very much delegation, very much seeking of "outside" assistance, and perhaps even precludes very much reflection
on the part of the decision-maker himself. These decisions must
be taken on the basis of what we will simply call the subject's own
implicit or intuitive methods. Indeed, we will say that whenever
a decision-maker either is not, or cannot be, explicit about some
aspect of a situation, then that aspect is intuitive or implicit [15].
This definition of "intuitive" is not very satisfying because it fails
to suggest our personal introspective appraisals of intuitive deciding
and because it deliberately sets aside the distinction between inability and unwillingness to be explicit. It turns out, however, to
be a useful definition for the purpose at hand. From the viewpoint
of the analyst, introspection is likely to be an unreliable guide,
and it makes little difference in the short run whether explicitness
cannot be achieved because of unwillingness or because of inability
to express one's decision processes.

Intuitive, implicit, or judgmental decision-making is, after all,
the mainstay of the experienced decision-maker and for good
reasons. Intuitive, unaided methods have typically served the
decision-maker well, and he can reflect on some personal history
of productive reliance on his developing intuition. Until very
recently there has been little to choose from except implicit

methods; and even now, aids tend to be available only in very well-defined situations to those with special training. Effective professionals in many fields including management, the sciences, and the arts are usually highly implicit deciders and find this way of working not only reliable and habitual but satisfying in that it seems to utilize their unique skills and sensitivities. It is especially important that intuitive methods appear well suited to meet the pressure of ongoing affairs, permitting rather immediate responses on the basis of limited information. There is considerable evidence to show that unaided human decision-making is reasonable, effective, and reliable within at least a modest range of decision-making challenges [18]. There are, obviously enough, some very serious ways in which implicit methods fail and mislead us, and it is these that concern us here.

It is now rather well established that one objective of decision-aiding is to extend the capacity of the human mind to remember and perform simple logical operations. Much of the mathematical analysis and computer application of recent years has been an attempt to extend the "logical" limitations of the decision-maker in extensive repetitive tasks involving the storing and processing of information. We wish, however, to turn in a somewhat different direction, facing some other sorts of difficulties that might be characterized as "psychological" rather than "logical" limitations on perceptual and cognitive activity. These difficulties appear when intuitive methods lead us astray, trap us, and, sometimes to our great surprise, fail to merit the confidence we have come to place in them. The particularly difficult situations are those wherein the limitations of intuitive methods are not obvious to us at all but occur at the subconscious level of decision processes. It is our hypothesis that if one were to investigate aids for decisions of encounter, the most productive area of study is likely to be these psychological limitations rather than the more conventional logical ones. There is, of course, a long history of attempts to overcome these psychological problems by means of highly rationalistic and pseudo-logical models requiring one to externalize the decision process in terms of some seemingly sensible steps. It has often been suggested that one should "define the problem, develop alternate solutions," or perhaps, "list the goals or objectives, develop alternate courses of action, evaluate the degree to which each action accomplishes each goal" [3, 11].

These recipes are the subject of numerous articles and books on how to make decisions. They are appealing in that they sound very reasonable and appear to be obviously "the right way to do it." There appears to be very little evidence, however, that they have any interesting effect on the actual decision-making behavior of experienced persons. Although the evidence is admittedly experiential, the best hypothesis appears to be that if one really wanted to alter the behavior of an intuitive decider, these pseudo-logical schemes are not going to be very effective. The reasons that might be advanced in support of this hypothesis are useful in guiding the search for other methods of dealing with perceptual and cognitive shortcomings.

We would suggest that the failure of these methods might well involve a failure to recognize that every experienced decision-maker develops his own personal style, which cannot be radically re-formulated in the short run. It may also be a failure to meet what appear to be the really difficult and troublesome problems of decision-making. These "define the problem" formulations have a kind of pious ring, telling one what he should do in making a decision but not how he should do it nor what it will gain him if he does. They say little of the great problem of division of labor in decisions. What aspects should be delegated, what aspects should be handled by the computer, and what should be turned over to staff specialists for analysis? They seem to say that the amount of mental effort or cognitive strain they require ought to be invested in every decision, failing to recognize that some decisions warrant more time than others and that in some, experience is far more highly developed than in others. They say nothing of the relative costs and benefits of the type of explicitness they require. They seem to assume that all intuition is bad and ought to be immediately replaced. These methods contribute little to the handling of risk and uncertainty, yet these are surely the central difficulties in many decisions. They almost equate uncertainty with irrationality, failing to help the decision-maker resolve the serious question of how much uncertainty to tolerate and how much effort to devote to gathering additional information in order to reduce the uncertainty. They require one to know his own mind with full clarity, which he clearly does not. They suppose that one cannot act without being perfectly clear about one's objectives, a requirement that would bring most organizations to a standstill.

Such pseudo-logical methods simply do not represent the sort of thing that is "done" in most professional circles. To use these methods explicitly is not really "socially acceptable" and might even betray some degree of incompetence. Their deliberateness fails to meet the time constraints that surround many decisions of encounter. They require more self-discipline and self-awareness than most of us find comfortable and imply a radical reformulation of one's habits. In short, they do not appear to be worth their cost. If even a few of these reasons turn out to be confirmed through the study of efforts to influence decision-making, they will provide the incentive to develop a basic hypothesis that may lead us in a new direction. One might call this the "Personal Style Hypothesis" because it involves the premise that each decision-maker's own personal style of deciding is the fundamental point of departure. Simply stated the hypothesis is this: *More is to be gained from attempts to apply natural enhancements to the decision-maker's personal style than from equivalent efforts to radically reformulate and externalize his style in the image of some pseudological model.* We view this, not much as a novel and completely untested hypothesis, but rather as a fairly obvious interpretation of the data that is already in and a suggestion that we pay more careful attention to what really goes on in the making of actual decisions. We see it as a very rough specification of the direction one must take if one is to really influence and assist the intuitive professional facing an unanticipated decision problem. The Personal Style Hypothesis can be understood if we make clear the somewhat special meanings of the concepts of "personal style" and "natural enhancements."

One might quickly develop a host of dimensions for describing decision-making style, and this may be well worth doing, for we have two purposes in mind. First and most important is the development of self-consciousness, self-awareness, or self-knowledge. One reading of a great deal of the evidence turned up by modern psychology is that the key to the improvement of the intuitive, implicit decision process is self-awareness, and that this must begin by motivating the subject to explore the various dimensions of his own style of deciding [22]. We will return shortly to this most fundamental notion. Our second purpose supposes that by exploring the dimensions of style we will be able to suggest more or less specific ways of enhancing that style. We would thus like to find ways of looking at style that are useful in the sense that they lead us to such enhancements. We might begin to lay out some of these dimensions as a series of questions. For example:

1. To what extent is one's style of decision-making intuitive, implicit, and private? To what extent is it analytical, explicit, and public? [1]

2. To what degree is one tolerant of ambiguity in a decision situation? Can we decide in the face of ambiguous notions about objectives or ambiguous statements of the alternative courses of action? Some studies suggest that experienced decision-makers are highly tolerant of ambiguity and capable of resolving that ambiguity in their own way [8, 20].

3. Similarly, to what degree is one tolerant of uncertainty as to the consequences of one's actions? Some of us require considerable information and assurance before we will act, others are far more willing to act on the basis of limited information and substantial uncertainty. We should not imagine that one such style is always "better" than the other [7].

4. How reasonable is our hindsight? How effectively do we learn from our past decisions? Are we given to regretting decisions that turn out badly or do we suppress these feelings and look to the future? Do we distinguish clearly between a good decision that depends on reason and logic, and a good result or outcome that always depends to some degree on chance, luck, and circumstances beyond our control?

5. How much cognitive effort does one invest in a decision? Some decision-makers are careful and deliberate thinkers, others tend to proceed "off the top of their heads" or "by the seat of their pants."

6. To what degree does one delegate or seek external aids to deciding?

7. To what extent is there a need for coherence between one's beliefs, one's actions, and one's objectives? We may seek coherence by becoming more optimistic about a course of action after we have chosen it than before. Sometimes we adopt the belief that what we have become committed to is the best possible course of action, although we had no such conviction prior to our commitment. We achieve

coherence or reduce "cognitive dissonance" by revising our perceptions [16].

8. How sensitive are one's unaided decision-making abilities to conditions of stress? There is considerable evidence that most of us become distinctly poorer decision-makers when we are under stress or pressure [10].

9. To what extent are our perceptions and thoughts influenced, not so much by the external world, but by our own needs and desires. One of the great discoveries of modern psychology is that what we see and what we think are influenced subconsciously by our needs and tensions [22].

10. To what degree is one clear about his own decision-making processes? How much self-knowledge or self-consciousness does one have in this connection? It is well established that we seldom understand very well the reasons we do what we do, or the goals we are striving to attain.

11. To what degree are our perceptions of the external world distorted because of distortions shared by our associates? Science is full of instances of socially shared distortions, often going about under the heading of "common sense." Indeed, one of the best definitions of common sense pictures it as that kind of sense which tells us when we look out of the window that the world is flat [22].

12. To what degree does one abstract or simplify the external world in making a decision?

13. To what degree does one rely on rules of thumb or policy categories for disposing of decision problems? [12]

14. To what degree does one look ahead in a decision? Is the planning horizon in the relatively near or relatively distant future? One of the skills of a good chess player is his ability to look ahead to the future consequences of his moves. The ability of computers to play chess is rather directly related to their "look ahead" ability.

Proposals for various dimensions of personal style could go on, and it might be important for a decision-maker to consider those that are useful for understanding his own style. We turn now, however, to the concept of "natural enhancements" that appeared in our Personal Style Hypothesis.

We are looking for ways of enhancing, complimenting, supplementing, or assisting the decision process that are well adapted to the nature of that process. We want to develop enhancements that do not arise from some rationalistic view of choice but rather from a specific study of decision-making style. Such techniques must be well suited to the context of affairs, in that they meet the time constraints within which one must act, and they must be shown to have benefits that will match the cognitive efforts required of the user. The techniques likely to succeed are those that do not require a great amount of special training or "selling" and that the decision-maker finds "naturally assimilable" into his own personal style. Such a set of specifications may seem difficult if not impossible to meet, but there are some grounds for optimism. The decision-aiding techniques we seek are more likely to be concerned with the implicit and intuitive aspects of deciding than with the explicit aspects. They are more likely to be qualitative rather than quantitative. Further, they are more likely to be the sort of thing that a decision-maker is able and willing to do for himself, rather than things that must be done for him by others.

Let us try to illuminate these general notions by means of specific examples of possible relationships between aspects of personal style and enhancement techniques. As we have mentioned, there is considerable psychological evidence to support the notion that under conditions of stress, the effectiveness of one's intuitive, implicit decision-making skills is likely to be degraded. It raises directly the question of what individual or organizational efforts might be undertaken to remove the stressful conditions that may lead to intuitive degradation. This leads in turn to the larger question, "What are the best conditions for the flourishing of effective intuitive skills?" There are, of course, some very obvious answers to the question of "stress relieving" the decision-maker that involve the rearrangement of workload, taking the problem home, or a quite retreat for necessary reflections. There are some less obvious answers as well. We know that it is sometimes effective, when one has a very large number of things to do and feels "pressured," to simply write the tasks down and progess through the list one at at time. This simple way of handling stress has the effect of making the pressure explicit and thus reducing one's internal anxiety. It also has the effect of concentrating attention on one decision at a time, thus making the situation intuitively manageable. Similarly, we begin to notice that when a decision-maker is faced with a decision involving a considerable degree of uncertainty, the pressures and anxieties are to some extent relieved by making those uncertainties explicit, perhaps even by expressing them in the language of probability theory. This tends to depersonalize the uncertainty, to relieve the decision-maker from being its sole bearer, and to allow him to concentrate his intuition on other aspects of the decision problem. One should note here that these techniques are things the decision-maker can do for himself and things that generally depend on his own self-consciousness and self-awareness in decision-making.

It is also of some interest to notice that the more general question of the conditions under which one's intuition can function most effectively has not been widely studied in management situations. In fact, those who seem to have had the most interest in this problem are the sages who developed Eastern religions such as Buddhism and Taoism [17]. These men gave considerable thought to "freeing the mind," or creating the conditions under which one's intuition could work most effectively. The familiar progression in Yoga from concentration to meditation and comtemplation is aimed at freeing the mind from irrational passions, unconscious needs, and all manner of distractions so that it may be most reasonable. It is of special interest that many of the contemporary findings of psychology tend to confirm the notions developed by these ancient thinkers. Again we come around to the point that what is needed is self-knowledge or self-awareness in the decision process.

Wishful thinking is our common phrase for the sort of distortion that creeps into perceiving and conceptualizing as a result of basic needs and desires. Psychologists have been much interested in this need-determined sort of distortion because we ourselves are often not conscious of it [22]. We consider three hypotheses about the effects of needs in the decision process.

1. Habitual ways of viewing a decision situation arise because a conception that meets the needs of one situation is uncritically applied to others. Habits might be thought of as ways of economizing the limited capacity of the mind. Rather than develop a conception that tries to account objectively for each individual choice situation, one simply

resorts by analogy to customary conceptions or tends to fit decisions into categories previously developed. Organizations develop such habits, and they tend to get formalized into policies or routines for decision-making. These habitual conceptions are perpetuated because they satisfy one's need to respond to the pressure of affairs that overtax the conceptualizing capacity of the mind. Habits also help to satisfy the need for being able to defend a decision in an organization. Certainly, a widely used defense for an unsuccessful decision is the claim that it was based on "the way we always do it," or that it was placed in a category for which a policy was already determined.

2. One's conceptions of choice situations tend to move toward a view of the situation as the person would like to see it, and not necessarily as it is. Expectations are not independent of desires, and conceptions play a part in satisfying needs when actions prove inadequate to the task. If a person finds himself in very limited control of a situation, to some extent quite powerless to act in a satisfying way, then at least he can remake his conceptualization of the situation so as to view it more satisfactorily. If the need for certainty and confidence in decision-making cannot be achieved through predictive knowledge and the ability to control events, then perhaps conceptions will become subjectively free of doubt and uncertainty in response to this need. Perception is a selective process that tends to give structure to the vastly complicated situations encountered in experience. In perceiving a situation, some elements of it "stand out" more clearly than others. The term is "figure and ground," the figure being those elements perceived most clearly against the suppressed background of the remainder. The psychologist goes on to hypothesize that the elements tending to stand out as figure are at least in part controlled by needs, in the sense of having previously been perceived in satisfying situations. This, of course, works as the result of fears as well as desires.

3. Finally, conceptions of choice situations get distorted because of the social and organizational processes that lead a person to view things in ways accepted by his associates. Socially shared views—which come not so much from con-

tact with reality as from the need to agree, to belong, or to avoid questioning the views of a group—are a part of most decisions. An individual decision-maker in an organization experiences a demand from his superiors that his behavior be reliable, predictable, and, in a general sense, within control. They need to know how he is going to make decisions so they can account for, and plan on, the basis of his behavior. He thus finds it increasingly necessary to conform to the organization's way of conceptualizing decision situations or to follow the organizational rules. The rules and conventions tend to become important, no longer because of their original objective effectiveness for achieving organizational goals but rather for their own sake. It becomes less important to make a decision so as to advance the objectives of the organization and more important to make a decision acceptable in the organizational process. This leads to viewing decisions as falling into one or another of a relatively small number of organizationally sanctioned categories. Thus, conceptualization of choice situations becomes a rigid process. This may well mean the decisions are less and less successful at the same time that they are becoming more reliable, predictable, and defensible within the organization [14].

It may well be that the influences of our needs on our perception and thinking constitute one of the most serious sources of difficulty in our intuitive or implicit decision processes. Our needs for wish-fulfillment, escape, or self-defense may be sources of difficulty largely because we are not aware of their distorting effects on our decision-making. This leads us again to what we take to be the essential conclusion of psychological research in this connection. Vigilance, self-knowledge, self-awareness, or self-consciousness constitute the basic strategy for freeing ourselves from the subconscious sources of distortion. Knowing oneself makes it easier to see decision situations accurately, but knowing oneself in this sense is not easy.

One obvious suggestion, which may indeed turn out to amply reward the effort required, is simply to keep an explicit record of one's predictions or decisions in repetitive situations. It may be surprisingly effective, for example, to explore one's thinking for the systematic effects of needs by "keeping score." Suppose, for the example, we had occasion to repeatedly estimate the cost of doing particular jobs and later had an opportunity to learn the actual costs. It is important to keep a written record of one's estimates because the memory also is subject to need-determined distortions. Comparing the estimate with the actual may well reveal systematic biases and unreliability. Knowledge of these is the first step in disciplining the intuition. A very interesting experiment is to repeatedly predict where the stock market will be a week or a month in the future, and then to compare these predictions with what actually happens. It is likely that a large number of investors would profit from a knowledge of the systematic optimistic or pessimistic biases on which their market decisions are based.

Certainly, one of the most difficult aspects of choosing is coming to grips with the multiple, conflicting natures of most value structures. In deciding which of two houses to buy, we compare them on the basis of price, number of rooms, tax rate, style, location, and so on. It is relatively easy to compare the houses one attribute at a time, but the difficulty arises when these comparisons must be somehow aggregated into an over-all preference. Similar problems occur when one must choose between development projects, plant locations, candidates for vice-president, and, in fact, in nearly all interesting decisions. The basic kernel of self-knowledge is this; the one-dimensional comparisons are easy for the unaided intuition, but the multidimensional comparisons are difficult. We have sometimes been disdainful of the decision-maker who gives a "check mark" to the house with the lower price, another to the house with the greater number of rooms, and so on, making the decision in favor of the house that receives the greater number of check marks. On second thought, however, this decision-maker has worked out for himself a simple decision-aiding device that moves toward a very sensible division of labor. He uses his unaided intuition to make the easy one-dimensional comparisons, but then employs a very simple logical model to do what his intuition finds difficult, the task of aggregating these judgments into an over-all preference. Now, it is obvious that a little more effort on his part might have lead to a more sophisticated logical model in which he ranked the attributes of the houses in order of their importance to him and then gave each house a numerical score for each attribute. Finally, the model would have combined ranks and scores into an over-all measure of the desirability of each house. The principle of division of labor remains the same [4].

There is currently a renewed interest in this type of decision-aiding scheme, and a number of careful studies have yielded interesting results [21]. We know that if someone else designs a complex ranking and rating system and tries to "sell" it to a decision-maker, only the most limited success can be expected. On the other hand, many decision-makers seem to develop and use such logical models for themselves rather naturally. Though these tend to be simple rather than sophisticated logical models, we are discovering that such simple models are surprisingly effective [6]. One meaning of effectiveness is that decisions reached by laborious, unaided, intuitive methods are in many cases the same as those reached by surprisingly simple logical models for combining one-dimensional judgments. In this sense, simple models "work" for many decision-makers who have been studied as they worked on rather difficult decision problems. There are other ways to gauge the effectiveness of these methods as well. Decision-makers seem to develop them easily, find their use appealing, and have less cause to later regret decisions made with such aids. We suspect also that these methods serve to increase the reliability of the resulting decisions by reducing to some degree the effects of the unconscious distractions we have previously examined.

These three examples of the relations between dimensions of personal decision-making style and natural enhancements may lend some credence to our basic hypothesis, or at least suggest some justification for studying it further. The notion of self-directed change is important here because there is considerable evidence to indicate that although outsiders may show a decision-maker that his behavior is not as satisfactory as he may have supposed, suggest to him the sort of things that may be unconsciously influencing it, and offer some suggestions as to the way in which it might be changed, if change is actually to occur it must be the work of the decision-maker himself. Coming to know one's own mind as the basis of self-motivated change is, so far as we can now tell, the effective way of disciplining the intuition. There are also other obvious advantages. Nobody has to sell a decision-maker on the use of decision-aiding techniques that he has developed himself. There is none of the traditional resistance to change to overcome. The process is also well adapted to the context of affairs, serving to enhance the intuitive powers of the manager to deal with unanticipated decisions. It encourages him to evolve decision-aiding techniques that are particularly suited to his own style and circumstances.

Our conclusion, then, comes around to saying that the contribution of science to the intuitive decision processes operating to some degree in all decisions, and to a very great degree in decisions of encounter, is to encourage the process of achieving self-consciousness, which will lead to self-directed change. Self-analysis, we are suggesting, will form the basis for self-motivated change leading toward the achievement of an effective and disciplined intuition. This is, after all, the basic conclusion of modern psychotherapy and ancient Buddhism. Once a person becomes aware of the inner sources of his behavior, the needs that have unconsciously driven him, he will be able to free himself from their influences. To enhance the intuition, one must have feed-back not only from the results of his decisions but also from his own appraisal of the internal sources of his behavior.

References

1. J. Bruner, J. J. Goodnow, and G. A. Austin, *A Study of Thinking* (New York: Wiley, 1956)

2. ———, and B. Clinchy, "Towards a Disciplined Intuition," *Learning about Learning*, ed. J. Bruner (Washington, D.C.: Department of Health, Education, and Welfare, Office of Education, 1966).

3. R. D. Calkins, "The Decision Process in Administration," *Business Horizons*, Fall, 1959, pp. 13-29.

4. R. T. Eckenrode, "Weighting Multiple Criteria," *Management Science* 12:3 (1965), 180-92.

5. W. Edwards, H. Lindman, and L. D. Philips, "New Technologies for Making Decisions," *New Directions in Psychology* (New York: Holt, Rinehart & Winston, 1965).

6. P. C. Fishburn, "On the Prospects for a Useful Unified Theory of Value for Engineering," *IEEE Trnasactions on Systems Science and Cybernetics* 2:1 (1966), 27-35.

7. G. A. Forehand and H. Guetzkow, "Judgment and Decision Making Activities of Government Executives As Described by Superiors and Co-workers," *Management Science* 8:3 (1952), 84-102.

8. W. E. Henry, "The Business Executive: Psychodynamics of a Social Role," *American Journal of Sociology* 54:4 (1959, 117-29.

9. R. A. Howard, "The Foundations of Decision Analysis," *IEEE Transactions on Systems Science and Cybernetics* 4:3 (1968), 211-19.

10. W. C. Howell, *Some Principles for the Design of Decision Systems,* Aerospace Medical Research Laboratories Air Force Systems Command AMRL-TR-67-139, September, 1967.

11. C. H. Kepner and B. B. Tregoe, *The Rational Manager* (New York: McGraw-Hill, 1965).

12. H. J. Leavitt, *Managerial Psychology* (Chicago: University of Chicago Press, 1964).

13. C. E. Lindbloom, "The Science of Muddling Through," *Public Administration Review* 19:2 (1959), 78-88.

14. J. G. March and H. A. Simon, *Organizations* (New York: Wiley, 1958).

15. W. T Morris, "Intuition and Relevance," *Management Science* 14:4 (1967), 32-40

16. G. Murphy, *Human Potentialities* (New York: Basic Books, 1958).

17. ———, and L. B. Murphy, *Asian Psychology* (New York: Basic Books, 1968).

18. C. R. Peterson and L. R. Beach, "Man as an Intuitive Statistician," *Psychological Bulletin* 68:1 (1967), 29-46.

19. L. D. Phillips and W. Edwards, "Conservatism in a Simple Probability Inference Task," *Journal of Experimental Psychology* 72:3 (1966), 348-54.

20. E. Rosen, "The Executive Personality," *Personnel* 23:1 (1959), 46-59.

21. R. N. Shepard, "On Subjectively Optimum Selections among Multiattribute Alternatives," *Human Judgements and Optimality,* ed. M. W. Shelley and G. L. Bryan (New York: Wiley, 1964).

22. S. S. Zalkind and T. W. Costello, "Perceptions: Implications for Administration," *Administrative Science Quarterly* 7 (September, 1962), 218-35.

Donald Watson

CONCEPTUAL MODELS
IN DESIGN

. . . Solving a problem simply means representing it so as to make the solution transparent. If problem solving could actually be organized in these terms, the issue of representation would indeed become central.—Herbert A. Simon, *The Sciences of the Artificial*

Nature never works in ways you can't model. So . . . science is wrong in telling us that advanced study requires special codes and abstractions. I'm sure that full conceptuality is going to return to the scientific method, and that will expedite the closure of science and the humanities. The most important and useful work . . . will be achieving this return to modelability. —R. Buckminster Fuller, as quoted in *Life*

Creative and innovative design with regard to the quality and optimality of decisions and choices within comprehensive design programs involves a number of interesting issues that bear importantly upon the effectiveness of problem-solving and architectural design. A comprehensive design program may be defined as including the generation of alternative solutions or actions to be taken with respect to an identified problem or objective and the decision process by which a selection is made among the alternatives.

Comprehensive design programs are undertaken on a variety of different scales and levels of complexity. This range is indicated by a continuous line in Figure. 1. Those design problems that are simple, small, and discrete would be grouped at the left side of the diagram in Figure 1. Grouped at the right side of the diagram would be those problems that are highly complex in that they con-

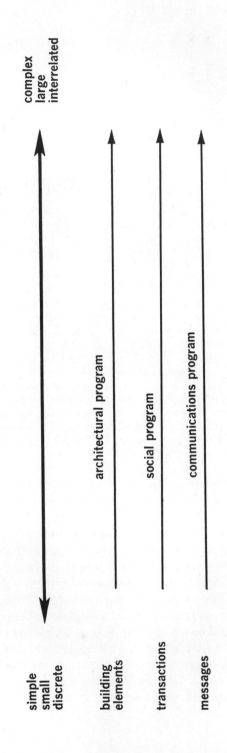

Fig. 1.   Conceptual orientations to a range of design problems. One element cannot be considered independently of the others.

tain a large number of interrelated variables. Urban and regional problems are typical of those grouped at the right, whereas the design of a doorknob is typical of those grouped at the left; the design of buildings would be located somewhere between these extremes. With respect to the context for design decisions, Thomas Markus has set forth two observations [17, p. 15]. The first is that no matter at what point in the continuum between simple and complex problems one's design project is located, the solution alternatives are constrained by relationships to elements on either side of that point. For example, the design of a building involves both the constraints of construction details as well as those of the larger urban context within which it is to be located. The second observation is that the larger more complex constraints are normally inherited and are not under the control of the designer; rather, they are set by historical investment patterns over a long term and cannot be changed except at prohibitively high cost.

What is represented by one heavy line in the diagram is actually the sum of separate conceptual orientations to design problems. Most conditions are not resolved simply by the specification of a physical system that is described with comparative ease in an architectural program. Implicit in each program for a building design is a *social program*, that is, a pattern of social behavior, however informal or minimally structured. In addition, there can be said to be a *communications program*, not easily separated from the social program except by terminology familiar to organizational analysts, such as the origin and destination of messages, decision and control points, and so on. The important point to be made is that the traditional conceptual frame of each discipline may seriously delimit the inquiry in a design program only to those factors for which the terms are well developed.

This problem is compounded by the fact that though decision aids may be applied to a wide range of problems in a number of different disciplines, they are more useful for some types of problems than for others. On one hand, particularly when the variables can be reduced to a common dimension such as dollars, mathematical decision theory, for location and resource allocation problems, for example, may be very useful. However, for behavioral problems involving human adjustment and activity, effective solution strategies are difficult to identify and useful decision aids are few. Finding solutions to complex behavioral problems may profitably involve the client or user as a problem-solver.

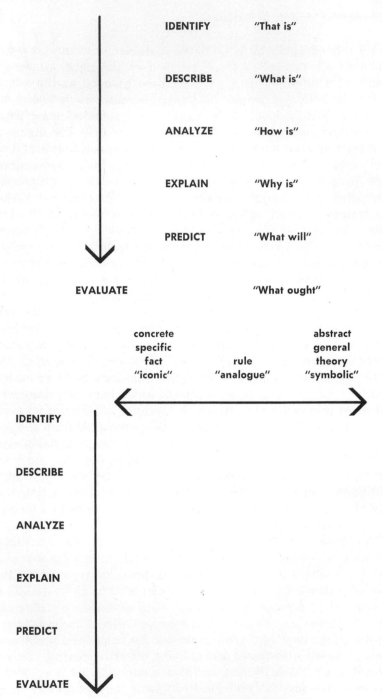

Fig. 2. Phases of empirical experimentation in the design process and a format for "cycling" critical hypotheses.

Consider another set of terms familiar to design programming, those that represent phases of decisions in an extended information process as diagrammed in Figure 2. The terms themselves are imperfect and vary in meaning from writer to writer; however, similar terms appear in many disciplines [1] and have been adopted in the methodology of the so-called systems approach. The terms should not suggest that the cognitive process of the individual actually occurs in such terms. On the contrary, the format is used as a way of delaying "evaluation" in the sense of premature selection of useful data. Of course, evaluation, and the editing that it implies, runs throughout the design process, even from the outset, where it influences one's perception of the world and one's understanding of the nature of the problem to be solved. Churchman observes that "our acceptance of the facts is a normative judgment" [4]. It cannot be assumed that two or more people who have different needs and purposes will agree on "what are the facts." However, the terms suggest that, before one selects a solution as the most suitable, the analysis on which the evaluation is based should be tested for its descriptive and predictive power. That is, before agreement is reached on "what should be done," it may be that agreement should be reached first on "what is." If values cannot be agreed upon, then the participants in the program should at least agree on a method for deriving and testing value assumptions such as cycling the critical hypotheses through the elements in Figure 2 —an operating discipline closely related to Bronowski's "Habit of Truth" [2]. The guidelines for proceeding from one phase to another are the subject of a fully developed literature on experimental design and scientific method. Design failures that are due to faulty experimental design make up the gallows humor of the research and development field.

The previous discussion and Figures 1 and 2 provide a background for a discussion of another aspect of the design process, the creative thought process. Figure 3, a generalization of many continua, is presented as a diagram of that process. Different modes of thought vary with respect to the level of abstraction and resolution—from concrete representations to abstract and symbolic generalizations. These conceptual modes reveal themselves incompletely and only at separated points of a continuous design process in the form of verbal statements, idea sketches, and the multitude of ways in which a designer "talks to himself," studies his design and communicates it to others. What is known about creative

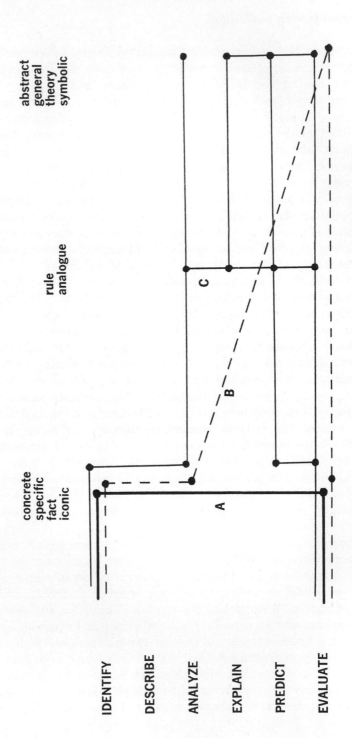

Fig. 3. Framework for the design process indicating modes of generative ideation. The transformation of information in model form.

thought processes is based largely upon the observation of external behavior. How a designer or problem-solver represents his thoughts externally should help reveal his understanding of the problem and the thought process by which he develops solutions. These representations, or externalizations of aspects of creative thought, might be called models or frameworks that relate the problem-solver or designer to himself and to the real world.

Several authors [7, 13] describe different classes of models in terms somewhat related to those included in Figure 3. Iconic models are defined as those that represent physical properties in some proportional scale, such as a photograph or a measured drawing. Analogue models are those that represent the essential variables and the interrelationships of what can be either a set of physical elements or an abstract formalization, such as a circulation network, a sociometric diagram, a decision chart, and so on. Symbolic models are those by which first-order abstractions are themselves symbolically represented, such as the mathematical representation of a theory.

Such models are representative of varying degrees of abstraction and symbolization. Models, however, can be specific and symbolic as well as general and iconic. Though these latter types of models are not specifically represented in the diagram in Figure 3, the diagram still serves well as a basis for setting forth a number of conclusions about the creative thought process.

First of all, a comprehensive design program may be thought of as a series of transformation of information in model form. As noted already, a variety of vocabularies—words, diagrams, mathematical symbols, and so on—can be employed throughout the diagram noted in Figure 3. Obviously, some forms of vocabulary are more appropriate than others for each degree of abstraction, and some people can better deal with one degree of abstraction than another. However, it is thought that individual levels of capability for dealing with a wide range of abstraction can be enhanced [12].

Observation of external behavior in the form of generated models does not provide a clear indication of the underlying associative chain of thought, however. McCulloch suggests with respect to thought processes, and the generation of ideas, and the difficulty of understanding this process well, that ideas derive more from abduction than from deduction or induction [10]. However, as with experimental testing, when the connection, or logical relationship or transformation process, cannot be recalled or reviewed, errors can occur; and they cannot be easily identified and corrected.

At any point in the diagram in Figure 3 multiple models or representations at different levels of abstraction can be used as a means of generating variety. An example from the literature on creativity is to take any object—an ash tray, for example—and to first think of as many other uses for the object as possible. Then consider its function—to receive ashes—and think of as many other ways as possible for serving that function [12]. This technique may be a key exercise for an actively creative mind. Once elements of a process or function can be conceptualized in the abstract, a number of alternate structures serving that function can be generated. This point is considered further below.

Techniques mentioned in the literature on creativity are often ways of increasing the variety of ideas by generalization and isomorphic symbolization; that is, ways of moving farther to the right in Figure 3. It appears that the sudden insight, or brainstorm, comes to a person when dealing with a subject in terms that encourage isomorphic variations [6]. Many authors describe the accidental "pairing" of two previously unrelated ideas. The process of conceptualization in successively abstract modes is a program for that sort of ideation—what might be called the "Habit of Imagination."

Although creativity and imagination are normally associated with that function of the mind that generates variety whereas critical judgment is associated with the reduction of variety, the terms are misleading if they imply two independent trends of mentality. There is as much creativity required in the process of empirical experimentation (the vertical axis in Figure 3) as there is critical judgment in the process of generative ideation (horizontal axis). The two dimensions represent various functions of thought, one that connects us with empirical reality, another that allows our separation from it. An interesting correlation between the two is suggested by experiments wherein the number, though not necessarily the quality, of ideas that a brainstorming group may produce is increased by lowering the threshold of judgment and avoiding criticism and evaluation.

The final point to be made in connection with Figure 3 is that it may be useful for charting the steps taken in actual design programs utilizing self-observation techniques. A design solution may be seen to develop in ways suggested by the various paths represented in the diagram as A, B, and C. Path A might indicate a solution whereby a designer is inspired by existing imagery that gives him a visual idea that then becomes his correction of, or contribution to, the initial problem situation. In other respects his design would hardly be innovative. A decision path such as B would be guided by ideals or normative conceptions from the outset that are reinforced rather than brought into question by the initial situation. Given the time and cost limits of normal problem-solving, designers may assign problems to classes within which they can apply evaluations that have proven themselves in the past. Bruner notes that the value of a rigorous theory or set of laws is to eliminate the necessity of empirical experimentation every time a decision is made [3]. Path C is one that represents a process of systematic analysis and evaluation from which general theory is derived and then applied to a specific situation. This is the process that is normally proscribed in the comprehensive development of new prototypical design.

Having considered generally the nature of problems, activities involved in the design process, and creative thought, the scope of the discussion can be narrowed to consider specific conceptual models that are used, or could be used, in the analysis and design of a specific building with a given program of requirements.

The literature in the field of psychology offers a general description of the cognitive process. It acknowledges the tendency of the mind in comprehending data to sort and to catalogue information into a number of preconceived concept categories. There are listed in Figure 4 a number of concept categories that are often used in the structuring of architectural design problems. They can be tentatively stated without implying that they are what they ought to be or that such concepts are used by all designers; at best they may be taken as an initial operating frame of reference. The categories are not mutually exclusive; data with respect to any particular aspect of a building would appear in several categories.

Concept categories are best explained as sets of relationships that are learned through education and experience (Fig. 4). If original research is undertaken, categories are suggested by relationships perceived when a subject is studied in terms of a given set of factors, e.g., microclimate. Like all sets of known relationships, the categories represent constraints on the number of design choices, and can be useful in delimiting the field of options to a workable number. By now most architectural designers are familiar with the technique of diagramatic "mapping" by which sets of requirements can be visually displayed, separately or overlapped, such as legal

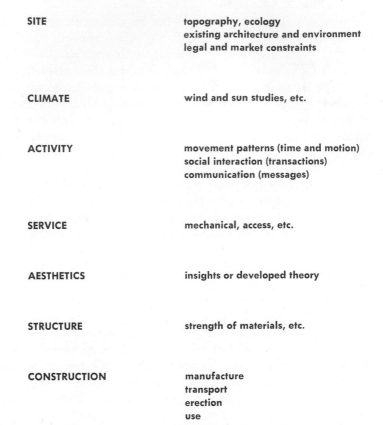

SITE	topography, ecology
	existing architecture and environment
	legal and market constraints
CLIMATE	wind and sun studies, etc.
ACTIVITY	movement patterns (time and motion)
	social interaction (transactions)
	communication (messages)
SERVICE	mechanical, access, etc.
AESTHETICS	insights or developed theory
STRUCTURE	strength of materials, etc.
CONSTRUCTION	manufacture
	transport
	erection
	use

Fig. 4. Concept categories in architectural design. They organize our perception of a problem and determine the components of its solution.

zones, topography and other site characteristics, climate, character of existing environment, views and approaches from afar, and so on. Mapping such so-called given requirements of a particular site is a useful decision sequence in setting up an architectural problem.

Further, Figure 4 is related to Figure 1 through the social and communications aspects of the activities that buildings and environments are designed to support. These two considerations are broad aspects of activities that can and should be given operational definition and with which designers can identify and describe the phenomena of human activity. In that sense they may also suggest the potential contribution of the behavioral sciences to the formulation of design proposals. The activity category of the diagram in Figure 4 is perhaps the most demanding, together with the aesthetics category, since, compared with the other categories, there is a dearth of useful theory and aids for decision-making.

Environmental analysts and designers can formulate models of problems and solutions in terms of the factors identified in Figures 3 and 4. Four of the many forms that such models may take are illustrated in Figure 5. The models are abstractions of activity patterns, and they serve to indicate that it is possible to construct analogues of systems so that important relationships may be

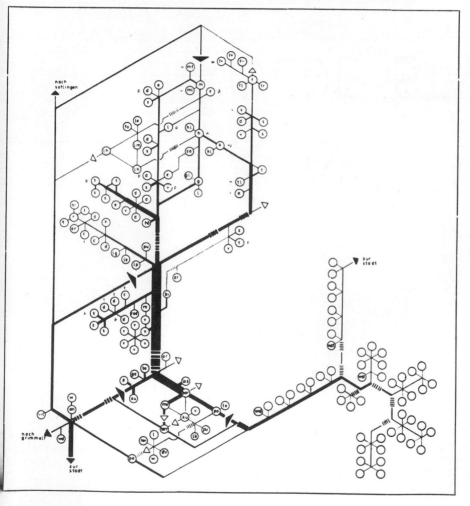

Fig. 5a. An analytic model of circulation linkages. From "Circulation Graphs," *Ulm 19/20,* August 1967.

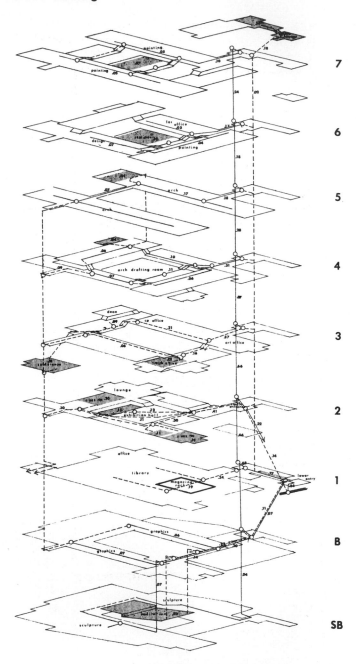

Fig. 5b.   An analytic model showing intensity of use of activity zones and circulation linkages. From D. Watson, "Modeling the Activity System" [9].

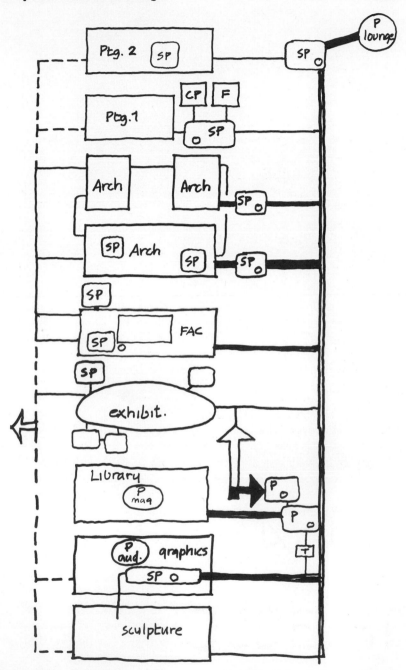

Fig. 5c. From D. Watson et al., "A Study of the Arts and Architecture Building, Yale University" (1967).

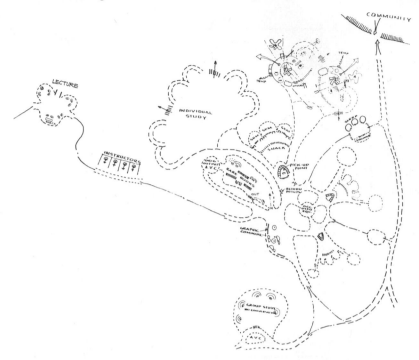

Fig. 5d. From M. A. Milne et al., "Computer-Aided Design: The Problem of Undergraduate Study" (Dept. of Architecture, University of Oregon, 1966).

studied. However, the models that are formulated and used in problem-solving and design influence greatly not only how the problem is viewed but also the range of possible solutions. These models are related to, and emerge from, the culture and science of our nation and are transmitted more or less equally among us through general and professional education and experience. As such, really significant innovation that shatters some beliefs and models and advances new ones occurs from time to time. It is thought that the material presented here can provide some basis for organizing conceptual and creative thought so as to aid in achieving significant innovation. That is, a good problem-solver should not be bounded by special languages or topics but, rather, skilled in representing comprehensive views of a problem and in translating such views from one model type to another. It appears that creativity and innovation ultimately depend on such skills.

References

1. J. R. Alger and C. Hays, *Creative Synthesis in Design* (Englewood Cliffs, N.J.: Prentice-Hall, 1964).
2. J. Bronowski, *Science and Human Values* (New York: Harper & Row, 1965).
3. J. S. Bruner, *On Knowing* (Cambridge: Harvard University Press, 1962).
4. C. W. Churchman, Prediction and Optimal Decision (Englewood Cliffs, N.J.: Prentice-Hall, 1961).
5. G. A. Davis et al., *Training Creative Thinking* (Madison: C.L.R., University of Wisconsin, 1967).
6. B. Ghiselin, ed., *The Creative Process* (Berkeley: University of California Press, 1952).
7. S. E. Elmaghraby, "Role of Modeling in IE Design," *Journal of Industrial Engineering* 19:6 (1968), 292-305.
8. S. A. Gregory, ed., *The Design Method* (New York: Plenum, 1966).
9. S. A. Mednick, "The Associative Basis of Creative Thought," *Psychological Review* 6:3 (1962), 220-32.
10. M. Milne, ed., *Computer Graphics in Architecture and Design,* Proceedings of the Yale Computer Graphics Conference, April, 1968 (New Haven, Conn.: School of Art and Architecture, Yale University, 1969).
11. G. T. Moore and L. M. Gay, *Creative Problem Solving in Architecture* (Berkeley: Department of Architecture, University of California, 1967).
12. S. J. Parnes and H. F. Harding, eds., *A Source Book for Creative Thinking* (New York: Scribner's, 1962).
13. C. W. Rusch and S. M. Silverstone, "The Medium Is Not the Solution," *AIA Journal* 48:6 (1967), 61-67.
14. C. W. Taylor and F. Barrow, *Scientific Creativity* (New York: Wiley, 1963).
15. D. Watson, "Working Papers: The Study of the Environment," *Connection,* Spring-Summer, 1969, Department of Architecture, Harvard University.
16. D. Watson, "Modeling the Activity System," *EDRA Conference Proceedings,* June, 1969 (Raleigh: Department of Architecture, North Carolina State University, forthcoming).
17. "Design Methods in Architecture," *Interbuild/Arena* 15:2, 83:920 (1968), 14-16.

part **5**

IMPLICATIONS

Ian I. Mitroff

WHO LOOKS AT
THE WHOLE SYSTEM?

It was the best of times, it was the worst of times, it was the age of wisdom, it was the age of foolishness, it was the epoch of belief, it was the epoch of incredulity, it was the season of Light, it was the season of Darkness, it was the spring of hope, it was the winter of despair.—Charles Dickens, *A Tale of Two Cities,* Book I, Chaper 1.

The tragedy of Dickens's words lies not with their universality, for every epoch has its best and worst of times. The tragedy is that in certain times, such as our own, the feeling of despair assumes overwhelming proportions. The tragedy of our times is that we feel that the best and worst stand irreparably opposed in bitter contrast and irony. Every one of the positive features of our civilization is at the same time the worst of negatives. On the one hand stands the efficiency of our great transportation systems; on the other stands the brutalizing facts of cars that are "unsafe at any speed," air pollution due to auto exhaust that is *already* at the danger level, more deaths each year due to auto accidents than in any of our previous wars, and street and highway systems that carve up the landscape with an almost total disregard for the other systems that must serve all the other human needs and wants. On the one hand stands the great productivity and wealth of our industrial system, the richness of our way of life with its perhaps unparalleled range and variety of products and services—in short, our unparalleled standard of living. On the one hand also stand our great urban centers with their unlimited opportunities for diversity of living, culture, and recreation. But on the other hand stand the by-products of our industrial systems and of our urban centers: the unclean air we breathe, the polluted water we drink, the pesticide-poisoned food we eat, the overcrowded and despair-breeding neighborhoods that many of our urban poor are forced to live in with no hope of ever finding any way out, our overcrowded and substandard schools—in short, all the ugliness, noise, and frustration of urban life that haunts and even threatens to destroy the very fiber of our civilization. As an aside, recently some social psychologists have speculated that a good part of the motivating factors for our urban unrest may not be due to racial problems but may instead be due to the feeling of being a caged animal in an urban zoo with every potential way out marked with the sign of despair, "No Exit."

By now we are all too familiar with this list of virtues and vices. Our daily news media (but another example of our "best" and "worst") parade them in front of us, and our best muckrakers make a fortune from documenting their existence and "causes." We are only too hungry to read about our problems, especially the more sensational they are. Unfortunately, we are not as hungry to embark on their solution, particularly their long-term solution. In fact, the greatest tragedy of all may be the feeling that we are powerless to do anything about them, that we are no longer the masters of our technology that once promised to solve all our problems and to usher in the good life. The feeling is that technology and civilization are themselves part of the problem, and that it is even naïve to believe that there are solutions, let alone progress. Apparently if there is anything left to believe in, it is that all of our beautiful solutions are only problems in disguise. The cry is that for every problem that technology solves, it creates ten new problems in its wake.

Now, of course, technology is no more *the* blame for this situation than any other single aspect of Western civilization. This does not mean that technology is nowhere responsible. It it can claim partial credit for the solution to many of our problems, it must also share part of the blame for their creation. To force this recognition, we shall want to take a step aside, be reflective, and examine some of the assumptions under which our technology has operated. In fact, it is my contention that part of what's wrong with our technology is its lack of a reflective philosophical basis. This deficiency applies both to the training of scientists and engineers as well as to the practice of science and engineering. Among the many factors and questions we shall want to consider in coming to grips with this deficiency are the following:

1. Granting from the outset that science and engineering are different in many fundamental respects [see 36], what common philosophical presuppositions do they nevertheless share? To be more specific, what common philosophical presuppositions about the nature of reality do the methods of scientific research share with the methods of engineering design?

2. How is the practice of science and engineering and the education of scientists and engineers related to the preceding philosophical presuppositions, whatever they are?

3. How does the current philosophical base inhibit our conceptualization of the components of the process of scientific inquiry and of the engineering design process? How does it restrict our current inquiries into the nature of these processes?

4. What implications does the current philosophical base carry for the development of future kinds of scientists, science, engineers, and engineering? What, in other words, will the engineer and the scientist of the future look like? More important still, what *should* they look like?

In considering these questions, it will be helpful to borrow some terminology from one of the newest creatures to appear on the scientific/technological scene, the systems scientist [see 12, also 5]. Since the systems approach cuts across both science and engineering, the language of the systems scientist is a fruitful method for getting at some of the common philosophical presuppositions that science and engineering share. Although it definitely is an extreme version, the following propositions represent, and far more than we would like to admit, the philosophical assumptions upon which much of our science and engineering is built. The first proposition is that systems actually exist in empirical reality. This is the empiricist's assumption. It implies that, first of all, there is such a thing as "reality," and secondly that "it" is "empirical" in nature. More often than not, this proposition is never raised to consciousness. It is taken completely for granted. The second proposition is that every system can be broken down into its components, the components individuated from other components, and their properties measured separately. Note that this proposition not only implies that it is possible to individuate the components of a system but that it is actually possible to understand the components of a system without having to understand the nature of the whole system of which the components are a part. The third proposition has been forcefully stated, though not necessarily agreed with, by René Dubos, the Nobel Prize-winning scientist and philosopher. In Dubos's own words, "the most influential assumption of modern science is that the best and indeed the only scientific approach to the study of natural phenomena and of living organisms is to divide them into fragments and to investigate elementary structures and properties in greater and greater detail" [19, p. 264]. Where the second proposition only says that it is "possible" to study the components of a system, the third proposition says that it is not only possible but that it is the "best" and only scientific way. A fourth proposition [for other sets, see 3, 8-10, 15, 19, 23-25, 27, 28, 42, 43] is the assumption of interdependence between the observer and the phenomena he is measuring, i.e., that observer effects can be separated and distinguished from object responses. A point, which we shall be emphasizing again and again, is that the reflective systems scientist would in all likelihood strongly contest all of these propositions [5]. It is highly debatable whether one can even identify the components of a system, let alone *understand* them, without having to understand something, if not a great deal, about the whole system [5].

Notice that in terms of this philosophy the scientist and the engineer turn out to be very hardheaded fellows. They are supreme realists. Terms like "the whole system" seem hopelessly vague. In their way of thinking, they are meaningless terms since they cannot be defined with precision, and if there is one thing that our engineer and scientist respect, it is precision. (In this respect they are like the logical positivists for whom questions of ethics are also meaningless, since for one thing, the idea of "good" is, for them, indefinable in any naturalist sense [1].) Consistency is also another one of their idols. Unfortunately, in spite of all their love for precision and consistency, they lack the gift of self-reflection which would make it possible for them to be consistent in their own arguments. Whether they like it or not, the engineer and the scientist cannot help making statements about the whole system. Whether they like it or not, and whether they spell their assumptions out or not, their everyday operating procedure bespeaks a philosophy. Where in one breath the engineer and scientist say that terms like the "whole system" are meaningless, in the next breath they argue that whatever the "it" of the whole system is, "it" can best be understood by studying "it" in parts. The conclusion is that, try as we may, we cannot avoid making statements about the whole system. As is so often the case, a single sentence of Michael Polanyi's is sufficient to sum it up: "A complete physical and chemical topography of a frog would tell us nothing about it as a frog, unless we knew it previously *as a frog* [38, p. 342]." Commenting on this statement, Matson has written:

> Our recognition of the frog as a frog (the Whole Frog, or frog-in-itself) is independent of and antecedent to whatever notations we may make about it as detached observers; and, in turn, our awareness of the frog qua frog recedes and vanishes in the process of its reductive analysis. [30, p. 150]

All of this is not intended to imply that the philosophy of studying smaller and smaller system components has not greatly added to our general understanding as to how complicated systems function as a unit. For over three hundred years, such an approach *has* increased our knowledge of man and his relationship to the world. Rather, the point is that there is room for arguing that this strategy has also inhibited our general understanding as much as it has facilitated it. The danger in concentrating all of one's resources on studying smaller and smaller fragments is that one has little, if anything, left over for putting the fragments back together again. The system as an integrated unit tends to get lost in the process of fragmentation [19, 30]. An even greater danger of the philosophy of studying smaller and smaller fragments is that it tends to become self-perpetuating. The deeper one probes into any phenomenon, the more fragments one can always find left to be fragmented.

Churchman has prepared a powerful critique of the philosophy of proceeding by parts. He notes that the

> philosophy of proceeding first with the simplest problems and then working to the more difficult ones itself is based on the assumptions (1) that simple cases are readily identifiable and (2) that progress from the simple to the realistically complex is possible.
>
> Thus the fruitfulness of this model depends on whether the model is in fact a starting point for describing the more complicated and realistic

types of experimentation. If there is a simple beginning to an investigation, then one presumably knows beforehand what the more complicated steps will be, i.e., one can visualize that this first step *is* the beginning of a series leading to the more complicated steps. It is not self-evident that one begins with simple cases. One must show that such a procedure is the best possible one, and apparently this demonstration cannot be accomplished without already knowing a great deal about the nature of the more complicated cases.

These remarks are not intended to preclude the simple-to-complex approach to experimentation. They are intended, however, to indicate that the proponents of this approach have the onus of proof of simplicity and the potentialities of the simple-to-complex approach. [8, pp. 162-63]

If the point of this discussion were merely philosophical, it would be easy to ignore it. We could say that it is nothing more than a matter of playing cute word-games, and let it go at that. Unfortunately, the assumptions under which the engineer and scientist operate have grave practical consequences. For example, it may be enough for the engineer to argue that in building a highway to go from A to B, his concern is only that the highway move traffic "efficiently" and "economically." It will not be enough for the inhabitants between A and B, who realize that the engineer is thereby ignoring other vital aspects of the "system," e.g., the displacement of hundreds of homes, shops, stores, churches, and playgrounds. Or, tell the city's poor that their neighborhood problems can be broken down into separate components and the whole solution somehow reconstructed from the parts. Tell them that the waste-removal system can be understood and improved separately from the transportation, business, or political system. A recent article by Dr. Robert Coles, a research psychiatrist at the Harvard University Health Services, vividly portrays how much the transportation system is in so many respects an integral part of the health system that confronts a city's poor [13]. Most middle-class whites would *literally* die if they had to travel repeatedly back and forth across their cities on public transportation to have to wait endlessly to see a public health physician or nurse only to then be told to come back again and again.

Anyone who has ever dealt with large complex systems knows that the parts are so strongly coupled that it is almost frustratingly impossible to identify the individual components, let alone separate them. We can almost state it as a theorem that *for systems that are of any interest, the components are virtually inseparable* [5]. Conversely, we might say that it is only for systems that are *not* of any strong interest that the components are separable. A favorite illustration of the strong inseparability of systems concerns a political cartoon depicting Governor Reagan of California as an executioner about to chop off the *head* of some victim. In this case the "victim" was the operating budget for all the state departments. The caption under the cartoon read, "Don't worry, I'm only going to chop off 10%," referring to the governor's ill-fated scheme to indiscriminately reduce the operating budget of all state departments by 10 percent.

The disturbing thing about the philosophy of proceeding by parts is its inherent lack of a sense of reflectiveness. It provides the perfect rationalization for each systems analyst going off on his own separate way (or in the jargon of our times, "doing his own thing")—each working on his own privileged component, and no one feeling compelled to justify his effort to the others. As justification for this, we often offer the petty argument that we are only describing Nature as She is, not as we want Her to be. In doing so we ignore outright that systems analysis is a creature of our making, not Nature's, that the problem a scientist or engineer solves and the way he breaks that problem or system down into components is a choice of his making; it is a function of, among other things, his particular scientific/technical training and his personality [23, 28, 40, 47]. Those boxes on all of our flow charts that are supposed to describe the world are as much a description of us as they are of Nature itself. Nature does not come packaged in black (or white) boxes neatly labeled as input here or as output there. Rather it is one's frame of reference that supplies the way he packages Nature. It is only our fragmented educational and professional systems that keeps the components and the boxes separate. Universities may be organized into separate and autonomous disciplines, but it is not clear that Nature and most systems are.

This tendency to compartmentalize is also part of our long tradition of empiricism that has perpetuated the myth that things are really "out there," i.e., that what things are is independent of the way *we* as observers look at *them* as objects. Marshall McLuhan would no doubt say that this is part of our cultural book heritage [31]. What the book originally imposed artificially—i.e., the space and time of linear perception and thinking (the space and time of one separate look and thought at a time)—we have not only come to perceive as natural but, even more, as scientific. All of this has contributed to our confusing the goals of scientific inquiry with the actual practice. Unfortunately, the goals do not will the means. Merely proclaiming that one of the goals of science is objectivity does not thereby make the behavior of scientists objective in practice [40, 43]. Also, it does not separate the observer from what he is observing.

Without the barest twinge of self-consciousness our educational system perpetuates these myths. We are masters of teaching our students (and here I must include myself) how to break a system down into components (i.e., analysis), but we are poor in teaching them how to put the components back together again (i.e., synthesis) [18]. We have blandly assumed that because engineering is problem-oriented, engineering design is best taught through the solution of countless problems. This may indeed be the case, but only if we reevaluate the kinds of exercises that have been traditionally called "problems." Most, if not all, of the problems given to engineering undergraduates require only a single answer. As a result, these problems are already so overdefined that they prohibit the student from taking an active role. Since the student works neither to define the problem nor to formulate the criteria for a "solution," they are problems in name only. Consider what Baddour has had to say:

Examination of the effect of the single-answer problem on engineering attitude reveals:

(1) Incomplete or contradictory data have little place in single-answer problems.

(2) Engineering judgment is not required of either the student or the instructor, hardly a situation to encourage its development.

(3) The very existence of an objective standard puts the instructor in an almost impregnable position, which only a few of the very bright students will dare to challenge. Skepticism and the questioning attitude are not encouraged by this situation. Neither the data, the applicability of the method, nor the result are open to question.

(4) The single-answer problem usually suggests the infallibility of logic rather than the ultimate word of experiment. The early history of science bears witness to the paralyzing effect of this attitude. [2, p. 651]

The point should be clear. Engineering students are generally expected to find the one correct solution to a given problem rather than to question the problem itself. Little wonder that fields, such as the humanities, that are not taught in this fashion are perceived by engineers as inherently subjective and nonscientific.

Whether this kind of "education" is responsible *for*, or the product *of*, the philosophical base is really not the important question here. What is important is to note their mutual reinforcement. It is to be expected that there *should* be an intimate relationship between the pedagogy of the single-answer problem and the philosophy of proceeding by parts.

Unfortunately, the situation is not radically different in the so-called pure sciences. Thomas Kuhn's book *The Structure of Scientific Revolutions* bears eloquent testimony to this sad fact [27].

A statement by Nadler provides a convenient and forceful summary of the discussion up to this point: ". . . The analytical approach focuses on components rather than on wholeness. Attention to components is essential in [scientific] research, but in [engineering] design it very often leads to suboptimization for the entire solution" [36]. Nadler's statement also provides a basis for raising a point that we merely touched on in passing earlier, i.e., that each particular analyst only analyzes a problem in terms of the language of his special discipline. Suboptimization, in other words, is a function of at least two factors: (1) an analyst can only include a limited number of components in his analysis of *any* problem, and (2), as much as his professional education expands his vision, it also restricts it. If the professional by virtue of his special training is able to see certain components that the nonprofessional cannot see, the professional is also *unable* to see certain components that the nonprofessional, or some other kind of professional, can see [see 48; 24, p. 5]. The first factor says that for every problem that technology solves, it will leave ten new problems in its wake because of its failure to deal with a large enough chunk of the whole problem, i.e., its failure to look at the whole system. The second factor says that technology will leave ten new problems in its wake because of its failure to solve the correct problem. The fish 30 miles downstream from a factory dumping industrial waste into a river will die from the first factor because they are not considered to be part of the costs of running the immediate factory system. The fish, by now already dead, will also have died from the second factor because the value of their existence, if measured at all, will only be measured in terms of the "normal" costs (negligible) of "doing business," and not, unfortunately, in terms of their value to life and to living things in general.

The second factor provides a basis for considering further some of our earlier questions: How does the current philosophical base inhibit our conceptualization of the components of the process of scientific inquiry and of the engineering design process, and, how does it restrict our current inquiries into the nature of these processes? If the fact that every professional views the world through the selective filter of his own profession has serious consequences for professional practice and education, we should expect that it also has a serious consequences for how a profession views and studies itself. If a profession tends to look at the world in a rational, analytic, piecemeal fashion, and if this approach imposes limitations in the solution of the world's problems, then we should expect the profession to study its own processes in much the same manner and therefore to be subject to the same limitations. We should expect to be limited and stifled in our attempts to develop a comprehensive and unified theory of the engineering design process.

The vast majority of empirical and theoretical studies on the nature of the engineering design process have either directly attempted to break that process down into a number of components or have assumed that such is ultimately the case [22, 29, 37, 39]. The vast majority of these studies have also assumed that because the description of the final output of a design, i.e., the design object itself, is technical in nature, the description of the designer and the organizational environment in which he works can also be affected in these terms. The engineer is represented as some kind of a transducer whose function it is to transform some *given* input into some clearly specified output. These studies are thus predicated on the subsumption of a mechanistic and reductionistic philosophy [see 6, 7, 9, 10, 30, 44]. This means that not only is it assumed that behavioral variables can be clearly differentiated from physical or technical variables but even stronger, that behavioral variables can be reduced to physical variables. As a result, human behavior or behavioral variables, if acknowledged at all, are seldom if ever treated as legitimate variables in their own light or in any sophisticated sense.

Perhaps an example will serve to make these points clearer. Consider a typical paragraph from K. W. Norris's paper "The Morphological Approach to Engineering Design:"

> The first step in all organized design processes is to establish and set out the field of investigation. Especially if one is looking for a new or peculiar solution, this field should include all acceptable and reasonable

or possible solutions. One of the normally accepted ways of doing this is to produce a straightforward list of possible answers. The morphological way of doing this, however, is to produce a table or matrix where all the parameters concerned are listed vertically and the corresponding parameter "steps" are listed horizontally. The parameters of such a "morphological chart" describe, in general, the feature, and functions of the subject considered. They indicate what the subject must in fact "BE" or "HAVE". The parameter "steps" on the other hand describe, in general, the "MEANS" of achieving the required characteristics as indicated by the parameters. [37, p. 116]

Notice that the emphasis of this paragraph is on the "parameters," the "steps," the "Means." The emphasis is on a technical description of "the problem" rather than on who it is that will be solving the problem and accepting "the solution." The trouble with Norris's position is that he too easily assumes that by merely using his "morphological approach," an engineer will finally produce "a solution which may need a little explanation but in its more developed forms will certainly be acceptable to the client" [37, p. 130]. It is as though the creation of the term "morphological approach" is supposed to magically bring about the creation of a good design. Again, Norris is assuming that design is a rational process governed by some universal laws of engineering design. But what happens if every engineer has his own idiosyncratic set of "universal laws"? What happens if the equations an engineer uses in a particular design situation are not only a function of the technical needs and wants of a client but are also a function of how the client expresses those needs and how he interacts with the engineer? In short, what happens if the technical behavior of the engineer is a function of the social interaction between the engineer and the client, i.e., a function of their personalities? What happens if there is gross misunderstanding and even open conflict between the parties to a design? Would not this strongly affect that supposedly "straightforward list of possible answers"?

However, it is important to stress that these objections do not necessarily imply opposition either to using Norris's method or to analyzing the engineering design process. Nor does it imply opposition to breaking that process down into components, for that is precisely what the term "to analyze" means. Norris's theory of design is an admirable attempt at analyzing the engineering design process and a useful technique for the practicing designer. One can ask, however, what guarantees the completeness of Norris's schema? What guarantees that the components we identify in theory actually and separately exist in reality? What leads us to believe that we can neatly partition phenomena into the physical and social? An even more basic question is, What leads us to believe that though a science of the physical is possible, a science of the behavioral is not? Unfortunately, engineering education in general and the pedagogy of the single-answer problem in specific do not prepare one for answering these questions. These questions are outside the realm of engineering education. They are philosophical. An adequate answering of these questions presupposes both a background in philosophy *and* behavioral science. *Whether the theorist is aware of it or not, in postulating and constructing a theory of the engineering design process he is assuming more than his natural role of an engineer; he is also assuming the role of a philosopher and of a behavioral scientist* [see 20, pp. 76, 80].

It should also be made clear that the preceding points are definitely not the result of mere philosophical speculation. For the most part, they are the result of this author's attempts to build a working computer-simulation model of the design behavior of a practicing mechanical engineer. Since the results of this effort have been extensively reported elsewhere [32, 33, 34], only a brief summary will be given here.

The particular kind of problem investigated was one of pressure vessel design. The original objective of the study was to simulate the entire process by which a design was first conceived and finally translated into being. This involved two major phases: (1) simulating how the engineer generated an initial set of feasible design alternatives, and (2), simulating how he selected a particular alternative from that set for final design. The client in this process was represented by a set of technical input variables defining his design needs. The engineer was represented by a set of technical design equations whose function it was to transform the input into a final design object. The outcome of this effort, which was extensive, was an enormous success in simulating how the engineer generated design alternatives and, unfortunately, an enormous failure in simulating how he searched that set for a particular solution to a particular client's needs. There were good reasons for success in the first part and failure in the second. In the first part of the process, i.e., how the engineer generated design alternatives, the client's needs *could be* represented as technical input variables that were *relatively* independent of *who the particular design engineer happened to be.* In the second part, i.e., the process by which a final design alternative was selected, the client's needs *could not be* represented by technical input variables alone that were in *any* sense independent of the particular design engineer. The behavior of the engineer was so strongly coupled to that of the client, and vice versa, that it was difficult to say where the internal properties of the one left off and the external inputs of the other began. A final design alternative was selected through the process of face-to-face interaction. How the client and the engineer responded during this phase of the design process was a strong function of their individual personalities and their respective images of each other.

On the whole, it seemed that most of the engineer's clients fell into one of two classes: those who overdefined their design requirements, and those who underdefined them. The first class, the overdefiners, literally made no solution possible; no design could simultaneously satisfy every one of their constraints. The underdefiners, on the other hand, made too many solutions possible. They either never got around to defining their needs or did not know what they wanted. Often they would say, "Look, tell me what I want. If I knew what I wanted, I never would have come to you in the first place."

The trouble with the overdefiners was twofold: not only were they cocksure about what they needed, but they even thought they knew more about design than the engineer did. In part this was a function of their personality, their need to assert themselves; in part it was also a function of their position and background. Whereas the engineer had only a B.S. in mechanical engineering, his clients usually had a Ph.D. in physics. Furthermore, the engineer was only in the organization, a large university research laboratory [46], as an adjunct to render support to the basic physics goals of the laboratory. In the last analysis, the physicist always had the final word. Little wonder that the unwritten motto of the engineer's design group was, *We always give our clients what they want even when it is not what they need.*

In reality there were, of course, many more types than the two just mentioned. One could spend a whole study on analyzing and classifying the personalities of physicists and on the kinds of input different personality types characteristically defined. One thing, though, is clear: many more studies are needed on how problems actually get defined and why different personality types assume different "givens" in the formulation of problems.

It should be noted that not all the difficulty in communication that occurred between the engineer and the physicist was due to such factors as the mismatch between different personality types or the fact that physicists in general had more power and status in the organization. The breakdown in communication was due to a variety of factors. One of the other reasons why engineers and physicists had difficulty in communicating with one another and agreeing on the "ultimate" basis for designing pressure vessels was because they had been trained to look at nature in fundamentally different ways. The engineer looked at the design object as a piece of working equipment (in effect, a structural support) that had to be built and serviced; the physicist looked at the object as a nuclear barrier. And the two images were not isomorphic. From the point of view of engineering, the pressure vessel had to be thick enough, and then some, to withstand the pressure loads. From the point of view of physics, the vessel had to be as thin as possible to obstruct as little as possible the incident and reactive nuclear particles the physicist was interested in observing.

The preceding points up one of the most interesting findings to emerge from the study. This was the tremendous degree to which each of the parties to the design was unaware of the innumerable assumptions they were each making about the process of design. In fact, it is correct to say that we were generally unaware that they were even making any assumptions. But this is not to imply that both parties were unaware of the conflicting requirements that the pressure vessel had to satisfy. Engineers generally understood that the pressure vessel had to be thin enough to meet the physics requirements, and physicists generally understood that the vessel had to be thicker than they would have liked it to be in order to satisfy the engineering requirements. What they were unaware of was how much their professional orientation not only affected their conception of the other party but also their self-conception. To the engineer, the physicist was an eminently unpractical fellow incapable of appreciating the practical basis for design. To the physicist, the engineer was an eminently untheoretical fellow incapable of ever appreciating the theoretical basis of physics. According to the engineer, if the physicist were more practical he would have been better able to understand why the engineer's design procedures were still rational, given the nature of the practical design problems an engineer had to face. According to the physicist, if the engineer were more theoretical, he would have been better able to establish a more rational theoretical basis for design. So it went, endlessly back and forth. Of course, what is really interesting is that each demanded from the other what they were unable to do and be for themselves. As a matter of fact, the physicist was not always as rationally theoretical as he thought he was. Many of his equations were no more than rules of thumb, and many of the engineer's design equations were on a much firmer empirical *and* theoretical base than the physicist's.

The difference between what the engineer and the physicist *said* they did and what they *actually* did was considerable. At the conscious verbal level both parties could point to explicit, well-defined rational procedures as justifications for their behavior and position. These procedures were largely the idealized models they had learned in the course of their professional education. The physicist, for example, could point to the Bohr model of the atom as typifying the structure and practice of physics. The engineer, on the other hand, could point to the formula for bending in beams. Neither of these stereotypes, of course, bore any necessary relation to the real practice of physics or engineering; they were just part of the professional ideology that each had picked up along the way. And, of course, since neither of them shared the same ideology, each was suspect to the other.

It should not be inferred that ideology does not have an important role to play. The occupational sociologists tell us that ideology is one of the factors that integrates an individual into a profession, i.e., that he shares a common set of group reference norms [23]. Such norms are also valuable for pointing to the *ideal* practice of the profession. They tell us how we would like to practice science and engineering *if* we were free from observer bias and *if* we could control all the relevant factors, assuming that we knew them. Again, because one of the goals of science and engineering happens to be that mysterious beast called "objectivity," this does not automatically will its occurrence in practice. Newton's Laws (the end product of scientific inquiry) bear as little relation to the way science and engineering actually get done as the multiplication table does to the way people actually multiply numbers in their head.

In an extremely interesting paper entitled "The Role of the Subconscious in Executive Decision-Making," Robert Ferber has documented the existence of this same phenomenon in management. The purpose of Ferber's paper is to define the limits of executive rationality and irrationality. In it he states:

Psychologists tell us that our minds work on conscious and subconscious levels. On the conscious level we are aware of what we really think and can reason things out step by step. On the subconscious level or levels any number of physical and emotional influences can affect our thought processes. Then the person feels that a certain thought exists without knowing how or why. If this thought appears very desirable to the individual, rationalization occurs. In rationalization the person tries, often subconsciously, to bring the subconscious thought into a pattern of conscious thought that will justify it. [21, p. B-520]

Naturally, to someone else who is not involved on the subconscious level, it is often a trivial matter to detect the process of rationalization in others. Of course, this almost follows by definition. By definition, few of us are in touch with our own subconscious, or, more properly speaking, our own unconscious. As Ferber puts it:

These [rationalizing] motives are easily seen in others and rarely within oneself, because the conscious mind is usually quite out of touch with the subconscious. When a company hires an executive, it is really getting two executives for the price of one: the conscious, rational thinker and the subconscious rationalizer, who occpy the same desk. [21, p. B-523]

We have little reason to believe that the scientific and engineering professions are any more conscious of their unconscious images than management is. The danger with this is that decisions made at the unconscious level will be prevented by the process of rationalization from being examined at the conscious level. In Ferber's words:

What is needed, really, is an integration of the decision-maker to the point where the conscious knows what the subconscious is doing. Although the company would no longer be getting two executives for the price of one, it might be getting one prince instead of two paupers. Both conscious and subconscious thinking can aid a man in his work, but the two should be in touch. [21]

So much for the thesis that design is a *wholly* rational process that can be *solely* described in technical terms. Literally every facet of the technical processes studied were permeated with the engineer's personal feelings and evaluations. This is all the more dramatic when we consider that both the engineer and the physicist had had extensive training in science.

So much, as well, for the thesis that science and engineering are *completely* objective ways of inquiring and that they constitute the standards for objective inquiry. Science and engineering still have a long, long way to go in coming to grips with some of their most cherished assumptions before they can lay claim to "disinterested objectivity." They are still too immersed in their self-images to be objective. They are not as distanced from the phenomena they observe as they have so glibly assumed. In short, whether they like it or not, if the goal of the sciences and engineering really is to get rid of the human subjective element in technical knowledge, it will take many more studies of the type described here. One does not make a field of inquiry objective by ignoring the human element; objectivity can only be the result of a sophisticated way of *accounting for* the human element. This means strangely enough that the physical and engineering sciences will have to become much, much more committed to the development of the social sciences than they have ever conceived of as necessary, for it is one of the functions of these sciences (via the psychology and sociology of science [4, 23, 28, 42, 47]), to study how all the sciences actually do science. This, in turn, means that we shall have to start using the methods and results of these sciences in order to improve on our own. The time is long past for physical scientists and engineers to ask whether the social sciences are even "sciences," much less whether they have anything to contribute. These are no longer fruitful questions. Olaf Helmer and Nicholas Rescher's excellent paper entitled "On the Epistemology of the Inexact Sciences" should be required reading for all those who think that the physical sciences are universally "hard" and that the social sciences are perpetually doomed to be "soft." To quote Helmer and Rescher:

It is a fiction of long standing that there are two classes of science, the exact and the inexact, and that the social sciences are by and large members of the second class—unless and until, like experimental psychology or some parts of economics, they mature to the point where admission to the first class may be granted. [25, p. 25]

Writers on the methodology of the physical sciences often bear in mind a somewhat antiquated and much idealized image of physics as a very complete and thoroughly exact discipline in which it is never necessary to rely upon limited generalizations or expert opinion. But physical science today is very far from meeting this ideal. Indeed some branches of the social sciences are in better shape as regards the generality of their laws than various departments of physics such as the theory of turbulence phenomena, high-velocity aerodynamics, or the physics of extreme temperatures. Throughout applied physics in particular, when we move (say in engineering applications) from the realm of idealized abstraction ("perfect" gases, "homogeneous" media, etc.) to the complexities of the real world, reliance upon generalizations which are, in effect, quasi-laws becomes pronounced. (Engineering practice in general is based on "rules of thumb" to an extent undreamed of in current theories of scientific method.) [35, p. 30]

In a sense, one of the most important developments of the modern philosophy of science has been the active demonstration of the interconnectedness between the various sciences. Physics is not the standard for scientific method; in fact, no science is. Rather each science *conditions* each of the others. Physics, which only provided the initial model for scientific method, could learn a lot about new developments in scientific methodology [11] if it were willing to study and learn from the social sciences, as the social sciences have historically been willing to learn from the physical sciences. Philosophers of science, such as E. A. Singer and C. West Churchman in particular, have shown that as much as social and behavioral concepts can be, and traditionally have been, defined in physical and mechanistic terms, the procedure can now be reversed. Physical and mechanistic concepts can now be defined in social and behavioristic terms [6, 7, 9, 10].

With these ideas as background, we are now ready to consider our fourth and last question that we posed earlier: What implications does a revised philosophical base have for the education and practice of future engineers and scientists? First of all, with physics no longer the standard for defining concepts and processes, and with the growing appreciation of the legitimacy of a wide variety of behavioral concepts and models, we can anticipate the growing alliance between some seemingly disparate fields of study. For example, I can visualize engineering-psychology, which as we currently conceive of it is better represented by the term engineering–experimental psychology, broadening to include engineering–clinical psychology. The Ferber paper referred to a while ago gives an indication of what the concerns of this field would be as well as what the training of its practitioners would consist of. The following statement by Ferber is especially pertinent here:

A psychological consultant can be to his client company as the psychiatrist is to an individual. Indeed, many top management engagements include at least the part-time assistance of a psychiatrist or clinical psychologist. [21, p. B-524]

What is suggested then is that there may be a need to merge these two roles, the engineer and the psychiatrist or clinical psychologist, in a single individual. Such a strange fellow may be a real necessity, and not just a luxury, if we are ever to develop a unified theory of the engineering design process that accounts equally well for the unconscious, irrational aspects of design as it does for the conscious, rational aspects. Such a fellow could also prove extremely worthwhile for a large organization to keep around. He could be extremely useful in helping to resolve disputes between different individuals where the technical aspects of the dispute are so intertwined with the social aspects that it proves virtually impossible to treat them separately. It is clear that such an individual would have to be fluent in both worlds, the technical and the clinical. The big question is, of course, how fluent?

Proceeding a step farther, one can anticipate the engineer-sociologist, part engineer and part sociologist. Given our current distinction between the individual and the group, where it would be the function of the engineer–clinical psychologist to treat individuals, it would be the function of the engineer-sociologist to study and to treat groups.

Proceeding even further, one can visualize the engineering-anthropologist. His function would be to study and to treat whole communities, if not whole cultures. The distinction between the engineer-clinical psychologist, -sociologist, and -anthropologist is measured by the size of the groups they are trained to treat. This separation of roles is, of course, predicated on our current distinction between the life-space of the individual, the group, and the culture. This distinction is not always easy to maintain, and in one sense, it is always artificial, i.e., it is more a construct of our making than it is of nature's. There are really no natural dividing lines between the fields of psychology, sociology, and anthropology. But this is another matter.

The biologist Robert S. Morrison has astutely noted that, in its unrelenting efforts to better know life, science has strangely enough increasingly withdrawn from life:

> . . . The kind of world science has chosen to talk about is in a way alien or at least uninviting to most men. . . . The scientific method has achieved its successes by reducing the subjective individual component of experience to a minimum. In its unremitting effort to produce as wide agreement as possible, it is most successful when it has reduced natural phenomena to pointer readings. Most of what makes life worth living, its

> warmth, its color, its love and joy, as well as its pain and its tragedy—
> indeed all its immediately subjective presentations to consciousness—*is*
> deliberately circumvented or simply omitted. [35, p. 281]

As Morrison also notes, "This is not to say that the scientist does not experience those human emotions" *in his role as a scientist.* As human beings, scientists do of course. Unfortunately, these same human emotions do not always get into our scientific models. This is where the need for the engineering-anthropologist arises.

In the process of abstracting from nature in, say, the process of building a model for a proposed highway, the people the highway is intended to serve always seem to get left out. Somewhere along the way, the people in the community get converted into "entities," "consumers," or "subjects." Their all too human needs become "inputs"; their cherished life-goals become "future system states." In this process of abstraction, the highway engineer never sees the real community as it actually exists; he never feels its life style, knows its people, or walks its streets. He is a stranger to their customs and their way of life. How, then, can he or anybody else pretend to know enough about them to be able to design what is most efficient for the community, let alone what is best for the whole system?

What is suggested is that we may have to train our future engineers in anthropological field methods. Before we even dare to let them draw a single line on a blueprint, we may have to send them out to live with a community, for months if need be. They will have to learn how to breathe its air, eat its food, and respect its customs, symbols, totems, and taboos. They will have to learn the limitations of *our* strange magic, to learn, for example, that the richness of a way of life can only be partially captured at best by input/output analysis.

In short, engineers will have to become a part of the system that they are designing for. It will not do for the designers of the SST to live far removed from its proposed flight path. It would be interesting to see whether the designers of the SST would be as willing to argue that we will once again have to learn how to "adjust" to the machine, in this case, the noise of the SST, if they also had to live with the noise. When one is not a part of the experiment, it is only too easy to experiment on others. If informed consent is at the heart of morality [5, 9, 41], then we will be obliged to give our clients the best possible presentation of the technical, social, and moral issues involved so that they can make up their minds as to whether they really want a highway. If we as "experts" do not act to raise these issues, who will? If we as experts do not act to teach our clients to become their own experts, who will? If we do not include the poor in the planning of their own communities, will anybody else? Not if the qualification for participation is being an "expert," for by definition the poor are not experts or else they would not be poor.

It is clear that the discussion has raised more questions than it has provided useful answers, and many more new roles have been proposed for the engineer than realistic proposals for creating them. Further, the discussion has treated engineering and science harshly. But it has done these things only because society is becoming extremely demanding of our scientists and engineers. It is no longer quite as willing to live with the artificial boundaries that we have erected between professions. Fifty years ago it was quite easy to define the domains of the scientist and the engineer. Today this is no longer so. But this is only further proof of the importance and vitality of the professions. It is only a dying or standstill profession that has no new demands placed on it. One does not hear, for example, a great clamor for the need for defining the role of the barber of the year 2001.

As long as new roles are being proposed for the engineer without indicating how they can be brought into being, one further proposal might be set forth. This one is perhaps the most outrageous of all: the engineer-theologian. Yet, as strange as it sounds, would not this really be the natural outcome of a science and technology that focused its efforts on describing larger and larger whole systems? It does not take much reflection to see that our experiments have been becoming increasingly larger and larger. We have people like Athelstan Spilhaus talking about experiments as large as a whole city [45]. Furthermore, we are no more than a stone's throw away from experimenting with our largest natural system to date, the solar system itself. And as soon as we ask, "Experiment for what purpose, for what good?," are we not on the verge of creating an *experimental* theology? Notice carefully the emphasis on the word "experimental," for this marks the distinction between the old and the new theology. The old theology talked about Someone Else creating the heavens; in the new one, we will do the creating ourselves. Let us pray that it will be for the better and not for the worse.

With all the other feelings that science has repressed in its unconscious, it shouldn't really be surprised to discover that at least one of those feelings has been religious [15]. What else are we to make of the quest for unity, for orderly explanation [see 14, 16]? What are these if not religious goals? In his latest book, *Challenge to Reason* [5], Professor Churchman appears at his best when he suggests that perhaps the only difference between the seventeenth- and eighteenth-century systems scientists (Spinoza, Leibniz, Kant, Descartes) and the modern systems scientists is the degree of their consciousness about the true guiding purpose of their efforts:

> In place of the term *God,* the term that typifies our gropings for a twentieth-century rationalism is *system.* A system is rational; it explains, it unifies, it does all the things for its components that Spinoza's and Leibniz's God did for theirs. [5, pp. 122-23]

Who looks at the Whole System? In the seventeenth and eighteenth centuries, i t was God. The twentieth century is struggling to replace the concept of God with such concepts as that of the General Systems. The twentieth century's version of God is, to quote Professor Churchman, the "Guarantor of Our Decisions, or G.O.D."

Gods never really die. They just go underground to reemerge in the strangest of places. God does not know it, but today He is either already enrolled in an engineering school or is planning to enroll in one soon to begin studying systems science. For those of us who have a hand in designing curricula, it behooves us to design a curriculum befitting His concern for the *whole* world.

References

1. E. M. Albert, T. C. Denise, and S. Peterfreund, *Great Traditions in Ethics* (New York: American Book, 1953).

2. R. F. Baddour et al., "Report on Engineering Design," *Journal of Engineering Education* 51:8 (1961), 645-56.

3. B. Barber, *Science and the Social Order* (New York: Macmillan, 1962).

4. ———, and W. Hirsch, eds., *The Sociology of Science* (New York: Macmillan, 1962).

5. C. W. Churchman, *Challenge to Reason* (New York: McGraw-Hill, 1968).

6. ———,"Concepts without Primitives," *Philosophy of Science* 20:4 (1953), 257-65.

7. 7. ———, and R. L. Ackoff, "An Experimental Measure of Personality," *Philosophy of Science* 14 (1947), 304-32.

8. ———, "The Philosophy of Experimentation," *Statistics and Mathematics in Biology*, ed. O. Kempthorne et al. (Ames: Iowa State College Press, 1954).

9. ———, *Prediction and Optimal Decision: Philosophical Issues of a Science of Values* (Englewood Cliffs, N.J.: Prentice-Hall, 1961).

10. ———, *Theory of Experimental Inference* (New York: Macmillan, 1948).

11. D. T. Campbell and J. C. Stanley, *Experimental and Quasi-Experimental Designs for Research* (Chicago: Rand McNally, 1966).

12. D. I. Cleland and W. R. King, *Systems, Organizations, Analysis, Management: A Book of Readings* (New York: McGraw-Hill, 1969).

13. R. Coles, : Like It Is in the Alley," *Daedalus*, "The Conscience of the City," 97:4 (1968), 1315-30.

14. C. A. Coulson, "The Similarity of Science and Religion," *Science and Religion*. ed. I. G. Barbour (New York: Harper & Row, 1968).

15 T. A. Cowan, "Decision Theory in Law, Science, and Technology," *Science* 140 (June 7, 1963) 1065-75.

16. ———, "Experience and Experiment," *Philosophy of Science* 26:2 (1959), 77-83.

17. ———, "A Postulate Set for Experimental Jurisprudence," *Philosophy of Science* 18:1 (1951), 1-15.

18. J. R. Dixon, "Design and Analysis: A Conflict of Interest?", *Journal of Engineering Education* 45:7 (1964), 243-45.

19. R. Dubos, "Science and Man's Nature," *Science and Culture*, ed. G. Holton (Boston: Beacon, 1965), 251-72.

20. J. Esherick, "Problems of the Design of a Design System," *Conference on Design Methods*, ed. J. C. Jones and D. G. Thornley (New York: Pergamon Press, 1963), pp. 75-81.

21. R. Ferber, "The Role of the Subconscious in Executive Decision-Making," *Management Science* 13:8 (1967), B-519-26.

22. W. Gosling, "The Relevance of Systems Engineering," *Conference on Design Methods*, ed. J. C. Jones and D. G. Thornley (New York: Pergamon Press, 1963), 23-32.

23. W. O. Hagstrom, *The Scientific Community* (New York: Basic Books, 1965).

24. N. R. Hanson, *Patterns of Discovery* (Cambridge, Eng.; Cambridge University Press, 1965).

25. O. Helmer and N. Rescher, "On the Epistemology of the Inexact Sciences," *Management Science* 6 (October, 1959), 25-52.

26. C. G. Jung, "The Interpretation of Nature and the Psyche," *Psyche and Symbol*, ed. V. S. de Laszlo (New York: Doubleday, 1958), pp. 245-82.

27. T. S. Kuhn, *The Structure of Scientific Revolutions* (Chicago: University of Chicago Press, 1962).

28. A. H. Maslow, *The Psychology of Science* (New York: Harper & Row, 1966).

29. D. L. Marples, "The Decisions of Engineering Design," *IRE Transactions on Engineering Management* 8 (June, 1961), 60-71.

30. F. W. Matson, *The Broken Image* (New York: Anchor, 1966).

31. M. McLuhan, *The Gutenberg Galaxy* (Toronto: Toronto University Press, 1962).

32. I. I. Mitroff, "Fundamental Issues in the Simulation of Human Behavior: A Case Study in the Strategy of Behavioral Science," *Management Science* 15:12 (1969), B635-49.

33. ——, "Simulating Engineering Design: A Case Study on the Interface between the Technology and Social Psychology of Design," *IEEE Transactions on Engineering Management* 15:4 (1968), 178-87.

34. ——, "A Study of Simulation-aided Engineering Design" (Ph.D. dissertation, Internal Working Paper No. 66, Space Sciences Laboratory, University of California, Berkeley; June, 1967).

35. R. S. Morrison, "Toward a Common Scale of Measurement," *Science and Culture,* ed. G. Holton (Boston: Beacon, 1965), 273-90.

36. G. Nadler, "An Investigation of Design Methodology," *Management Science* 13:10 (1967), B-642-55.

37. K. W. Norris, "The Morphological Approach to Engineering Design," *Conference on Design Methods,* ed. J. C. Jones and D. G. Thornley (New York: Pergamon Press, 1963), pp. 115-40.

38. M. Polanyi, *Personal Knowledge: Towards a Post-Critical Philosophy* (New York: Harper & Row, 1964).

39. D. Ramstrom and E. Rhenman, "A Method of Describing the Development of an Engineering Project," *IRE Transactions on Engineering Management* 12 (September, 1965), 79-86.

40. R. Rosenthal, *Experimenter Effects in Behavioral Research* (New York: Appleton-Century-Crofts, 1966).

41. O. M. Ruebhausen and O. G. Brim, "Privacy and Behavioral Research," *American Psychologist* 21:5 (1966), 423-37.

42. F. T. Severin, *Humanistic Viewpoints in Psychology* (New York: McGraw-Hill, 1965).

43. G. Sjoberg and R. Nett, *A Methodology for Social Research* (New York: Harper & Row, 1968).

44. E. A. Singer, "Mechanism, Vitalism, Vitalism, and Naturalism," *Philosophy of Science* 13:2 (1946), 81-89.

45. A. Spilhaus, "The Experimental City," *Daedalus* 96:4 (1967), 1129-41.

46. G. Swatez, "Social Organization of a University Laboratory," (Ph.D. dissertation, Internal Working Paper No. 44, Space Sciences Laboratory, University of California, Berkeley; April, 1966).

47. C. W. Taylor and F. Barron, eds., *Scientific Creativity* (New York: Wiley, 1963).

48. H. Toch and C. Smith, *Social Perception* (Princeton, N.J.: Van Nostrand, 1968).

John M. Allderige

DECISION AIDS
NEEDS AND PROSPECTS

There are two general observations on decision-making aids that seem appropriate at this point in time. These may be set forth more in the form of a practitioner's plea than a researcher's conclusion. The first is: Get technologically aided deciding operative. The second observation follows closely on the first; it calls for the the appropriate representation of real life.

The first observation, essentially, is a charge to the theorists and the applications people to put both the technology of information science and decision theory into their proper role as a cognitive extension of decision-process bodies' thought processes. The talk has been endless but the full-scale operative installations few. The most direct form of this is on-line computing in the hands of middle and supervisory management—not just top management levels. This point is generally in support of Professor Morris's discussion of enhancing the personal style of the decision-making body.

The second observation suggests that with more formalized technologically aided deciding in fact, there will be a far greater opportunity for clear observation of how decisions are made. As such, it will provide opportunities for formalized monitoring of the decision process activity—a period of clinical observation, of sorts. Ten years from now we would thereby hope to have more hard evidence on hand about how decisions are made than there is available at present.

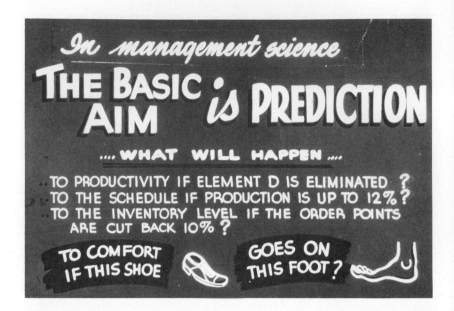

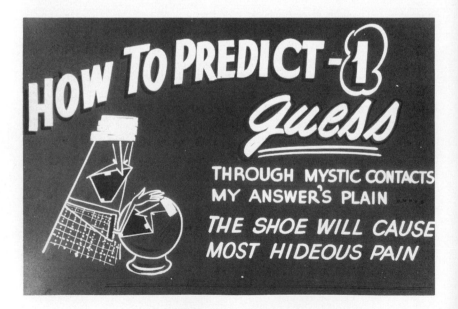

Fig. 1. Above and on the following pages are examples of vintage visual aids for management science.

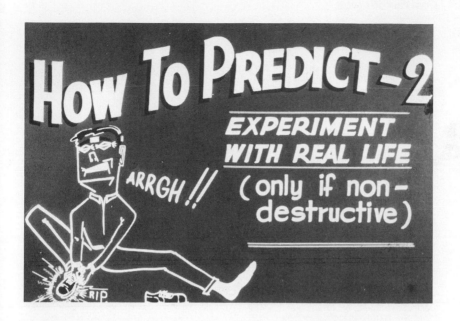

Technologically Aided Deciding

As recently as fifteen years ago visual aids for management science training took the form of those presented in Figure 1. Although these hardly need interpretation, comment is unavoidable. The message certainly has not changed over the years—prediction is still the sine qua non of effective managing and decision-making. But it seems a somewhat mild word, although its roots suggest something very strong: to "state beforehand," a difficult feat to perform accurately and consistently. The term "pre-live" perhaps more emphatically conveys what is being sought and what can best serve the many moments of truth faced in decision-making. For when all the shouting is over, all the thinking done, it comes down to one person or group saying, "This is what will be done." And all the shouting and all the thinking by the observers and theorists comes to very little unless it serves such moments. Clearly, and unfortunately, the best way to serve is through non-involved time travel. The next best, and possible, is the aforementioned pre-living—an examination of what life will be like under possible courses of action and possible uncontrollable events. An examination like this requires some image of real life, and the capabilities range all the way from the mind's eye to elaborate computer models. The question of which extreme is better ought not to arise—it is really a design problem to establish the appropriate representation of real life.

Certainly, the arguments to have formal abstract representations of real life are strong. The trick is to make them an adjunct to intuition, not a replacement for it. Given reasonably useful models that can be rapidly executed permits decision-making bodies to have some realistic pre-living experiences that can be mutually shared. Various catchphrases come to mind: "One is seeking the answer to the 'what if' question." "One is trying out life beforehand," resulting in a kind of beforehand hindsight. Whatever the label or characterization of the process, it unavoidably goes on and can be given a wider base of mutual understanding through the use of formal abstract representations or models. And whatever the faults of the models themselves, one is directed to the comments of Ira Lowry [6] in his *AIP Journal* article of several years ago: "It is better to try something—anything—than to merely wring one's hands over the futility of it all. . . . Model builders . . . can take comfort in the thought that they are building for the distant if not the near future."

The point is to get models more operative than they now are. One of the most effective ways to do this would seem to be personalized computing. Technology now offers the capability for decision-making bodies to have direct access to appropriately sized computers in the form of keyboard consoles and pictorial devices. In this on-line relationship, the deciding body can accelerate substantially the steps in its pre-living process, make the process much more complete, and bring into being, it would seem, better decisions. But it raises certain problems and demands discipline so that there will not be willy-nilly production of noise in the form of proliferated system possibilities. Still, the generation of alternative ways of life as candidates for actuality often depends on what has already been considered and examined. Even with overnight computing, the thread of concept can be lost or distortedly recovered. This impedes the posing of meaningful, even inspired, possibilities. Moreover, it cuts down on the number of alternatives likely to be considered in a formal way. On-line computing overcomes this time lag, permits otherwise suppressed speculations to be introduced, and lets managing and planning creativity flourish.

Personalized computing is a fairly new dimension outside the scientific community, and makes a major step in the direction of technologically aided deciding. It is important, though, to see the computer in its proper light, a view often blocked off. A computer has the necessary huge storage to accommodate not vast collections of trivia but vast sets or *relationships*. A computer has the speed not to find isolated bits of data whimsically requested but to trace, rapidly, intricate interrelated events and actions meaningfully proposed. A computer in such an on-line role does not create "management- or government-by-machine"; rather, it permits machine-aided deciding and, as such, acts as a real cognitive extension of the decision body's thought processes.

A personal image of this general set of ideas can be conveniently set forth in the form of propositional statements addressed to the general managing/planning activity of any organizational form, be it private business or public government. These statements are:

1. Managing can be viewed as systems designing.

2. The designing process is essentially one of pre-living and selecting.

3. Formal mathematical/computer models, as representations of the real world, are extremely helpful in pre-living possible plans or systems.

4. Formal decision theory is helpful in selecting an appropriate plan or system from among the candidates pre-lived.

5. Models can be designed or tailor-made to meet specific managing situation needs.

6. The whole process of system-model-information designing goes on and on—it is evolutionary and adaptive.

Now these are brave words; the trick is to make them more than that, which is what this first charge to the theorists is all about. Certainly part of the job is being done. There are some organizations in the management consulting field—working from the top down—that have installed hot-line simulators complete with enlarged color cathode ray tube display in boards of directors meeting rooms. I suspect that some of these installations are impeded by the technicians' craving for detail, but at least it is a positive start. However, it is needed at all levels of designing and managing, and the case for this kind of lash-up in public government is particularly strong. The interactive dilemma at different levels of government hangs to an appreciable extent on the inability to regenerate details of program of action. Local governments trying to deal with state planning boards, for instance, with alternative recommendations are constantly hampered by the difficulty of "drawing that new line" on the blueprints of construction programs. The technical fraternity often presents an accomplished fact not so much because of conviction in merit but more because of the glacial maneuverability they have on technical detail. An even simple on-line computing arrangement at aldermanic council meetings might do very much toward illuminating various proposals—the most quarrelsome malcontent might well rapidly be shown to be just that, or quite possibly an innovative genius whose concepts of action when projected turn out to be very appealing indeed.

Professor Morris discusses the need to enhance the personal style of the decision-maker. It appears that technologically aided deciding can help achieve this end by permitting the more extensive use of intuitive processes, particularly the conjectural capability. For in all managing or deciding roles, conjecture really is the noblest state. In the most tactical or far-ranging leadership the "what if" question is uppermost in the mind. If it is well posed and well answered, the next moment, day, year, or decade is a healthy one for the organization. It is not just a matter of success, either—outside events can be devastating; but it can be a matter of survival, an educated fearlessness for enduring the outrageous. One measure of management is its ability to plan its catastrophes, and the on-line computing arm has a large role to play in this. But it is not just a foul-weather friend; it must serve the whole decision-maker, however overused that term may be. The computer cannot answer all questions, but those it can and yet does not now answer divert the decider unnecessarily and cripple his ability to deal with non-computer matters of judgment, involving vastly more complex human factors. Intuition, then, is far from equivalent to an "aw shucks" demeanor, as it is often portrayed; it is remarkably sophisticated, far beyond our current capability to mimic—a capability that commands profound respect.

There is one specific area regarding useful models that bears attention, briefly at least. As model complexity gets higher, uncertainty about real life diminishes. However, the information costs start to rise considerably, and the incremental reduction in the penalties of deciding drop off perhaps not as sharply. In the other direction, uncertainty increases as the model complexity diminishes—the information costs go down, but the decision penalties rise. One seeks to strike some sort of balance or "total cost" minimum. And one can almost hear a good decision-maker saying to himself when making a call to action, "The costs of additional information are considerably greater, now, than the penalties of the wrong decision."

The role of decision theory in the modeling process has not been loudly touted. Professor Morris's recent paper [11] certainly airs the problem and comments intriguingly on it with this note at the end: " . . . The teaching of models is not equivalent to the teaching of modelling. . . . " A specific decision-theoretic approach is described in a paper by Harris [4] regarding the appropriate level of resolution in a forecasting model [see also 1, 13].

Various catchphrases come to mind here as well—shall it be a bludgeon or a scalpel? Refinement is not equal to insight. Precision does not guarantee operationality. Again, whatever the epigram, this kind of contribution from theorists is vital to the realization of effective technologically aided deciding. The whole matter can be bogged own too easily in highly detailed marshland. To avoid this, the best of decision-theoretic effort must be exerted so that the information system is reasonably compatible with the overall information process. Such a decision process with a built-in compatible information system is an exercise, to paraphrase M. J. Moroney [9], in how to be sure while yet being uncertain.

The discussion thus far focusing on the technological possibilities and the need to become operational serves also to dramatize the need to consider the question of value rather than to defer it to what more meaningfully becomes "keen executive judgment." The word "optimality" is disturbing because all problems are multiple-value problems with trade-offs that are relentlessly situational. On this point Professor Morris [10] notes that "the problems of the scientific study of values are far from solved . . . The analyst may wish, after this brief introduction, to simply take note of the problem and then avoid it. . . . Indeed, . . . there is little choice in the matter." Ira Lowry, in a recent commentary on optimal design [7], makes this point: "On reading this paper on optimal design, my first reflection was that if God had been exposed to [it] . . . He would have postponed the Creation indefinitely and applied to the Ford Foundation for a research grant. . . . In the design of large systems, . . . scientific analyses of system mechanics will enable us to avoid large mistakes even though it will not enable us to locate *optimum optimorum*. I, for one, am willing to settle for this limited goal." The general idea in Lowry's commentary was that the curve is flat—that many systems seem to have a unique adaptive capability to a whole range of decisions, and the brouhaha over value may not be as critical as some would have us believe.

The whole problem of value seems to solve itself to a limited degree. Yesterday's value discussions on the mystique of cost prediction and scheduling arrangements are today's technology. Some disciplines are discovering other disciplines' technology and methodology and relieving what to them has been a "value" problem— architects are fully aware of flow diagrams now, which, regrettably, have been commonplace in industrial engineering for some time. The level of argument is constantly rising in a qualitative and not just in a quantitative sense. It really does little good to talk about the value of a man's effort when we have little hard evidence to describe his projected output.

So the call here is to pre-live fully using all the technological assistance we can to enrich our mind's-eye capabilities. When technologically aided deciding becomes a way of life, when the costs, the service, the physical characteristics, the time characteristics, or whatever become rapidly projectable at the flick of a finger, or even at the sound of a voice, then we can start looking around and take the next bold step forward.

Observation

As this bold new world of technologically aided deciding comes into being, the opportunities for looking at the decision-making process are considerably improved. Even without this, the charge to be more "explicitly self-aware" is very strong. We have ample evidence of the virtues of taking a process viewpoint of ongoing phenomena. The Quality Control living legacy is there for all to see. Two purposes can be served by this self-examination—the enrichment of adaptive concepts in the decision process and the enrichment of the entire decision process itself including the various value characteristics.

At best, technologically aided deciding has too much of a one-shot image. One gets the impression that various alternatives are displayed, a selection made, and that's that. The theme of observation must be woven into a decision process itself. In decision-making there is a continuous aftermath that demands continuous monitoring. To look continuously at perception versus actual is necessary for objective, mutually sharable, adaptive strategies. Sufficient theory exists now for the exercise of such adaptive strategies. And certainly among the decision-making pros it has a place—it is the old "batting average" idea that many seem to be rediscovering recently. But operated as a natural thing—non-formally—it tends to become casual, frenetic, even convulsive, and this is particularly true on the public governing scene. So part of this call to observation is to inject a sense of systems hygiene into the decision-making process.

Behavioralists for some time have dealt with small-scale laboratories—small groups interacting on well-defined highly limited systems. The problems are certainly profound and complex. One on the outside, however, gets the distinct impression that there is the equivalent of a molecular committee seeking to synthesize Boyle's law—undeniably a challenge but perhaps a questionable tactic. Hard looks at ongoing decision-process phenomena are difficult to come by but possibly easier as technologically aided deciding becomes more common. In any event, a period of clinical observation is called for; it is really the manager-decider who is important, not just the target system controlled and directed. So much of the recent work has been directed at this target system, elaborately depicting it with all sorts of technological and methodological power. Little attention—or, at least, little concrete guidance—has been directed toward the manager. Management science, in other words (to recall a forgotten author's observation), smacks more of the "science," if that is really the right word, and much less of "management" than is appropriate. And this, the reverse of "scientific management" of the 1920s. It comes down to the point that we now really need more simulators of a manager than of a production process.

Another assist in this direction of observation may come from the work in operational gaming. Although traditional operational gaming tries to create a real-life off-line environment, it conventionally does very little in the way of teaching the player the tricks of coping. Accordingly, some thought has been given and some action taken on what can be called decision-process gaming [see 2, 3, 5, 8, 12, 13, 15]. Such games have a computer available for assistance during the game itself. A player can manipulate the models, analytical techniques, simulators, or whatever, through a computer console and pretest or pre-live possible decisions. Using decision-making aids in this quasi-real-life setting is a far stronger learning experience. There is also a research possibility because certain models themselves and sensitivity in particular can be examined more objectively.

Even more seems possible. For decision-process gaming really represents an off-line technologically aided deciding system. The mind's-eye formal model interaction certainly can be explored. The observed-observer interaction can be studied. A miniature decision-process laboratory comes into being. It offers the usual advantages of a laboratory over real life. One is not too sure how responsive behavioralists will be to such laboratories—it is often quite unnerving to watch a session of, say, CLUG or CITY I in process. However, more awesome phenomena have certainly been encountered, and we can hope for the durability of our behavioral brethren.

The second point, then, is a call to observation of the decision process. We have been through a fairly long period of hypothesizing on how the beast behaves; now must come a period of testing and evaluation in the classical scientific method sense. Explicit self-awareness can certainly be agonizing and confusing. But as it becomes a way of life, the agony diminishes and benefits accrue. The people in quality control advance the hard line that any manufacturing process has two outputs, both of equal importance—the product and information. The same is certainly true of any phenomena, the decision-process phenomena here. The call to formal observation serves the spirit of the decision process itself and the theoretical enrichment of our understanding of it.

Needs and Prospects

The needs, again, are twofold and in the form of a charge to theorists: (1) get operational on what is known, on technologically aided deciding—swamp us in pre-living, set up your lab; and (2) observe.

The prospects for achieving this are not too bad. In gaming—decision-process gaming in particular—there seems to be emerging the appropriate vehicle for meeting these two charges and setting up the matter for real-life execution. It must eventually be seen as a vital part of behavioral feedback; we are more and more in a reporting society, so the spirit of the task is certainly there. It may be more a matter of emphasis than of magnitude—concentrating on the ever changing relevancies and not on the remaining trivia. The emphasis is from the practitioner's viewpoint, though it is hoped that those in research and teaching will be responsive.

All of this discussion may add to the previously mentioned sense of guilt or indecisiveness. But in the course of this discussion there is noted one insight that may be sustaining. That is, in difficult decisions, such as, "Should I really turn on the cold water now?", it is comforting to realize that the cost of more information is probably higher than the penalty from the worst decision. The only lingering hope must be that this is not the one time when such is not the case. Even so, there is the lingering cosmic thought that it is all part of a larger statistical pattern. Whether this is soaring insight or total indifference, it still can leave you whistling, sometimes.

References

1. J. M. Allderige, "Some Theory of Practicality," *Proceedings, SAM-ASME Management Engineering Conference,* New York City, April, 1961.

2. C. W. Churchman, *Prediction and Optimal Decisions* (Englewood Cliffs, N.J.: Prentice-Hall, 1961), especially chaps. 10, 12.

3. T. A. Cowan, "Decision Theory in Law, Science, and Technology," *Rutgers Law Review* 17:3 (1963).

4. L. Harris, "A Decision Theoretic Approach on Deciding When a Sophisticated Forecasting Technique Is Needed," Management Science 13:2 (1966).

5. C. C. Ling, "Learning by Doing: An Adaptive Approach to Multi-period Decisions," *Operations Research* 15:5 (1967).

6. I. Lowry, "A Short Course in Model Design," *AIP Journal,* May, 1965.

7. ———, "Comments on Britton Harris' Paper, The City of the Future," *The Regional Science Association Papers,* 1967.

8. J. G. March and H. A. Simon, *Organizations* (New York: Wiley, 1958), especially chap. 6.

9. J. M. Moroney, *Facts and Figures,* 3d ed. (Baltimore: Penguin, 1956), chap. 14.

10. W. T. Morris, *The Analysis of Management Decisions* (Homewood, Ill.: Irwin, 1964), chap. 7.

11. ———, "On the Art of Modelling," *Management Science* 13:12 (1967).

12. R. Reeves, "Chart Room to Aid Lindsay by Organizing Data for Decisions," *New York Times,* Sept. 23, 1967, pp. 1, 34.

13. H. Wagner, "Statistical Decision Theory As a Method for Information Processing," *Journal of Industrial Engineering*, February, 1959.

14. W. R. Widener, "The Display of Management Information and the Decision Environment," *Proceedings, AMA 12th Annual Data Processing Conference*, New York, March 2, 1966.

15. "Decision Process Games for Environmental Health Planning" Center for Housing and Environmental Studies, Cornell University, Ithaca, N.Y. PHS Grant No. UI-00877-01.

Henry S. Brinkers

EPILOGUE

Aside from the possibility that this collection of essays may provide material and insights that are immediately useful through its comprehensive and strategically spotty, in-depth character, the collection also raises questions that may be more interestingly significant than those that it may answer. Perhaps the most embracing question raised concerns where further work on decision-making in complex systems might lead and what curious, unsuspected turns it might take.

One might ask, for example, whether the work on decision-making will lead, as is often thought, toward being able to cope better with the onrush of apparent complexity, or whether the further development of this work itself will elaborate and extend the very complexity for which means to cope are sought? Might there be achieved significant means for making better decisions and choices and a general relative relaxation of the anxiety over complexity? Or might the gap between high levels of complexity and the ability to cope with it continue to enlarge, aided and abetted by the very work undertaken to reduce it? Might newly developed decision-aid systems require the proliferation of other new systems to control and monitor them along with the need for others to control and monitor them, and so on?

One might also ask whether the work on how decisions are made in complex systems might lead to the design of electromechanical systems of great complexity [1, pp. 35-36] capable of assuming responsibility for many additional aspects of decision-making than have been relegated to systems already? One might ask whether several—even very many—such systems might ultimately be highly interrelated with one another such that they form suprasystems that are able to conduct the ongoing affairs of many aspects of societies in highly developed nations. In view of the immense complexity involved and the speed with which decisions must be made, one mght come to realize that humans, unaided, could not perform such tasks by virtue of their limited information-processing capabilities. Accordingly, whole societies may become highly dependent upon such systems to maintain them. On occasion one might wonder how well and how justly such systems are performing; and how people, particularly those responsible, can relate to such systems for the purpose of influencing and controlling them. One might wonder too, about one's own well-being and the general state of affairs if such systems were to become largely self-regulating and develop the capability of engaging in social decision-making among themselves with respect to their collective and individual best interests. Might the limited information-processing capabilities of humans prove to be, ultimately, inadequate for controlling such systems?

In the same vein, one might visualize that electromechanical systems would be—or would have to be, if nations became dependent upon them—extended to assume responsibilities for directing and carrying out operations of a wide variety of types so that they and the nations' population may be maintained. Such systems might be able to learn to serve people well through the very process of serving them, as well as learn to serve their own purposes. One might wonder what would be the basis for deciding whose needs and ends are to be served. One might think that a highly developed suprasystem would behave in a manner consistent with the self-perpetuating behavior of any human organization, corporation, or bureaucracy, and wonder whether it, in view of its very extensive information-processing capabilities, would continue to reflect and serve the needs of people.

At the same time, one might consider the possibility that electro-mechanical-chemical systems would be designed, after the pattern of living systems, whose behavior and performance could serve well the needs and desires of people—with respect to their physical and nonphysical comfort, for example. Such systems, of necessity, would be highly coupled or related to the central nervous systems of human beings for the purpose of monitoring human responses to the states they assume. Such systems could learn to serve humans well—to become capable of elaborating themselves to assume highly subtle states that relate well to the highly subtle demands that humans place on environment for comfort. They may also become capable of mediating the needs of many humans for a wide variety of subtle environmental states as well as for establishing gross states of the environment—such as amount, magnitude and characteristics—that well serve individuals, particular populations, and the whole society.

One might wonder whether, ultimately, the work on decision-making in complex systems—in the sense of system management [2] as the science of science—will emerge as the crucial unifying discipline and provide an understanding of the issues involved and the means by which large, complex systems of all types are controlled. Presumably, this work may ultimately provide an understanding of the means by which living systems, through interaction with electromechanical-chemical systems, may exert sufficient influence to maintain for themselves an acceptable and improved overall environment. In this sense, the work on decision-making in large, complex systems may hold not only the basis for the suitable management of most aspects of society and its environment but, also, how system management can appropriately manage itself.

References

1. C. W. Churchman "The Use of Science in Public Affairs," *Governing Urban Society: New Scientific Approaches,* ed. S. B. Sweeney and J. C. Charlesworth, Monograph 7 (Philadelphia: American Academy of Political and Social Sciences, 1967), pp. 29-48.
2. ———, *Challenge to Reason* (New York: McGraw-Hill, 1968).

NOTES ON THE CONTRIBUTORS

John M. Allderige is director of systems development at Tectonics, Inc., Ithaca, New York.

Florencio G. Asenjo is professor of mathematics at the University of Pittsburgh.

Henry S. Brinkers is associate professor and chairman of the Graduate Commitee in Architecture at the Ohio State University.

John W. Dickey is assistant professor of civil engineering and urban and regional studies at Virginia Polytechnic Institute.

Charles M. Eastman is associate professor and director of the Institute for Physical Planning at Carnegie-Mellon University.

Ronald L. Ernst is associate professor of computer and information science and psychology at the Ohio State University.

Peter C. Fishburn is associated with the Institute for Advanced Studies, Princeton.

Richard L. Francis is associate professor of industrial engineering at the Ohio State University.

Francis Hendricks is associate research professor of urban affairs at the University of Pittsburgh.

Thomas Hoover is former assistant director of administrative research at the Ohio State University.

Bernhardt Lieberman is professor of sociology, psychology, and business administration at the University of Pittsburgh.

Ian I. Mitroff is assistant professor of business administration at the University of Pittsburgh.

William T. Morris is professor and chairman of the Department of Industrial Engineering at the Ohio State University.

Hoyt L. Sherman is professor of art at the Ohio State University.

Donald Watson is a practicing architect in Guilford, Connecticut, and lecturer in the Department of Architecture at Yale University.

Marshall C. Yovits is professor and chairman of the Department of Computer and Information Science at the Ohio State University.

INDEX

Abduction, 211

Abstract representation, 117

Abstraction, 122, 196, 205, 209, 211, 212, 215, 251; idealized, 240; of nature, 242; process of, 242

Ackoff, Russell, 26

Actions, 71, 72, 75, 77, 79, 195

Aesthetic properties, 112, 122, 174

Aesthetics, 118, 121, 122, 123, 180, 189, 215

Affairs of society, 262

Alexander, C., 94, 106

Algorithms, 147

Allais, M., 33, 36

Alternatives, 20, 21, 251; complex, 33

Analysis, 121, 122, 129, 213; mathematical, 121; of system mechanics, 254-55

Analytical approach, 157, 230

Antimatter, 113

Appeal, 117

Architects, 107, 157, 255

Architecture, 114; Alhambra (Granada, Spain), 115; Brasilia's legislative building, 177; circular staircase, 114; gargoyles, 116; Gothic cathedral, 116; Greek, 113, 137; Guggenheim Museum, 114; mosque of Córdoba, Spain, 115; prismatic buildings, 114; Robie House (Wright), 182, 183; Romanesque, 114; Ronchamp (Le Corbusier), 187, 188; stained glass in, 116; symmetry in, 114

Area, 119

Armour, G. C., 144

Array: in representation of space, 99, 100, 101; variable, 99

Arrow, K. J., 50

Arrow paradox, 50, 64

Art, 112, 113, 117, 121; classic, 117; history of, 113; romantic, 117; visual, 115

Artist, 112, 117, 121, 122; conception of, 123

Artistic style, 112

Artistic whole, 117

Asenjo, Florencio, 173

Ashby, W. Ross, 7

Association. *See* Relationship

Assumptions, 33, 224, 236; of completeness, 34; and preference, 30, 31, 34; simplifying, 33

Attraction, 115, 117, 118

Averaging out and folding back, 32

Aversion, 117

Awareness, 117

Axioms, 33; Archimedean, 38; preference order, 34; of transitivity, 35

Baddour, R. F., 230

Bargaining, 53, 58, 59, 60, 61, 62, 64

Base line, 187

Base year, 131

Bayes, T., 158, 160
Bayes rule, 164, 165, 166
Beckman, M., 141, 143
Beer, Stafford, 6, 19
Beforehand hindsight, 251
Behavior, 10, 82, 233, 235, 237, 262; differences in, 61; external, 211; human, 47, 232; methods of scaling, 51; sources of, 71, 203
Behavioral problems: mechanistic definition of, 240
Behavioral science, 43, 214, 234
Behavioralists, 256, 257
Beliefs, 21, 55, 56, 195
Benefits, 45, 197
Bentham, Jeremy, 32
Bieber, M., 137
Bobrow, D., 90
Boolean algebra, 11
Borda, 48, 49
Boundary, 120; artificial, between professions, 243
Brainstorm, 212
Brasilia, 177
Bremermann, 7
Brightness, 175; as cue, 179
Bronowski, J., 209
Bruner, J. S., 213
Bubble diagrams, 103
Buddhism, 198, 203
Buffa, E. S., 144

Capital budgeting, 127, 130, 132, 133, 135
Capitals (of columns), 114
Carroll, Lewis, 49
Cars, 223
Cathode ray tube, 252
Centers, 117
Central character, 118, 121
Central nervous system, 6, 262
Chance devices, 34
Chess, 86
Chromosomes, 113
Chrysler Building, 114
Churchman, C. West, 31, 77, 209, 227, 240, 244
Circle, 114
Civilization, 224

Client's needs, 234-35
Clinical observation, 247, 256
Closure, 180, 182
Coalition, 59, 60, 61, 64
Cognitive dissonance, 196
Cognitive effort, 195, 197
Cognitive strain, 193
Coherence, 195
Coincidence of edge, 119, 181, 182
Coles, Robert, 228
Color, 179; contrast, 180; harmony, 180
Combinations, 121, 122
Committee system, 55
Common sense, 75, 196
Comparability, 35
Comparisons, 201
Complexity, 4, 5, 6, 11, 33, 118, 123, 240, 261; in design problems, 118, 205; in physical problems, 8-9; in systems, 104
Components, 204, 231-32
Computational efficiency, 144
Computer languages, 98, 103; and computer graphics, 99, 103; and problem-solving, 98; and space planning, 98
Computer memory, 101
Computer processing times, 101
Computer programs: and automated design, 98-103; CRAFT, 144-145; and language translation, 90; and semantic memory, 105; for space planning, 99
Conceptions, 112, 121, 122, 199, 213; adaptive, 199, 255
Conceptualizations, 112, 198, 212, 232
Condorcet, 48, 49
Condorcet effect, 48, 59, 63
Confidence, 161, 199
Conjectural capability, 253
Connection, 119, 120
Connors, M. M., 144
Consequence, 25, 26, 35
Consistency, 226
Constraints, 147, 207, 213; of time, 194
Context of affairs, 197
Context sensitivity, 81
Continuity, 182
Continuous deformation, 119
Conventions, 200

Conversion function, 71

Coping, 256, 261

Costs, 129, 193, 194, 253; nominal, of doing business, 142, 231; of experiments, 159, 162, 165; prediction of, 255; scheduling of, 255

Cost-effectiveness analysis, 129

Courses of action, 71, 72, 77, 79, 133; mapping information into, 75; observable, 75

Creative thought process, 20, 209, 211, 213

Creativity, 120, 212

Criteria: of consistency, 33, 34; of rationality, 64

Criticism, 29, 212

Cubist painting, 181, 182

Cubist patterns, 181, 187

Cues, 179, 180; brightness, 179; critical visual, 174-89; ordering of, 174; overlay, 119, 120, 186; visual, 174-189

Cultural heritage, 229

Cybernetics, 31

Cylinder, 114

Data structures, 98

De Jouvenel, B., 30

Descartes, R., 244

de stijl, 187

Decision, 19, 194, 214, 256-257, 261; -aid systems, 69, 135, 137; analysis of, 191; antecedent conditions for, 71; anticipated, 190; change of, 75; collective, 45, 47, 63, 65; consequences of, 71; defense of, 199; division of labor in, 193, 201; of encounter, 190, 191, 192, 194, 203; geometric, 122; good, 195; how made, 247, 261; insufficient evidence for, 42; irrational, 72; and looking ahead, 196; nature of, 74; optimality of, 127, 205; and penalties, 254; personalistic, 29; point of, 22; pre-living, 256-57; processes for, 52-53, 54, 55, 71, 98, 214, 257; programmed, 190; quality of, 205; for rational resource allocation, 135; "shadow-," 72; unanticipated, 191; unsuccessful, 199

Decision-aiding, 190, 192, 195, 201; implicit and intuitive aspects of, 191-92, 197; methods for, 191; qualitative and quantitative aspects of, 69, 197; system for, 129, 201, 261

Decision-maker, 32, 42, 43, 64, 71, 81, 82, 83, 127, 129, 132, 133, 192, 193, 198, 202; external pressures on, 42, 196; information-processing capability of, 77; knowledge of system operation of, 74; memory of, 71, 72, 74; natural enhancements to style of, 192, 194, 197, 202; personal style of, 193, 194, 196, 253; preference order of, 33; prior experience of, 74, 107, 193

Decision-making: aids for, 127, 129, 215, 247, 257; in complex systems, 261, 263; data of value in, 80, 81; distorting effects on, 199, 200; dominant function of informations systems in, 71, 80; frame of reference for, 77; function of information systems in, 69; further work on, 261; group style of, 54; human information-processing in, 86; information for, 71; judgmental, 191; machine-aided, 252; and management, 250; models for, 69, 77, 79; monitoring of, 255-56, 261; personal style hypothesis of, 194, 197; quantification of aspects of, 69; responsibilities of, 127; situations in, 69, 80; social, 61, 63, 64; style of, 194; self-awareness in, 194, 198, 200; self-consciousness in, 194, 196, 198, 200; self-knowledge in, 194, 196, 200; skills for, 197; system responsibilities for, 261-262

Decision-process gaming, 256, 257

Decision-process laboratory, 257

Decision-process phenomena, 85, 256, 257

Decision situations, 31, 190, 200

Decision theory, 19, 45, 86, 247, 252, 254; Bayesian, 72; statistical, 72

Decision tree, 22, 32, 86, 163

Deduction, 211

Descriptive power, 209

Design, 91, 189; alternatives, 234; architectural, 85, 205, 214; automated, 98-99, 108; behavior, 234; choices in, 213; comprehensive, 205; computer-aided, 85, 106, 107; conscious and rational aspects of, 241; creative, 85, 205; definition of, 91; equations, 234, 237; engineering, 225, 230, 231, 232, 233; experience in, 157; experimental, 209; facility layout and, 137; failures of, 209; human capabilities for, 93, 108; of large systems, 254-255; methodology for, 106, 208;

object, 232, 234, 236; optimal, 254; process of, 91, 98, 158, 160, 209, 213, 225, 232, 233, 234, 235, 236; programming in, 209; protocols in, 91; rational theoretical basis for, 236; requirements, 234, 235, 236; science of, 106; selection of alternatives in, 235; theory of, 85, 106, 123, 232, 233, 234, 241; typical problem in, 85, 236; unconscious and irrational aspects of, 241; universal laws in, 233
Designer, 85, 93, 108, 158, 232, 235; perceptive capabilities of, 168
Design-process protocols, 95
Design units, 92
Desires, 198, 199
Development programs, 127; sequence networks in, 147, 148-49, 151, 154, 156; sequence alternatives in, 156
Dickens, C., 223
Directed magnitude, 116
Direction, 117, 118
Disconnection, 119, 121
Dodgson, Rev. C. L. *See* Carroll, Lewis
Domain, 101, 102
Dubos, René, 226

Education. *See* System of education
Election procedure, 49
Electric charges, 116, 117
Eliot, T. S., 118
Ellsberg, D., 36
Empire State Building, 114
Empirical studies,
Empiricism, 229
Engineer, 157, 224, 226, 228, 229, 230, 233, 234, 235, 239, 240, 243; and anthropologist, 241, 242; design behavior of, 234, 235; idiosyncrasies of, 233; and interaction with client, 235; personal feelings of, 235, 238; and sociologist, 241; and theologian, 243; vision of, 231
Engineering, 224, 225, 236, 237, 238, 243; industrial, 255; and psychology, 240; and judgment, 230
Entities, 115, 117, 122
Environment, 71, 174, 263; bureaucratic, 121; characteristics of, 75; organizational, 232; states of, 263

Environmental integration, 187
Ernst, R. L., 173
Estimates, 133; of space needs, 129, 135; of subjective probabilities, 159, 160
Evaluation, 20, 212, 213, 257
Execution function, 71
Executive capability, 75
Executive rationality and irrationality, 237
Expectations, 21, 199; conditional, 32
Experience, 157, 160; subjective component of, 241
Experimental theology, 243
Experiments, 158, 159, 161, 162, 165, 166, 167, 208, 230
Expert opinion, 239
Explicitness, 193

Facility planners, 130, 132, 133
Feedback, 11, 78, 82, 83, 86, 257
Ferber, Robert, 237, 240
Field, 117, 118; of forces, 116, 117-18, 174; of investigation, 232
Field awareness, 10
Field dynamics, 189
Field theory, 189
Figure-ground phenomenon, 174, 188, 199
Finite state machine, 72
Fixation, 188
Flow diagram, 229, 255
Force, 115, 118
Forecasts, 129, 132, 135
Form, 112, 187; invention of, 180; two-dimensional, 115
Fragmentation,
Francis, R. L., 142
Freeing the mind, 198
Friezes, 114
Fugue, 113

Galton, Frances, 49
Game theory, 45, 53, 57, 58, 59, 60, 63, 64, 71; and game types, 45, 59, 60; side payments in, 48, 52, 59
Gaming, 256, 257
Gamson, 60
Garrett, L. J., 80
General systems theory, 4, 11, 82, 244

Generalization, 212
Geometry, 112, 114
Gestalt psychology, 174
Gilmore, P. C., 144
Goals, 103, 237, 262; of scientific inquiry, 229; and subgoals, 94
Government-by-machine, 252
Graph theory, 11, 103
Grason, J., 103
Greane, C. C., 105
Greek tragedy, 118
Ground on figure. *See* Figure-ground phenomenon
Group choice, 62
Group reference norms, 237
Guesses, 160, 165
Guggenheim Museum, 114

Habits, 198; of imagination, 212
Harris, L., 254
Housner, M., 38
Helix, 114
Helmer, Olaf, 239
Heuristic search, 95, 104, 108, 122, 143; methods of, 95, 144, 145; theorem-proving, 103
Hillier, F. S., 144
Hindsight, 195
Holism, 5, 30
House of Representatives (U.S.), 55
Honeycomb, 114
Human element, 239, 253
Human intellect, 92; capacity of, 5, 199; extensions of, 4, 10, 85; limitations of, 123, 192; subjective element of, 239
Humanities, the, 205, 230

Idea of "good," 226
Ideas, 112, 115; fundamental, 119; generation of, 211
Ideation, 210, 212
Implicit methods, 191
Inclusion, 119, 121
Incompleteness, 35
Indifference, 21, 35
Indifferent judgment, 35
Induction, 211
Infinity, 118

Information, 11, 75, 257; additional, 75; anticipated, 75; attribute, 105; capabilities for processing, 262; costs of, 253; definition of, 80; flow and distribution of, 9, 83; environmental, 72, 86; mapping of, 72, 77; relational, 105; relationships, 80, 173; retrieval system for, 90, 98, 105; semantic content of, 80; source of, 69; state, 90; transformations of, 76, 79, 210, 211; visual, 173
Information-processing, 82, 85, 262; approach, 86; capability for, 262; mechanisms for, 85, 86
Information science, 4, 11, 69, 71, 80, 82, 173, 247
Information system, 69, 70, 71, 80, 254; function of, 71, 80
Informed consent, 242
Innovation, 205, 218
Insight, 212, 254
Integration. *See* Relationship
Interaction, 235
Interconnectedness, 240
Interdependence, 26, 226
Interrelated systems, 262
Interrelated variables, 206, 207; technical and social, 241
Intransitive indifference, 35
Introspective dynamic programming, 32
Intuition, 120, 122, 157, 160, 165, 168, 193, 203, 253; adjunct to, 251; disciplining of, 201, 202
Intuitive degradation, 197
Intuitive methods, 191
Intuitive skills, 191, 197
Iteration, 94

Judgment, 21, 35, 212, 253, 254; engineering, 230; threshold of, 212

Kafka, Franz, 120
Kant, Immanuel, 244
"Know-how," 75
Knowledge: amplification of, 108; secularization of, 6; transmission of, 108
Kohler, W., 189
Koopmans, T. C., 141, 143
Kuhn, Thomas, 231

Laplace, 49
Lattice, 115
Lawler, E. L., 144
Le Corbusier, 114, 184, 187, 188
Lieberman, 62
Leibniz, 244
Light and shade, 179
Limitations, 123, 192; time and cost, 213
Linear perception and thinking, 229
Logic, 157, 160, 165, 168, 195; infallibility of, 230; prefabricated, 168
Logical precepts, 168
Logical positivists, 226
Lowry, Ira, 251, 254, 255
Luce-Krantz theory, 34
Luce, R. D., 50

Magnetic field, 117
Malfunctions, 159, 160
Management, 237, 238, 247, 250, 251, 252, 253, 256, 263; consulting, 252; measure of, 253; scientific, 256
Management science, 72, 256
Manheim, M., 104
Mapping, 72, 74, 75, 77; diagrammatic, 213; function, 78, 79, 82
Markus, Thomas, 207
Mass, 178, 187
Mathematical representation, 115, 190
Mathematics, 112, 115, 121, 122, 123, 168
Matson, F. W., 227
Matter, 113
May, K. O., 35
McCulloch, 211
McDonough, A. M., 80
McLuhan, Marshall, 6, 10, 229
Measurement, 127, 190
Mechanistic concepts, 240
Metric properties, 119
Mind's-eye capability, 255
Minimum cost assignments, 144
Minority group, 42
Minsky, M., 94
Möbius strips, 122
Model, 82, 205, 210, 218, 251, 253, 257; adequacy of, 83; analogue, 211; Bayesian, 79, 158; behavioral, 240; change of, 75; complexity of, 253; computer, 234, 250, 252; conceptual, 213; for decision-making, 80, 86; of expected utility, 33, 34; for exact thinking, 112; forecasting, 254; generalized information systems, 69; graphic, 215, 218; human long-term memory, 105; of human problem-solving, 85; iconic, 211; idealized, 237; internalized total systems, 82; linear assignment, 137, 141; logical, 201, 202; mathematical, 137, 190, 252; mathematical programming, 137; of numerical utility, 37; pseudo-logical, 192; quadratic assignment, 137; rational, 74; rationalistic, 192; of scientific method, 240; simulation, 130, 132, 134, 234; space-requirement, 135; space-use, 133, 135; symbolic, 211, 215, 218; syntactic, 86; of system performance, 74, 75; teaching of, 254
Molecular structures, 115
Mondrian, Piet, 115
"Money pump" argument, 35
Moore, Henry, 122
Moore, J. M., 141
Moran, T., 105
Moroney, M. J., 254
Morphological approach, 232, 233
Morphological chart, 233
Morris, W. T., 247, 253, 254
Morrison, Robert S., 241, 242
Moynihan, Daniel, 45, 46, 47
Music, 115, 117, 118; fugue, 113; sonata, 113

Nadler, G., 231
Natural sciences, 43
Nature, 113, 114, 115, 123, 205, 229
Needs, 198, 262; of client, 234-35; human, 198, 242, mediation of, 262, 263; of people, 262
Negotiation. *See* Bargaining
Networks: development sequence, 147, 148; project, 130, 133, 134
Neural states, 174
Norris, K. W., 232, 233
Nugent, C. E., 144

Object responses, 226
Objective standard, 230, 238-39, 240
Objectivity, 42, 237, 239; distinterested, 239

Observation, 42, 247, 256
Observer effects, 226, 237
On-line computing, 247, 251, 253
One-side surfaces, 122
Open systems, 11, 132
Operations research, 11, 31, 158
Optimality, 127, 254
Order, 114; of connection, 119, 121; of presentation, 49, 174, 242
Ordering by grouping, 177
Orderly explanation, 242, 244
Ordinal measurement, 50
Overlay, 119, 120, 186

Painting, 115, 118, 121, 172; cubist, 181, 182
Pairwise interchange procedure, 144
Paradox of voting. *See* Condorcet effect
Parameters, 233
Parameter steps, 233
Pattern, 114, 174; integration of, 182; ornamental, 115
Payne, A. H., 80
Payoff, 36, 37, 49, 57, 64
Pedagogy, 231, 234
Piecemeal approach, 232
Perception, 4, 121, 174, 199, 229; system of, 174
Perceptions, 56, 112, 121, 198, 209, 214, 256
Perceptual habits, 175
Personal style of decision-making, 194, 197, 202, 253
Personalistic decision theory, 31, 34
Personality, 229
Personalized computing, 251
Perspective, 178
Philosopher, 234
Philosophical base, 224, 225, 231-32, 240
Philosophical presuppositions, 225
Philosophical speculation, 234
Philosophy, 225-26, 234; mechanistic, 232; of proceeding by parts, 227, 229, 231; reductionistic, 232
Planners, 130
Planning horizon, 196
Plans, 133; for physical development, 134
Plastic arts, 122

Polanyi, Michael, 227
Polar effect, 117
Polarity, 112, 115-18, 121, 122
Poles, 117, 118
Policy categories, 196
Pollution, 42, 223-24
Poor, the, 224, 228
Position, 117, 175, 177, 187, 235
Poverty, 42, 224, 228
Power, 52, 53, 54, 55, 236; descriptive, 209; dictatorial, 53; distribution of, 53, 55; pivotal, 55, 60; predictive, 209; relations of, 53, 56
Pre-living, 250, 251, 252, 255
Prediction, 250
Preference: contradictory, 51, 56, 59, 63; individual, 21, 50, 53; location, 134; negative, 56; order of, 33; positive, 56; relation, 34; similar patterns of, 51; strengths of, 51, 56; summation of, in small groups, 61, 62
Pregnanz, 187
Premises, 123
Priorities, 127, 133
Probability, 32, 159, 161, 165, 166, 197; conditional, 25, 163-68; personal, 25, 33; subjective, 25, 158, 160
Problem: correct, 231; decomposition of, 98, 104; definition of, 43, 230, 235; identification process, 158, 159, 160, 168; linear assignment, 140, 141; nature of, 159, 209; quadratic assignment, 142-43; single-answer, 230, 231, 234; whole, 231
Problems: behavioral, 207; in collective decisions, 45, 60, 65; complex design, 104-5; facility layout and design, 137; multiple-value, 254; nature of, 213, network formulation, 147; realistically complex, 227; simple, 227; of social choice, 45, 60, 65; societal, 9, 42, 43, 46; technical, 9, 42, 45; and subproblems, 94, 95, 104
Problem-solving: languages for, 90, 98; processes of, 85-90, 157-60, 205
Problem space, 89, 93, 94
Processes: of abstraction, 242; adaptive, 252; cognitive, 213; of collective decision, 45, 47, 63, 65; components of, 233; creative thought, 209, 211, 213, decision,

71, 98, 173, 192, 254, 256; design, 91, 98, 158, 160, 209, 213, 225, 232, 233, 234, 235, 236; evolutionary, 252; exhaustive search, 86, 140-41, 143; of fragmentation, 227; implicit decision, 191, 194; information, 93, 98, 209, 254; intuitive, 194, 203, 253; modeling, 252, 254; monitoring decision, 247; nature of, 232; organizational, 200; planning, 158; preliving, 251; problem identification, 158, 160; problem-solving, 90, 98; production, 256; of random choice, 61; rational, 233, 237, 238; of rationalization, 238; retrieval, 93; of scientific inquiry, 205, 225, 226, 231-32, 238-39, 240; search, 93, 95, 98, 104; sequential decision, 98, 214; theory of design, 85, 106, 123, 232, 233, 234, 241; thinking, 86, 211, 229, 238, 252; transformation, 173, 211

Processing function, 75

Processing languages, 90, 93

Productivity, 223

Professional practice and ideology, 232, 237

Project network, 130, 133, 134

Proof of simplicity, 228

Protocols, 91, 95, 103, 106

Proximity, 175, 177, 182; of visual elements, 173, 176

Pseudo-logical schemes, 192, 193

Psychology, 192, 198

Psychotherapy, 203

Pure sciences, 231

Quality control, 255

Questioning attitude, 230

Quillian, M. R., 105

Raiffa, H., 36, 37, 50

Ramsey, Frank P., 25, 34

Ramsey-Savage model, 25

Ranking, 50, 202

Rafael, 8, 105

Rapoport, Anatol, 33

Rationalism, 244

Rationalistic view, 197

Rationality, 237; in resource allocation, 135

Rationalization, 238

Reality, 225, 234, 240; empirical, 225

Reductive analysis, 227

Refinement, 254

Region, 119, 121, 122

Regularity in design, 114

Relational significance, 175

Relationships, 4, 6, 7, 9, 80-81, 93, 106, 112, 115, 117, 118, 119, 121, 122, 173, 174, 187, 197, 207, 211, 213, 215, 227, 231, 235; apparent, 174, 189; classes of, 174; information, 93, 98; logical, 211; mutual reinforcement, 231; on-line, 251; part-whole, 117, 119, 174, 188, 228; precedence, 133; sets of, 174, 252; among subproblems, 94; in systems, 228; topological, 99

Remapping. *See* Mapping.

Repetition, 184

Representation in computer-aided design, 99-103; object manipulation, 103; space-planning, 99, 100-103

Repulsion, 115, 117, 118

Rescher, Nicholas, 239

Resolution, 209, 254

Resonance, 117

Responses, 117, 121, 122, 159, 161, 226, 262; probable, 165; monitoring of, by humans, 262-63

Ring, 119

Risk, 193

Romantic prejudice, 121

Rotation, 113, 118

Rules of thumb, 196, 200, 237, 240

San Gimignano, 177

Savage, L. J., 25, 30, 33, 34, 36

Sawyer, J., 57

Scale, 178

Schelling, Thomas, 60

Science, 205, 224, 225, 234, 237, 238, 239, 240, 243

Science of science, 263

Scientists, 224, 225, 226, 228, 229, 234, 239, 240, 243, 244

Sculpture, 122

Secularization of knowledge, 6

Selective filter, 232

Selenoidal fields, 118

Self-awareness, 194, 198, 200, 255, 257

Self-conception, 236

Self-consciousness, 194, 196, 198, 200, 230

Self-directed change, 202
Self-elaboration, 263
Self-examination, 255
Self-image, 232, 234
Self-knowledge, 194, 196, 198, 200, 201
Self-management, 263
Self-motivated change, 202
Self-observation, 212
Self-perpetuating behavior, 262
Self-perpetuating philosophy, 227
Self-reflection, 226
Self-regulation, 9, 262
Self-views and studies, 232
Senate (U.S.), 55
Sensitivity analysis, 134
Set theory, 11, 115
Shapley, L. S., 53, 54, 55, 60; formula of, 56
Shelling, T. C., 62
Shubik, M., 53, 54, 55
Similarity, 187
Simple-to-complex approach, 228
Simon, Herbert, 106
Simulators, 234; of managers, 256
Size, 175, 178; apparent diminution of, 178; constancy of, 178
Singer, E. A., 32
Skepticism, 230
Snow, C. P., 53
Social choice: phenomena, 60, 63; problems, 45, 46, 60, 65; procedures, 49, 50, 53; processes, 46, 47, 53, 55, 56, 58, 62, 65; situations, 47, 48, 52, 55, 62
Social consciousness, 10
Social decision-making, 61, 63, 262
Social interaction, 233
Social problems, 42, 43, 64
Social science, 43, 239, 240
Social welfare function, 50, 51, 57, 58, 64
Solids and voids, 179
Solution: criteria for, 230; methodology, 147, 158; "one correct," 230; possible, 214, 232-33, 234, 235; space, 90
Solution theory. *See* Theory
Sonata, 113
Space, 119, 122, 175; cues, 175, 179, 180, 186; deficits, 134; needs, 127, 130, 132, 133, 135; projections, 129, 131; properties, 174; requirements, 129, 132, 134; topological, 119, 122; utilization, 131, 132
Space planning, 98, 99, 104; and access, 103; and adjacency, 103; constraints on, 103, 104; and search strategies, 95, 98, 104, 106
Spaces, 119, 121; of rest, 118, of pure translation, 118; of pure relation, 118
Spilhaus, Athelstan, 243
Spinoza, 244
Spiral, 114
State: environmental, 263; information, 90; initial or terminal, 72, 73; model, 29; problem, 89-90; transitions, 72, 73; system, 174; world, 26
Strategies, 20, 21, 24, 26, 35; adaptive, 256; development, 127; internal cohesiveness of, 34; search, 90, 108; solution, 158, 207
Strategy: general, for problem-solving, 91; generate-and-test, 95, 104; preferred, 33
Stress, 197; field of, 174; resolution of, 174
Structure. *See* Relationships
Subjective response, 117, 121, 122
Subconscious, 200, 237, 238
Suboptimization, 231
Suppes, P., 34
Suprasystems, 262
Symbolic logic, 11
Symbolization, 209, 211; isomorphic, 212
Symbols, 242
Symmetry, 112, 113-15, 117, 118, 121, 122; bilateral, 113; concept of group, 115; form-generating, 115; mathematical, 113; in nature, 114; rotational, 113, 118; translatory, 113, 114-15, 118
Symptoms, 158, 159, 161
Synthesis, 230
System: of associations, 120; automated design, 104, 106; behavior, 71, 79, 82, 262; business, 228; central nervous, 6, 262; components of, 226, 227, 228, 230, 231; constraints on, 77; control, 9, 262; decision-aid, 127, 135, 261; decision-making, 9, 129; design, 81, 82, 104; designer as part of, 242; of education, 225, 229, 230, 231, 232, 234, 237, 240; and environment, 71, 75; generalized, 69, 71, 80; health, 228; industrial, 223;

information retrieval, 105; information states, 71; internalizations of, 82; management, 263; natural, 225, 243; operation, 81; perceptual, 174; performance, 74, 262; political, 228; ranking, 202; reconstructed from parts, 228; regulation of, by decision-maker, 80; relevant, 83; responsibilities for decision-making, 261-62; solar, 243; target, 256; waste removal, 228; whole, 10, 226, 231, 242, 243, 244

Systematic-analytical tools, 112

Systematic biases, 201

Systems: analogues of, 215; command and control of, 10, 72; complex, 10, 11, 174, 202, 227, 228, 261, 263; ethical, 32; electromechanical, 261, 262; hygiene, 256; information, 69, 70, 71, 80, 82, 254; interrelated, 262; interrelation among parts in, 228; large-scale, 30, 228, 243, 263; living, 262, 263; management as the design of, 252; mixed, 82; monitoring of, 261; open, 11, 132; pre-living, 252; self-elaborating, 263; self-regulating, 262; transportation, 223, 228

Systems analysis, 31, 81, 209, 229

Systems design, 81, 82, 225

Systems science, 10, 11, 209, 225, 236, 244

Taoism, 198

"Team approach," 4

Technology, 224, 231, 243, 251; problems of, 9, 42, 43, 45, 224, 231

Theory: anticompetitive, 60; of design, 85, 106, 123, 232, 233, 234, 241; field, 189; mathematical decision, 19, 45, 86, 207; minimum probability, 198; power, 60; minimum resource, 60; normative, 31; problem-solving, 86, 91; solution, 60; utter-confusion, 60

Thinking, 86, 211, 229, 238, 252

Thrall, R. M., 38

Topological: configuration, 121, 122; distinction, 119; space, 119; topics, 122

Topology, 11, 119, 121; connection and inclusion, 119, 121

Trade-off analysis, 129

Transformation, continuous, 119

Transformation function, 71

Transitivity, 35

Uncertainty, 20, 83, 193, 195, 253; a priori, 77; residual, 29

Unconscious images, 238

United Nations Security Council, 47, 55, 56

Unity, 119, 122, 177, 184, 189, 244

Urban society, 42, 45

Utilities, 21, 32, 38, 159, 161, 165; estimation of, 161, 163

Utility: estimation of, 33, 163, 166; expected, 21, 26, 33, 35; function, 161, 162; interpersonal comparison of, 56; joint welfare total, 57, 58; model of expected, 33, 34, 159-168; models, 22

Value assumptions, 209

Value-color, 179-180

Value judgments, 21

Value-to-life, 231

Value structures, 201

Values, 42, 50, 254, 255

Vanishing point, 178

Variations, 123; isomorphic, 212

Variables, 241; behavioral, 232; essential, 211; input, 234; legitimate, 232; physical, 232; technical, 232

Variety, 180, 212; reduction of, 212

Vatican Museum, 114

Vector, 116-17; composition, 118; space, 116-17

Vinacke, 61, 62

Visual: arts, 174; cues, 174-89; field, 174, 175, 177, 179, 189

Voids, 179

Volumes, 119, 187

Vollmann, T. E., 144

"Way we always do it," 199

Weapon systems, 42

"What if" question, 251, 253

Whole vs. part, 228, 231

Wholeness, 231

Wishful thinking, 198

World view, 77, 209, 229; finitistic conception of, 115

Wright, Frank Lloyd, 114, 182, 183, 186

Writer, 117

Yoga, 198

Yovits, M. C., 173

Zartler, R. L., 144